Dear Ken,

Thank you sincerely for all of your help & advice on the teaching of my recent course. I can only hope this provides an amusing distraction — or a good anecdote.

Sincerely,

Mark Faber

Rights of Passage

RIGHTS OF PASSAGE

The Passport in International Relations

Mark B. Salter

LYNNE
RIENNER
PUBLISHERS

BOULDER
LONDON

Published in the United States of America in 2003 by
Lynne Rienner Publishers, Inc.
1800 30th Street, Boulder, Colorado 80301
www.rienner.com

and in the United Kingdom by
Lynne Rienner Publishers, Inc.
3 Henrietta Street, Covent Garden, London WC2E 8LU

© 2003 by Lynne Rienner Publishers, Inc. All rights reserved

Library of Congress Cataloging-in-Publication Data
Salter, Mark B.
  Rights of passage : the passport in international relations /
    Mark B. Salter.
    p. cm.
  Includes bibliographical references and index.
  ISBN 1-58826-145-X (hbk. : alk. paper)
  1. Passports—History. I. Title.
K3273.S25 2003
341.4'842—dc21   2003041368

British Cataloguing in Publication Data
A Cataloguing in Publication record for this book
is available from the British Library.

Printed and bound in the United States of America

∞ The paper used in this publication meets the requirements
  of the American National Standard for Permanence of
  Paper for Printed Library Materials Z39.48-1992.

5 4 3 2 1

To Kate

Contents

Acknowledgments ix

1 Introduction: A Body, a Soul, and a Passport 1
   Security and Mobility 2
   Examining Our Papers 3
   Not-so-Hidden Agendas 6

2 Passports, Violence, and International Society 11
   Ne Exeat Regno 12
   Privateers, Princes, and Letters of Marque 16
   Colonial Space and Passports 20
   Description, Depiction, and Conscription 24
   Antipassports 33
   Conclusion: The Control of Violent Movements 39

3 Health and the Body Politic 49
   The Prince and the Plague 50
   Colonialism, Cholera, and Passports 55
   New Plagues, the New World Order, and the
      World Health Organization 63
   Conclusion: Health and the Citizen—Disease and the Stranger 69

4 Passports and International Society 77
   Formation of the Modern International System 78
   Citizenship, Immigration, and the Return of the Repressed 86

Machine-Readable Identity *93*
Conclusion: Protecting Whom from What? *95*

5 The Disappearance of Passports   101
   Bothers, Nuisances, and Passports *102*
   Schengen Again and Again *105*
   Passports in the Periphery *112*
   Conclusion: Integration, Not Freedom *115*

6 Borders, Frontiers, and Formalities   121
   The Frontiers of Sovereignty *121*
   Design, Space, and Interrogation *123*
   Translocality, Transversality, and the Persistence of Borders *134*
   Conclusion: Narrating the Border *142*

7 Conclusion: Passports, Identity, and International Relations 149
   Problems of Citizenship, Nationality, and Documentation *152*
   Constituting the Self as a National and International Actor *156*
   Taking the "Inter-" Seriously *158*

Bibliography   163
Index   183
About the Book   195

Acknowledgments

Much of the research for Chapters 1 and 3 of this book was made possible by a grant from the American University in Cairo (AUC), which allowed me to spend a wonderful month in London at the Public Records Office. AUC also supported the presentation of sections of the manuscript-in-progress at its own Research Fellows Seminar, the Pan-European International Relations Conference, and the International Studies Association.

My students at AUC suffered through endless detours into the realm of the passport and challenged many of my assumptions about mobility, identity, and security. I am grateful to them, as well as to all those people who told me their own passport stories. In particular, I would like to acknowledge my colleagues in the AUC Department of Political Science: Bahgat Korany has been a true mentor and colleague. I am fortunate to count Trevor Parfitt as both friend and colleague, and his support during the development of this book has been a real source of encouragement. I would also like to thank Jean Allain, Hayat Alvi, and Dan Tschirgi for their support and friendship.

The Norm Patterson School of International Affairs at Carleton University offered me their warm hospitality, which I much appreciate.

Nivine Nosshy and Heather Booth assisted in the final preparation of the manuscript. I would also like to acknowledge the hard work of Pamela Ritchie and Christine Miller. Peter Mandaville provided some extremely useful feedback at an important stage in the project.

I would like to thank Lynne Rienner, whose patience and faith in this project emboldened me to write the kind of book that is presented here, and also two anonymous reviewers of the manuscript for their thoughtful comments.

My deepest and dearest thanks go to my wife, Kate, whose care, support, and optimism made this project possible.

—*Mark B. Salter*

Rights of Passage

1

Introduction:
A Body, a Soul, and a Passport

> *A man consists of a body, a soul, and a passport.*
> —Russian proverb

> *Son, we live in a world that has walls, and those walls have to be guarded by men with guns.*
> —Jack Nicholson as Colonel Jessup, A Few Good Men

This book was originally prompted by a number of personal experiences. My grandparents insisted that my sister retain her British passport after our immigration to Canada, and her case was brought up in Parliament as an example of the danger of changing citizenship laws. I was once stuck between Canada and the United States because my (adopted) nationality and the nationality of the car I was driving differed (if it were not for an understanding border guard, I would still be circulating through the Blaine, Washington–White Rock, British Columbia, truck crossing). My grandfather's birthday was not recorded anywhere. He had to give a date of birth for his passport application to immigrate to England, which for most purposes became his "real" birthday. A colleague was unable to leave Egypt on a completely valid replacement passport because the original entry stamp was missing. As I started discussing my project with friends, family, and acquaintances, the passport was often involved in an important event in their lives: being the first member of the family in three generations to get a passport, the nationalities question of postcommunist passports in Lithuania, the differing passport regulations among countries. Passports and passport stories were an experience of the "international" that nearly everyone shared. The passport not only prompts questions of immigration, nationality, globalization, travel, and belonging but also connects the individual to the realm of the international.

Security and Mobility

Governments have two opposing motivations in regard to the international movement of people: to facilitate trade and international intercourse by opening borders and allowing travel; and to protect—especially after the September 11, 2001, terrorist attacks—the state, society, and economy by closing borders and restricting travel. Passports are the primary document that states use to regulate the permeability of their borders.

I make three main arguments. First, passports play a limited (and limiting) role in the identification of travelers; they can only derive their authenticity from other state-issued documents. Second, a passport does not guarantee security, either to the individual bearing it with regard to other sovereigns or to other sovereigns with regard to the traveler. Foreigners are always subject to the law of the state in which they are present (and though one's country of origin can make requests, its power is limited in another jurisdiction). Likewise, states are not protected from dangerous travelers, no matter how that danger is defined. Passports are issued as documents of nationality, not good character. As the September 11 attacks as well as Palestinian terrorists' evasion of Israeli security illustrate, strict document checks cannot guarantee safe borders. Third, there are two worlds of movement. In this post–Cold War, postmodern, postcolonial era, we see a bifurcation in the contemporary regime of international movement. Citizens of the developed North have a freedom of movement that is legitimated by domestic and international government structures. Citizens and refugees of the developing South, however, are restricted in their movements both domestically and internationally. As Amitava Kumar illustrates, the passport takes on differing functions in the North and South: "For those who live in affluent countries, the passport is of use for international travel in connection with business or vacations. In poorer nations of the world, its necessity is tied to the need for finding employment, mainly in the West."[1]

Passports are thus the material markers of identity that structure legitimate and illegitimate international movement. They are the evidence of nationality that we carry with us when traveling; among all government-issued documents, they traditionally have "high truth-claims" with regard to nationality, belonging, and citizenship.[2] And the passport provides a useful way to explore the intersection of the national and international.

Although travel is always dependent on material and social factors, at several points in history the size and possibilities of the world changed. Roman roads, the invention of the railroad, the airplane—all are moments when distances shrank.[3] But there are less tangible innovations that likewise changed the accessibility of the world: the consolidation of the state as "safe" space, the health passport (*billeta de sanità*), the conquering of colonies, the modern passport regime, the Schengen Agreement of the European Union (EU). The history of the passport in international relations traces the impact of these "soft" innovations on the movements of individuals in the world.

I have attempted to temper a straight chronological narrative by focusing on the concerns that prompted the invention of the passport: disease, violence, cooperation, integration, and control. Chapters 2 and 3 of this book cover the development of the passport from the perspectives of violence and health, respectively. Chapter 4 examines the evolution of the international passport regime. Chapter 5 considers those few cases in which the passport has disappeared or been replaced by other structures. Chapter 6 looks at the border issue, where passports are inspected and the state discriminates between safe and unsafe travelers. Chapter 7, the concluding chapter, provides an overview of the functions of the passport in the context of international mobility. My approach is not exhaustive; rather I try to tell an interesting story of identity, place, movement, sovereignty, and world politics.

Examining Our Papers

To set the stage, here I give an overview of the passport as a document. All passports remain the property of the government and must be surrendered upon its request. The form of the passport is global: the cover bears the name and often the crest of the national government. On the inside cover is a request by the state's foreign representative (the secretary of state or similar officer) to other governments that the bearer be afforded protection.[4] The inside pages bear personal information about the bearer: name, photograph, date and place of birth, and usually the date of issue and expiration of the passport itself. Various security devices attempt to prevent tampering; these might include lamination, stamps, special tamper-proof paper, or holograms. There are also pages for visas and entry and exit stamps.

Though earlier versions of the passport existed, the modern passport has remained largely unchanged in form and function since its inception in the 1920s. First, the passport offers proof of identity and nationality, but it cannot guarantee admission into foreign countries. (The national country's visa regime regulates admission; in many countries, visa requirements include a passport and "proof of sufficient funds" for stay.) Second, the passport often states explicitly the limitations of the granting country's possible role in the intervention in another country's sovereignty. The doctrine of sovereignty in international law is based on two principles: All states are legally equal; and no state has the right to interfere in the domestic affairs of another state. The passport illustrates both principles. The request by the foreign representative that another sovereign protect and assist the passport bearer serves as an admission of equality and noninterference. Once in another sovereign territory—regardless of the passport one holds—the issuing country cannot protect or intervene authoritatively. Thus, the passport offers only two guarantees (both of which are limited): identification of the bearer, and the place of repatriation.

The passport also illustrates the relation between the individual and the state and thus connects the individual to international law through the sovereign state.[5] Acting alongside international law governing immigration, diplomacy, and refugees, the passport makes two significant promises. First, it promises other sovereign states that the individual is a safe and legitimate traveler—because she has a home to which she can be returned. Second, as the Canadian Passport Office argues, for example—the Canadian passport "enables Canadians to travel freely and safely."[6] Each of these promises needs to be further explained.

Diplomats, businesspersons, travelers, and refugees all move between states, but they do so with different types of passports. The differences are not merely functional but ascribe a distinct international status. Take Canada as an example: Diplomats and government officials are issued a special type of passport that is green and signifies immunity under international diplomatic law; businesspersons hold a blue passport with forty-eight pages; regular travelers carry a twenty-four-page blue passport (this accounts for 98 percent of all passport documents issued by Canada); and refugees carry passports that state the bearer's identity but not the place of repatriation. Thus, if traveling on a green Canadian passport, one may bypass foreign customs interrogations and enjoy diplomatic immunity. If traveling on a blue Canadian passport, one may travel for business or pleasure, but must obey foreign laws. If traveling on a Canadian refugee document, one may travel anywhere but not necessarily return to Canada.

How can governments be certain that bearers of national passports are safe and legitimate travelers? First, passports purport to truly identify the bearer according to bureaucratic and juridical apparatuses. With reference to previous government documents and the personal investigation of the issuing passport officer, the government ensures other sovereigns that the identity of the passport holder is accurate.[7] Second, governments reserve the right to refuse to issue a passport if the applicant has committed, has been charged with, or has been convicted of an indictable offense.[8] Thus, the passport is intended to serve as a sovereign's assurance to other members of international society that the citizen being endorsed is safe (see Chapter 4 on the development of the passport under the auspices of the League of Nations).[9] Passports also serve to legitimate the movement of individuals, as illegal migrants by definition usually travel without proper documentation. In sum, the passport is a signal between states regarding the character and safety of the bearer.

Once issued, the passport places no obligation on foreign sovereigns to protect the citizen-traveler.[10] In fact, the legal doctrine of sovereignty proscribes the degree to which sovereigns can interfere in other jurisdictions. States cannot prevent application of foreign laws to their nationals if those nationals are under foreign jurisdiction. The only exception is diplomatic protection, whereby a state uses its international legal personality on behalf of a national who cannot find satisfaction in a legal case against a foreign state.[11] Spies, terrorists, and other problem actors cannot claim the protection of a sovereign abroad.[12] Thus, even the limited assistance and good offices that the passport affords are beyond the reach of the naturalized citizen in the country of his birth, if he holds dual citizenship. It is a fundamental tenet of sovereign statehood that foreigners are subject to the laws of the country in which they are present.[13]

What is the security function of the passport? It does not certify that the individual is not a past criminal—only that he is not wanted for any current crime. It does not certify that the individual is a safe traveler with enough funds for her journey or repatriation. It does not guarantee any assistance from the traveler's own government in a foreign country. I argue that the security function of the passport is twofold: it helps the state to regulate the status of "national" and to regulate repatriation. Passports, of course, also provide a way for immigration and customs officials to abridge their examination at the national frontier; examination of the document replaces the examination of the individual and his belongings.

Daniel Turack argues that

> passports are not usually issued for international use, but rather for usage at the frontier of the issuing state and outside its borders; they are not meant to be issued for use as certificates of citizenship. In some states a passport is not only essential for foreign travel but it has a critical function in control over exit and has been utilized for the protection of a state's internal security.[14]

The discourse of international law focuses on three aspects of international movement: the sovereign right to refuse or to determine conditions of legitimate entry; the right of individuals to leave and reenter their country and to have a nationality; and the sovereign obligation to protect and/or accept refugees.[15] This tension between sovereign power and individual rights reflects larger issues in international ethics between national and cosmopolitan ethical frameworks. In other words, do we have an obligation to all people or solely to people from our own country?

Passports directly reflect the continuing dominance of the sovereign state in world politics. International treaties that aim to reduce statelessness reflect the general acceptance of this norm of sovereign citizenship.[16] In this context, passports can be seen as part of the larger discourse of sovereign statehood and the life-world of international relations that the state engenders. Movement is strictly determined as legitimate or illegitimate at the will of the sovereign state, and whether mobility is considered legitimate or illegitimate is based on documents issued by the sovereign state. The sovereign state thus derogates to travel documents some of its authority to legitimate the subject and to control his movements.

Not-so-Hidden Agendas

A great deal of scholarship analyzes the dynamics of gender and immigration law. Feminist scholars and activists have pointed to the discriminatory labeling of women as dependants. This gendered dynamic was egregious during the Uganda crisis, when British immigration officials and passport legislation did not recognize women as legitimate heads of households, which circumscribed their ability to apply for British passports.[17] There is also a deeper gendered relationship at work. As Cynthia Enloe argues, "In many societies being feminine has been defined as sticking close to home. Masculinity, by contrast, has been the passport for travel."[18]

The passport application process also stresses paternity. The concern in colonial discourse about miscegenation, or race-mixing, is represented in laws and regulations concerning paternity, inheritance, and citizenship.[19] On the application form for a British passport, there are several references to legitimate and illegitimate children and the status that is accorded or denied as a result. For example, the British passport application form reads: "'Father' does not for this purpose include the father of an illegitimate child." National belonging is policed by acknowledgment of the father, a clear echo of imperial and postimperial worries about racial integrity.

The body of the king as the ultimate source of determination of citizenship—who is and who is not a true child of the *patrie*—haunts contemporary passport technologies. To obtain a British passport, one's identity and good character must be certified by a member of the upper classes.[20] Canadian passports follow a similar model in certifying identity and physical likeness by having a professional sign an applicant's photograph. U.S. passport applications have no such class dynamic but stress the inquisition of the subject by the passport agent. That agent stands in as a member of a professional class. In each of these countries, the recommender certifies that the applicant's identity has been the same for a period of five years, that the photograph provided is a good likeness of the individual, and that the applicant is of good character.

* * *

Anxiety about travelers is a central component of national security discourse, especially in light of September 11. At the time of the attacks, I was at Heathrow Airport waiting to board my flight to Cairo. My plane was the last one to take off from Heathrow before all air traffic was grounded. We waited an extra forty-five minutes on the ground because a BBC news crew had decided not to fly and their equipment had to be unloaded. Many travelers had decided that they simply did not want to risk travel that day. The terrorist attacks on the United States that day are a striking example of the dangers inherent in the movement of people. Governments across the world are now taking extra precautions and putting in place new security measures to fix the problems of terrorism and leaky borders. An international history of the passport is especially relevant in light of these events.

Notes

1. Amitava Kumar, *Passport Photos* (Berkeley: University of California Press, 2000), p. 20.
2. Benedict Anderson, "Exodus," *Critical Inquiry* 20 (Winter 1994): p. 323.
3. Paul Virilio, "The State of Emergency," in *The Virilio Reader*, edited by James Der Derian (Oxford, UK: Blackwell, 1998), p. 47.
4. P. Weis, *Nationality and Statelessness in International Law* (Germantown, MA: Sijthoff and Noordhoff, 1979), p. 225. Weis claims that "the passports of most other countries [other than the United States and the United Kingdom] do not contain such a request." However, this has become general practice since his contention was made.
5. United Nations, Department of Economic and Social Affairs, Population Division, "International Migration Policies" (New York: United Nations, 1998 (ST/ESA/Ser.A/161), p. 27.
6. Canadian Passport Office, "Business Plan, 1993–94" (Canada: Department of Foreign Affairs and International Trade, 1993), p. 2.
7. John M. Davis, "Passport Fraud: Protecting U.S. Passport Integrity," *FBI Law Enforcement Bulletin* 67 (July 1998): 9–13.
8. See Canadian Passport Order (SI/81–86), sections 9b and 10b, in *Canada Gazette* part 2, vol. 115, no. 12 (Ottawa: Queen's Printers, 1981), pp. 1852–1857. Also see the court decision *Vithiyababthan v. Attorney General of Canada* (available online at http://www.fja.gc.ca/en/cf/2000/orig/html/2000fca26262.o.en.html, accessed July 19, 2000); and United Nations, "International Migration Policies," p. 34.
9. As an aside, many nations, following Britain and Canada's lead, also restrict exit to those divorced parents who share custody of a child or are the providers of child support. Australian law in the 1960s and 1970s required a husband to prove his wife's permission for his passport application to protect women from being abandoned unknowingly. Robert S. Lancy, "The Evolution of Australian Passport Law," *Melbourne University Law Review* 13 (June 1982): 442. In these cases, the restriction of passports seeks the protection of a country's own citizens.

10. Stephen Smith, "Always Alone with a British Passport: Britons in Cuba Suspected of Being Spies," *New Statesman* (November 6, 2000): 31–32.

11. Weis, *Nationality and Statelessness,* pp. 226–227.

12. The passports of British naturalized citizens contain a special warning: "The general good offices and assistance of His Majesty's Representatives abroad cannot be extended to the holder when within the limits of the foreign state of which he was a subject or citizen prior to his naturalization unless he has ceased to be a subject or citizen of that state." Consular Instructions, 1921, p. 12 (FO 612 265).

13. Daniel C. Turack, *The Passport in International Law* (Toronto: Lexington Books, 1972), pp. 3–4.

14. Ibid., p. 19.

15. See Hurst Hannum, *The Right to Leave and Return in International Law and Practice* (Boston: Martinus Nijhoff Publishers, 1987); Clive Parry, ed., *A British Digest of International Law, Part 6: The Individual in International Law* (London: Stevens and Sons, 1965); Louis B. Sohn and Thomas Buergenthal, eds., *The Movement of Persons Across Borders* (Washington, DC: American Society of International Law, 1992).

16. United Nations, "International Migration Policies," pp. 40–41.

17. Robert Moore and Tina Wallace, *Slamming the Door: The Administration of Immigration Control* (London: Martin Robertson, 1975), pp. 47–51.

18. Cynthia Enloe, *Bananas, Beaches, and Bases: Making Feminist Sense of International Politics* (Berkeley: University of California Press, 1990), p. 21.

19. Ann Laura Stoler, *Race and the Education of Desire: Foucault's History of Sexuality and the Colonial Order of Things* (Durham, NC: Duke University Press, 1995), p. 67.

20. That is, by "a British citizen, or other Commonwealth citizen, who has known you personally for at least two years and who is a Member of Parliament, Justice of the Peace, Minister of Religion, Bank Officer, Established Civil Servant, professionally qualified person, e.g. Lawyer, Engineer, Doctor, School Teacher, Police Office or a person of similar standing." Notes for Form C1.

2

Passports, Violence, and International Society

> *A passport can be compared to an issue of Army equipment which the recipient uses but which is not his property, and which he is bound to return eventually.*
> —"New Caution on Passports: Liberal Peer's Anxiety," *Manchester Guardian*, 26 October 1955

The history of the state can be seen as a gradual taming of violence, from unpredictable, chaotic violence to regularized, orderly security. The control of people and territory is a vital part of this story. The current organization of the world requires the division of global space into discrete entities—states—that have distinct territories, populations, and authority. This politico-territorial order came into being in a process of political revolutions and slow bureaucratic accretion. One can point to other times in history, most notably the Middle Ages, in which the politico-territorial order was markedly different. During the Middle Ages, authority was not linked to specific territories but rather across spaces, classes, and functions. A guild might structure one's wage and work; the church might structure one's education and salvation; the feudal lord might structure one's land and local police; and the king might structure the general laws of the land. The emergence of the Westphalian state (named for the Peace of Westphalia in 1648), which prohibited rulers from interfering in the religion of other states, marks the ascendance of the sovereign in this competition for authority and legitimacy. A primary way that the sovereign "won" this battle for a state was by generating a monopoly on the legitimate means of violence. The control of movement in the Middle Ages marks the beginning of the sovereign state as an international actor—and of the formulation of the state as a safe domestic space and the outside as a dangerous international space.

Making war outside the state and making peace inside the state are major functions of the sovereign state, and the passport plays a crucial role in both. However, the sovereign state cannot act independently: a stable state requires an international system that recognizes the principles of noninterference and equality. In this chapter, I examine the passport as evidence of sovereign power and as a documentary attempt to project the power of the sovereign state toward other states. I also consider how the passport came to represent a guarantee of security, as well as the problems with that representation.

Ne Exeat Regno

The doctrine of *ne exeat regno* is interpreted in English common law to mean that no subject may leave the territory of the king without his specific permission. Rulers in the late Middle Ages and early modern period were often in competition with other forms of authority: ecclesiastical, local, and mercantile. A successful strategy for the concentration of power and legitimacy was to formalize relations of violence within the state. In competition with nobles and criminals whose violence was unexpected, the ruler might develop methods for implementing violence in regular ways and delegitimating other kinds of violence. This Weberian account of the state as the monopolizer of legitimate violence relies upon a bifurcation of space: safe domestic space, and unsafe international space. The only way that the burden of domestic violence is acceptable is if the alternative is worse (i.e., that the international realm is violence unmitigated by any sense of identity and/or stewardship). Medieval and early modern Europe were characterized by a space of overlapping and interconnecting authority structures.[1] Europe was a patchwork of territories and authorities: borders were hazy, unclear, and disputed. Boundaries reflected the limit of actual physical control rather than a juridical limit.

In administrative terms, then, a frontier was not territorial but instead described the limits of a jurisdiction (whether noble, ecclesiastical, or municipal). Even then, the overlap of different jurisdictions made it impossible to arrive at geographic precision in peace treaties. However, frontiers did not necessarily mean there were differences in politics and culture among independent political units.[2]

Therefore, the state evolved as a unit within a system of other states—the boundary of one state was the boundary of the adjacent state. Sovereigns defined their territory as the limit of their practicable or actionable authority.

The legal foundation for controlling the movement of populations is the right of the king to determine who may enter and leave his personal territory. Because the "principal duty" of a subject is to be "at the service of his king and country," being absent from the kingdom without leave of the sovereign was illegal.[3] The Magna Carta of 1215 represented the first general exception to this principle, allowing merchants to leave the country without specific leave.[4] N. W. Sibley argues that this indicates the presence of a previously existing common law rule that specific leave *was* necessary.[5] Merchants were the first exceptions to the requirement that all subjects obtain permission from the king to leave his domain. At the same time, permits were being issued in France and the Iberian Peninsula with more pecuniary intent.

The "safe-conduct instrument" (*sauf-conduit,* or *guidaticum*) was used to consolidate the ruler's monopoly of mobility and violence within a state's territory. It was the precursor to the passport.[6] The safe-conduct pass was a "letter of [patent] that included the name of the bearer and the purpose of his mission" and asked that the bearer not be hindered in his journey, often threatening punitive action if the safe-conduct pass was not provided.[7] Sovereigns used this instrument for two purposes: to protect envoys, and to create revenue. Before modern telecommunications and travel, a robust international society required a secure way to conduct diplomacy. Some of the earliest international treaties reflected the necessity of diplomacy and the safety of diplomats through diplomatic papers and safe-conducts. However, such protection was likely available only to high-ranking officials. Before extending protection to all citizens, the king exchanged surplus capital for coercion. By using safe-conducts, travelers were protected by the authority of the king and were not solely responsible for their own personal safety. This generalization of security—from self-protection to sovereign protection—led many to accept the idea that the king was the guarantor of safe movement and territory.

Safe-conducts protected merchants and deterred thieves. The safe-conduct pass is a clear example of the dual functions of the sovereign, assuring the security of his subjects within the national space through diplomacy and by exchanging wealth for protection. It came into use during the thirteenth century in Europe, in part because of the development of distinct territorial boundaries. As John Ruggie argues, "The notion of firm boundary lines between the major territorial formations did not take hold until the thirteenth century; prior to that date, there were only 'frontiers,' or large zones of transition."[8] By the sixteenth century, both territorial boundaries and the form and content of safe-conducts had been regularized and were similar throughout Europe.[9]

Janet Abu-Laghod describes how safe-conduct passes were central to the development of the Champagne market fairs. An essential part of the thirteenth-century world economy was the connection of northern European to Mediterranean economies. The safe-conduct pass, available for purchase by merchants from the ruler, guaranteed that any interference with the bearer would result in the wrath of the ruler. She illustrates one of the earliest usages of the safe-conduct pass: "The Counts of Champagne accorded to the merchants attending the fairs very active protection of their persons, their men and their goods. This protection began the day they set out for the fair."[10] The nobles used their existing military might to protect merchants traveling to the fair. Once the merchants made it there, the nobles extracted taxes, which were in turn used to pay for market police and for courts that ensured minimal order and the enforcement of contracts. In this instance, we see nobles indirectly exchanging coercion (safe-conducts and market police) for capital (levies, taxes, and market tariffs). The guarantee of safety while traveling to the fairs facilitated regular long-distance trade, which was a vital component of what J. M. Blaut refers to as "protocapitalism."[11] The decline of the fairs in the late thirteenth century was largely a result of the conflict between the nobles and the Capetian king, which disrupted the safe-conduct regime.[12] In effect, would-be kings made a bargain with the merchants and towns directly to exchange regular taxation for protection.[13] To make the nobles' promise unappealing to merchants, the kings disrupted the nobles' safe-conducts. The bargain of a centrally administered state taxation and policing system seemed more appealing. Thus, in this very early example, we see competition between two groups (nobles and kings) to guarantee safe movement, which enabled the protocapitalist system that funds the machinery of surplus extraction that is necessary to build the administrative structure of a sovereign state.[14] I do not want to argue that control of movement is a sufficient precondition of statehood, but it is certainly true that control of movement was a necessary precursor of the sovereign state.

However, governmental entrepreneurs used the safe-conduct pass for multiple ends, which were not entirely protocapitalist. Robert Burns describes how the safe-conduct pass (or *guidaticum*) became a tool of King Jaume in Arago-Catalonia in the early thirteenth century.

> The crown *guidaticum* might seem of limited application during normal times, but ingenuity and necessity soon multiplied them into a routine product of the king's chancery, to the profit of his treasury and the peace of his realms. The king gave such charters to high and low, men and women, Muslims and Jews.[15]

They had three functions: to extract capital from merchants and travelers; to foster the creation of new market towns; and to expand the realms into which the king might exercise sovereign authority. Importantly, *guidaticums* were issued to subjects and foreigners alike and bore no relationship to protocitizenship or nationality. For example, King Juame

> used them to protect commerce and foreigners, to lure settlers to the frontier, to facilitate the acceptance of criminals he had pardoned, to establish a market or fair, to reserve cases to his personal court, to serve an injunction so as to guarantee orderly judicial process, to protect debtors or the credit system, and to restore public order.[16]

The *guidaticum* served as a bureaucratic stand-in for actual physical force and, if obeyed, represented the vanguard of the sovereign's authority. Thus, King Juame used the *guidaticum* to generalize his sovereign presence even in his physical absence. The threat of force was associated not only with the peace of his realm but also in the smooth functioning of his economy and the administration of his justice.

Looking back on the safe-conduct system, it appears to indicate that the state had not yet gained its monopoly of violence within its borders. But the safe-conduct system also aimed to convince a king's subjects that the international or nonnational was more dangerous than the national. The sovereign protection racket was an acceptable exchange for king, merchants, and subjects.[17] The king monopolized not only the use of violence but also the threat of violence. The safe-conduct system also indicates the general perception of the amount of danger in the world and the potency of the king. It is interesting that a simple letter might act as a deterrent to subjects and foreigners alike.

Emmerich de Vattel, a prominent eighteenth-century international lawyer, distinguished the passport and the safe-conduct pass on the basis of the benign bearer who is not predicted to come to danger and the bearer who may likely come to danger.[18] The passport system can be seen as the extension of the safe-conduct system, a documentary tool that indicates the sovereign's reign and legitimizes the domestication of national space through a state monopoly of violence. (In the eighteenth century, a special *militärpass* was issued to "citizens capable of military service, in order to prevent desertion and enrolment in foreign armies."[19]) Military papers operate within the same logic. Military commissions confer on soldiers the sovereign authority to be legitimately violent.[20] Violence in the service of the king, or the king's economy, was authorized through the issuance of state documents. This notion of the passport, the state, and the international system is predicated on the notion of violence—either in its inevitability, as punishment for breaking the civil peace, or as a deterrent.

Privateers, Princes, and Letters of Marque

The distinction between legitimate and illegitimate violence is the foundation of the polis. A primary function of the state is to reduce violence within domestic territory. However, sovereigns were often not capable of deterring, or were unwilling to deter, violence in the international realm—defined in international law as the distance of a cannon shot from shore. An early realist, Georg Schwarzenberger, describes the heart of medieval international law as comprising three principles:

1. In the absence of an agreed state of truce or peace, war was the basic state of international relations even between independent Christian communities,
2. Unless exceptions were made by means of individual safe conduct or treaty, rulers saw themselves entitled to treat foreigners at their absolute discretion,
3. The high seas were no-man's-land, where anyone might do as they please.[21]

In addition to the lurking danger of the unknown, there existed the known danger of pirates and privateers who were a constant threat in the early modern period through the seventeenth and eighteenth centuries. In early modern Europe, the sovereign made domestic space safe by appropriating the legitimate uses of violence and international space violent and unsafe by commissioning privateers. The sovereign made market fairs safe for foreign traders by promising safe passage but could not make international trade safe on the high seas or in territories beyond the seas. Here I focus on letters of marque and the practice of privateering, which can be viewed as a kind of mirror of the safe-conduct pass. Although the safe-conduct pass promised a violence-free voyage for a fee, the letter of marque promised a voyage that *sanctioned* violence for a fee.

Letters of marque are decrees from sovereigns that legitimize attacks by privateers on enemies of the issuer (and for which the sovereign charges a percentage of the plunder). These letters were the inverse of safe-conducts: the sovereign authorized private violence (against his enemies), but only in the international realm (three miles from shore). Letters of marque were first issued by the English king in 1295, during the same time period as safe-conducts.[22] As with safe-conducts, letters of marque can be seen as part of the consolidation of the state as safe domestic space and the construction of international space as dangerous and violent. However, there is a pragmatic difficulty in distinguishing between pirates and privateers, the difference being the possession of a letter of marque. As Barbara Fuchs argues, "The trajectory from privateer to pirate is somewhat of a state fantasy in the first place—the pirates are always already there, before the state uses them and also once it no longer has any use for them."[23] Consequently, it was the document of the letter of marque that distinguished, legally if not actually, the difference between pirate and privateer.[24]

Jens Bartelson claims that piracy and privateering represent critical cases for "protosovereignty," by which he describes the transformation of ecclesiastical-based notions of sovereignty to "the polity-centred paradigm of rulership in the late Middle Ages."[25] Because piracy originates from nonsovereign territory (i.e., the sea), it is a threat that cannot be countered by the practice of sovereign protection of domestic territory. As Fuchs argues, "The pervasiveness of piracy fundamentally challenged state sovereignty at the margins, both on the coasts of England and in those territories, such as Ireland, even more tenuously under its control."[26] As piracy was outside of the territory of the state, likewise pirates were outside the authority of any sovereign and thus were nonsubjects. Pirates were described as being "of no nation or state . . . an outcast from the society of nations."[27] In fact, pirates were considered outside of the human community. As Hugo Grotius puts it: "A pirate is not entitled to the rights of war, but is the common enemy of mankind, with whom neither good faith nor a common oath should be kept."[28] And as Joel Baer explains, "A pirate was thought to be beyond the pale of civilized society and hence the lawful prey of any who could destroy him by foul means or fair."[29] Because the sea is outside any sovereign control, piracy is *outside the outside*. However, sovereigns needed to be perceived as controlling the problem of piracy as part of their larger roles (bringing order and limiting violent threats to the populace). Thus, sovereigns in Europe established laws and regimes creating an international legal structure that granted certain violent international actors legitimacy and made all other violent actors illegitimate. Ethan Nadelmann argues that "the regime against piracy represented the first global prohibition regime," although it did not fully mature until the nineteenth century.[30]

The connection of letters of marque to passports becomes clearer if we look at events in the seventeenth century. Sibley traces the "first occurrence of the term 'passport' in a treaty . . . to be the treaty between Great Britain and Demark, July 11, 1670."[31] This treaty cited the passport as proof of nationality. Throughout the seventeenth and eighteenth centuries, a ship, its crew, and its flag were likely of different nationalities, making discovering national status by examination of persons alone problematic.[32] The nationality of a ship was authenticated by a passport, also known as a sea brief and *certificat de nationalité*.[33] This documentation determined which rules of war applied to ship, cargo, and crew: it held a different legal personality (which itself carried dramatically different consequences) depending on whether it was a pirate, privateer, or envoy of a sovereign. The passport determined whether the ship could be the rightful victim of privateering, a rightful privateer, or a neutral vessel.

Thus it was legally and morally acceptable to sponsor nonnational violent international actors; previous to the nineteenth century, pirates and privateering had been legitimated—at least nominally—by the dominant powers. As Janice Thomson argues, "there is simply no question that piracy was a legitimate practice in the early European state system."³⁴ Over the course of the eighteenth century, sovereigns actively discouraged pirates and courted privateers. In this delimitation between legitimate and illegitimate actors, we see a nationalization of international space as sovereigns consolidated their authority as the sole legitimate arbiters of violence in the international system. This legitimation was accomplished by introducing antipiracy legislation and reducing the issuance of letters of marque to privateers. The U.S. and British governments offered pardons to pirates in the first decades of the eighteenth century and finally made all contact with pirates punishable by death.³⁵ In ceasing to subcontract violence, the official agents of the sovereign came to be the only legitimate users of violence in international society. By the eighteenth century, pirates were found "as distant as possible from the powers of the state."³⁶ Privateering had been not been used after the Napoleonic Wars, and the 1856 Declaration of Paris made privateering completely illegal.³⁷ Thomson summarizes: "Because it proved impractical to enforce a distinction between legitimate and illegitimate nonstate violence, states eliminated it altogether, abandoning the practice of exploiting nonstate violence."³⁸

The active use of private violence by states reflects the incomplete monopoly of violence. However, just as the territorial limits of the state are transcended by travelers, the efficacious limits of the state were demonstrated by the inability of states to control piracy. The presence of pirates and private violent actors, who were increasingly incorporated into the spatial geopolitics of states, was domesticated by the authorization by the sovereign to act on his/her behalf. The point of this example is to show how the geopolitics of the sea complicated the traditional narrative of safe domestic spaces and anarchical international spaces. Precisely, the extension of state mechanisms such as the *certificat de nationalité*, letters of marque, and sea briefs helped consolidate the role of the state in international waters, extending domestic authority into international law.³⁹ By the nineteenth century, international space within Europe was considered so safe that passports might even be dispensed with. The exchange between sovereign and subject was understood, the space of Europe domesticated. One may trace two commonly held notions of non-European space in the eighteenth century: it was a violent realm and a risky but potentially lucrative market. The task of the imperial sovereign was to make the risks acceptable and the profit accessible. The rise of national economies at the end of the eighteenth century, and the writings of Friedrich List, John Locke, Thomas Malthus, Jean-Jacques Rousseau, and others, indicated that expansion was seen as a necessary state activity. The passport and its precursors, the safe-conduct pass and sea certificate, were the leading edge of sovereign authority. The evolution of the early passport regime reflects the consolidation of the sovereign state itself. The passport marked the safety of the domestic territory as well as the equality of sovereigns. Crucially, the passport in the guise of letters of marque served to extend national personality into the international realm. In each of these cases, the passport did not guarantee security but constructed a particular politico-territorial order in which security was limited to the sovereign state. Because the colonies of the Great Powers also represented a complication of the domestic-international divide, I want to consider again violence and passports in the colonial scene.

Colonial Space and Passports

A primary argument of this book is that there are currently two worlds of travel—a zone in which travel is easy and requires few documents, and a zone in which travel is difficult and requires a great number of documents. International society during the nineteenth century was a precursor to this system, as travel within the colonies was more difficult and tightly regulated than travel within Europe. Another argument is that the passport plays a limited role in identifying individuals. The use of the passport as an identity document internally suggests two aspects of imperial discourse that are relevant to international relations. First, the colonial government was attempting to incorporate the colonized not as subjects but as objects of governance while marking them as different and dangerous. Second, the colonial government treated colonies as somewhere between safe national spaces and unsafe international spaces. Colonial commerce was not unlike privateering. Chartered companies, such as the East India Company and the Dutch East Indies Company, extracted resources and labor from the colonies using violence authorized by the Dutch or British Crown. As the sovereign state expanded to administer the colonies, the colonial space became similar to early modern Europe, in which the colonial government guaranteed the safety of traders and subjects.

Colonial governments used a variety of instruments to figure, map, and coordinate subject populations. The census, maps, anthropology, education, and urban planning were all used to extend control over the colonists' material life, spiritual life, sense of self, and political freedom. The passport was a primary document of movement control that figured the colonized in terms of race, class, gender, and complicity with the colonial project. Colonial subjects were also severely restricted in moving about their own country and the empire. Simply suggesting that colonized subjects required passports implied that they were dangerous—a theme that is repeated in the later history of the passport.

The colonial landscape complicates the traditional notion of state-centric geopolitics. Colonial territory represents a space that is the object of a continuous and always incomplete process of domestication. That space is neither the safety of the home counties nor the absolute anarchy of the high seas. Lord Dufferin, charged with reforming Egypt after the British took control in 1882, argued that his task was "to rescue the people from anarchy."[40] In effect, colonized space, though it constituted nearly 80 percent of the globe, functioned as a liminal space for Europeans. Colonial space was the space in-between. This in-betweenness justified violence, which lies at the heart of the tension of imperial discourse. The "civilizing mission" justified imperialism on the grounds that it improved the conditions of colonial subjects by reducing "savagery" and "barbarism." This domestication of colonial space would bring the benefit of European state-builders in pacifying the colony. However, to achieve that aim, violence was necessary. Specifically, colonial powers used violence to maintain colonial rule that would eliminate all other kinds of violence. This system can thus be understood as the *colonial economy of violence*.

The international result of this colonial economy of violence was the delegitimation of nonstate violence within the European state, the legitimation of interstate violence in the international scene, and the legitimation of violent rule in the colonial scene. Gerrit Gong describes how colonial ideology was embedded in the legal structure of international society. Precisely, there were three sets of international legal norms: those that applied between civilized states; those between civilized and barbaric states, where a non-Christian government existed; and those between civilized and savage states, where no competent government existed.[41] This trifurcated system of international laws was a reflection of colonial ideology. This construction of safe European space, dangerous international space, and insecure colonial space was also reflected in the mobility regimes of the time.[42]

There were three kinds of voluntary travelers during the nineteenth century at the height of European colonial rule: government agents, commercial agents, and tourists.[43] In the case of government agents (whether governors, bureaucrats, or soldiers), letters from the government describing their appointment to a particular position served as their passport. Commercial agents often carried a similar letter from company headquarters. However, tourists (unofficial non-state travelers) posed a problem. Europeans traveling in the colonial world were granted single-use passports to travel from one territory to another. In the nineteenth century, for the most part, such letters were written in French and were granted on the personal recognizance of the traveler to a consular official. The issuance of passports based on personal connections was a reflection of the class stature of many travelers before the late nineteenth century. These passports detail only the name of the person to whom the passport was issued, the date, the intended destination, and by whom the bearer was recommended.[44] The safety and security of the bearer were assured, or at least improved, by the special legal standing that Europeans enjoyed in many colonies. Europeans, rather than being subject to the laws of the Ottoman Empire (to use a famous example), were subject to European laws, European courts, and lighter sentences for like crimes.[45] It was the military and economic might of the colonial powers that stood behind every lone traveler. With the possibility of mass tourism opened by entrepreneurs such as Thomas Cook, greater numbers of international travelers required more travel documents. By the 1920s, the British Passport Office had a specific department solely assigned to issue the passports for Thomas Cook travelers.[46]

A pressing problem for colonial officials was not just the mobility and safety of the few adventurers or those under the care of Cook but rather the mobility and security of the many colonial subjects over whom they held a tenuous rule. The ways in which European governments attempted to control the liminal space of the colony lends a very interesting perspective to this history of the passport.

In Egypt, the British controlled a large portion of the rural population through documents. The British regime was an extension of the regime put in place by Mohammed Ali. Officials at the provincial, district, canton, and village levels were each required to assure that any movement by peasants (*fellahin*) was tightly monitored and controlled. The colonial government was not competing with local nobles, as in early modern Europe. Consequently, the shaikhs (i.e., the nobles) were in collusion with the British to control the movements of the peasants. As Helen Rivlin describes, a peasant "could leave his land only after [having] received the consent of his *shaykh* and after having obtained an identity card (*tadhkirah*)."[47] This control of the population was made necessary by the feudal system of landownership and the economic conditions under which the *fellahin* lived. The British faced unstable rule, wary of anticolonial revolts. The economic logic of imperialism required the mobilization of the vast stores of labor that the colonies promised. Under Mohammed Ali's feudal system, *fellahin* were required to serve their feudal lord. The corvée (unpaid labor) is a remnant of the feudal system in which peasants were required to give up some amount of labor to their lord each year for maintenance of his property. Demand for labor for the construction of the Suez Canal required large movements of unskilled laborers, controlled in part by local police.[48] The British continued the system of corvée and used it to make use of colonial labor availability. As the corvée system was phased out, it was replaced by a system of coolie labor. Mobility within British Egypt was controlled by a system of passes, issued by a police force concerned with the threat of revolution, escape, and insecurity. This system was a necessary part of the regime that "confined [villagers] to their native districts, and required them to seek a permit and papers of identification if they wished to travel outside."[49] As with other mobility regimes, the British regime controlled the rural poor far more carefully than it did the urban rich.

Another important aspect was movement between colonies. Historians suggest that trade *within* the empire was greater than trade between the empire and Great Britain. A vital feature of this interaction was the forced relocation of labor among the British colonies. This movement was for two main reasons: labor and government. Although the British government was the driving force behind the abolition of slavery over the course of the nineteenth century, the British were also responsible for a great deal of forced migration. English-speaking South Asians were brought to Africa to act as the "translator class" between the British rulers and the colonial population. However, as

Radhika Mongia relates, Indians were not allowed in Canada. She shows that the Canadian government's restrictions on Indian immigration occurred through secondary characteristics of race rather than through appeal to race directly.[50] When the attempted control of passports did not function to exclude Indians, the British imperial government implemented other forms of restrictions, such as literacy tests.[51] In other cases, Indians and Chinese were used throughout Southeast Asia as coolie labor.[52] However, the use of colonial subjects as laborers or translators in other colonies did not disrupt the racial hierarchy on which British nationality was partially constructed.

In using identification documents and transit passes, the imperial sovereign extended familiar governmental strategies, such as the passport that was already in use along their borders, to the liminal borderlands of colonial space. The use of passports was an integral part of colonial ideology, especially the marking of peoples as racial, national, and governmental subjects. The colonial government conscripted colonial subjects to increase wealth through the colonial market and to protect the state through war. In sum, there were four basic assumptions about travel in the nineteenth century: Travel within Europe was made safe through the implicit bargain between sovereign and subject; movement for the purposes of trade outside of Europe was dangerous; travel by non-Europeans was dangerous and required a great deal of governmental control; and travel within or among the colonies carried the inherent risk of violence. The passport did not act as a guarantor of security of the space but rather described the space as safe or dangerous. Passports within European space illustrated the safety of sovereign protection; passports outside European space illustrated the danger to the traveler venturing beyond sovereign protection. This division between safe and dangerous spaces was reflected inside Europe with World War I.

Description, Depiction, and Conscription

Conscription—the mobilization of all able citizen-subjects for war— was possible only with the development of a significant bureaucracy and policing system.[53] The enumeration, classification, and consequent mustering of citizens as troops was an invention of the French Revolution. Michel Foucault articulates the ways in which the French government attempted to mobilize all citizens for labor or war through methods of institutional control. In particular, Foucault highlights the notion of discipline in a variety of institutions, including the army, the school, the prison, and the hospital. And whereas Foucault concentrates on the architecture of power, and the power of architecture, John Torpey examines the ways that the French revolutionary regime used passports to control the "national" and "nationalist" populations, illustrating the full history of the passport within the French revolutionary period. I wish to highlight two interesting points from his analysis.

First, early in 1791 the revolutionary regime declared that all foreigners and merchants who departed France would require a passport issued from their own ambassador or the French foreign ministry.[54] The fact that passports were available from either national or foreign authorities illustrates how the identity that the passport certified was tied more to any government rather than to a specific or national identity. Second, the revolutionary regime used passport laws to police more assiduously those who were ideologically unreliable or marginal in society.[55] Although the French Revolution allowed greater mobility for some citizens, the policing of the population came to be figured in terms of revolutionary ideological terms rather than class alone. As Torpey states, "The term 'foreigners' therefore applied as much to those who opposed the revolution, regardless of their 'national' origins, as it did to persons not of French birth."[56] Passports were used in this context to define those who were foreign to the nation, either through birth or allegiance.

In August 1793, the republic decreed that "until the moment 'when enemies have been driven from the Republic's territory, all Frenchmen are permanently requisitioned for the service of the armies.'"[57] The recompense for permanent and complete mobilization was citizenship, an alien concept among the lower classes. As with the general control of the population during the revolution itself, the organization of some 1.1 million soldiers required a great bureaucracy that connected the issuance of passports for the purpose of military maneuvers and had the effect of linking passports to war and to citizenship.[58]

Borders were free and largely unregulated in the mid– to late nineteenth century. After the defeat of Napoleon and the reemergence of conservativism in Europe, passports became generally obsolete for the European elite, who self-identified primarily with being European and civilized rather than national and parochial. Once the dangers of the revolution and the masses were quelled, then Europe could be seen as a civilized sphere that rarely required passports.[59] British subjects on their grand tours viewed any documentary requirements as a source of bother and graft. Passports, which were often single-use letters from a member of the diplomatic corps, could be acquired in one country for crossing one border; other passports could be obtained from the next country, and so on. This disappearance of the passport will be studied in Chapter 5.

The period 1914–1919 was the prehistory of the modern passport, dominated by the military and economic consequences of World War I. The eruption of large-scale warfare on the European continent meant that European space was no longer safe. Europe was a violent, dangerous space, and states moved to control the movement of persons again. The British passport was adopted at the conference of the League of Nations in 1922 (see Chapter 3). Here I wish to look at the development of the British passport during the period 1914–1919.[60] Before World War I, British passports were single sheets and had been written in English and French since the nineteenth century; they asked that the bearer be given support at the request of the bearer's sovereign for a particular journey.[61] They were issued infrequently, often only to individuals known personally to the secretary of state for foreign affairs, senior members of government, or travelers in the colonies known to the consular staff.[62] Passports were issued for a single journey and could be issued only from British soil.[63] Identity in these nineteenth-century passports was certified by personal knowledge of a member of the upper classes.[64] Although military officers are not mentioned as official recommenders, in practice they were accepted by the passport office, often because they belonged to the upper classes by default. The extension of the bureaucratic state, as well as the issuance of birth certificates, were integrated into this system of verification, and by 1921 a birth certificate was required for all passports. However, at the start of the war, we see a wider issuance of military passes and passports. The military passes had no official name or authority and were called "travel permits" issued on behalf of the War Office.[65] Other passes, issued to aliens, have a murky past. E. R. Cowley, an immigration archivist, states, "I have been completely unable to establish definitely the circumstances in which Certificates of Identity for Aliens first came to be issued by [the] Immigration Branch, and I am fairly satisfied that any records which would have provided the answer have either been destroyed or mislaid."[66]

Most probably, the origins of the military pass were for aliens and military personnel traveling to the outlying islands of Wight and Man, and later for all military personnel going abroad.[67] Over the course of World War I, these passes were regularized into travel permits and finally adopted by the Immigration Branch of the Home Office. This possible origin of the pass marks the internal face of documents of identity, as well as the blurring of the distinction between internal travel among the British islands and international travel between England and France. Travel permits were a pragmatic solution to the new problem of movement, wherein governments could not assume that travelers were innocuous (even tourists were perceived as potential spies or refugees). As the Axis powers attempted to expand in Europe during the interwar years, the British government tried the same colonial methods of control of movement.

British passports were issued (as they are today) to the general public by the Passport Office, which is part of the Foreign Office. Form A (the general passport application form) changed over the course of World War I. In 1915, the passport was issued in most cases for a single journey only. As photography was not yet an entirely trusted technology, a physical description was required in addition to the photograph. Applicants described their age, profession, height, forehead, eyes (meaning color), nose, mouth, chin, color of hair, complexion, and face. Of the passport applications kept on file in the Public Records Office for 1916, there remains little variation in the self-descriptions.[68] Noses were "normal," "ordinary," or "large." Foreheads were "normal," "ordinary," or "high." Mouths were "normal" or "straight." Complexions were "normal" or "fresh." Setting aside two self-described aristocrats with Romanesque foreheads, aquiline noses, and "intelligent" faces, the descriptors are remarkably uniform.[69] The sole variation were five British subjects coming from Malta who were described as "dark." By mid-1915, photographs started to be attached but with no uniformity. By 1916, Form A was revised and photographs were required, with an endorsement by the recommender. Paul Fussell argues for the importance of the passport photo: "so small a phenomenon as the passport picture is an example of something tiny which has powerfully affected the modern sensibility, assisting that anxious self-awareness . . . the passport picture is perhaps the most egregious little modernism."[70]

The physical descriptions and photographs cannot by themselves verify nationality or loyalty. Visually, there is little immediate difference between the stereotypical German and Briton. The description itself could not verify the race, nationality, or safety of the traveler. The form itself, and the identity with the form, fixed the citizen's identity, and thus the form became the object of examination. With the widespread use of a similar passport format, the examination at the border came to be centered on whether *documents*—rather than the traveler herself— were in order. This trend continues today and represents a fundamental limitation of the passport system. Regardless of whether a passport is correct or fraudulent, it cannot guarantee the intentions of the traveler.

One way that early passport regulations attempted to gauge the intentions of the traveler was by requiring that the passport be endorsed by a member of the upper classes. The recommender certified that the applicant was known to him and was of good character. And though the class of the recommender was verified by reference to "Who's Who" guides, there was no attempt by the Passport Office to verify the recommender's recommendation.[71]

Applicants described the destination and purpose of their visit. Between 1914 and 1915, there was an examination of the potential destination of the traveler. Prior to 1914, applicants were required to state the purpose and destination of their visit and were issued passports valid for that particular journey. By December 1916, a similar question was answered, but the authorization of the passport had changed. Rather than authorizing a single destination, the passport was valid for "all countries except the zone of the armies."[72] The military was solely responsible for the control of movement inside the zone of the armies, whereas the Passport Office was responsible for controlling all movement outside the zone of the armies. Providing documentation to spies also indicated that some of the anxiety that prompted the widespread installation of the passport regime was well-founded. On December 22, 1916, we see the first issuance of a passport in a recognizable form: a folded sheet of cardboard, not paper, that included the coat of arms of the country, a photograph of the bearer, and an official standardized message from the secretary of state for foreign affairs.

The Passport Office provided a governmental solution to the broader problems of nationality and belonging. In the United Kingdom, the issuance of a passport is seen as an extension of the royal prerogative, delegated to the secretary of state for foreign affairs.[73] The British passport and Passport Office have no statutory foundation. British citizens have no right to a passport, yet a passport cannot be denied them. A British citizen cannot be required to show a passport precisely as proof of citizenship. The passport is simply the most convenient mechanism to do so. Furthermore, without a passport, the citizen has to prove to an immigration official that he/she is a citizen. Even though a passport is not necessary for either entry or exit in the United Kingdom, it remains the easiest way to access the bureaucracy of legitimate entry and identification. Thus, the functional or pragmatic rationale for the passport is to ease travel for British citizens; the government's rationale is to regulate and patrol nationality. This identification was certified in the late nineteenth century by the secretary of state or consul himself and in the early twentieth century through affirmation of identity and "character" by a member of the upper classes (a lawyer, doctor, minister, bank manager, Member of Parliament, etc.).

However, after World War I, when travel was encouraged to help redevelop and integrate the European economies, identity was certified through concordance with *other* governmental documents, such as a birth certificate or national identity card. This odd state of affairs stemmed from the common law origins of the passport. The right to issue a passport was derived from the common law right of the king to determine who may leave his realm (*ne exeat regno*), which was conferred to his secretary of state for foreign affairs. The refusal to grant a passport, which was made only "in the gravest circumstances," had to be defensible in Parliament.[74] However, there were several circumstances in which the Passport Office did deny passports or made the otherwise easy process difficult: cases where the passport officer suspects the traveler may require repatriation at the expense of the Crown; women and children; theatrical artistes, as part of the mandated duty to stop the white slave trade; and travels to some colonial territories under British mandate such as Egypt, Iraq, and Palestine.[75] The Passport Office thus played a paternal role in the issuance or refusal of passports. Travelers who were against the direct national interest were refused passports. The majority of those refused for political grounds were members of the Communist Party.[76] Two examples were anticolonial activists in India and Ireland.[77] Anticolonial activists represented the worst kind of illegitimate violence that threatened the government's precarious position in the colonies. Revolutionaries threatened unsanctioned violence, which disturbed the discourse of the sovereign's monopoly of violence. While it was extremely difficult for the Passport Office to refuse to issue a passport, they could significantly delay or hinder the process.

Britain used banishment to the colonies as a form of punishment throughout the eighteenth and nineteenth centuries, but the question of passports for the voluntary emigration of criminals arose in the early twentieth century.[78] Although the Passport Office checked the applicant against the "black list" of those sought for current crimes, it had no statutory right to deny the passport to dangerous travelers.[79] Because the Passport Office, as the agent of the secretary of state for foreign affairs and the agent of the sovereign, could not ask consular officials abroad to afford criminals "every assistance and protection," on police advice passports were not issued.[80] The threat of random violence that these individuals' movement represented was controlled through the passport. This assertion is proven in two cases. One British citizen was charged with falsifying information for the purposes of obtaining a passport. The Passport Office advised that due to the fact that he "has an unenviable reputation, is considered to be mentally unstable and has a criminal record . . . no passport facilities should be offered him."[81] In this case, the criminal was already abroad, having previously secured false papers. A second case involved a colonial subject whose criminal past was well known to the colonial government. Though the colonial (Gold Coast) governor-general had denied the passport, the subject was applying directly to the Passport Office. There are several interesting points about this case. First, neither the colonial government nor the foreign office distinguish between the rights of subjects born in the colonies and natural-born citizens of Britain with regard to the right to a passport.[82] However, the reputation of the colony was used as a reason for "special consideration." The director of the Passport Office, R. Bloore argued,

> When a British subject gets into trouble abroad it is true that the Consular Office concerned has to deal with the nuisance but not much damage is done to British prestige, whereas a native of a British Colony if he behaves very badly does, in fact, bring a certain amount of discredit on the Colony and prejudice[s] the position of other natives who are traveling on legitimate business.[83]

The danger to the market, and the British prestige of colonial traders, warrants a restriction of movement through the mechanism of the passport. Second, the Passport Office had no facility to deny a passport. As a consequence, we hear of the incidental strategies used by the office: "We, in fact, have hitherto done what we could in the direction of preventing undesirable characters, who have caused trouble already, creating further trouble and embarrassment to HM Consular Officers."[84] Thus, the Passport Office required a monetary deposit against possible repatriation, which had the function of excluding or restricting the travel of lower-class dangerous travelers. However, if the bearer was a "reformed" criminal, whose intention was not to commit crimes abroad but gain a new start, and this intention was guaranteed by a member of the upper classes, then a passport was issued.[85] Thus, the Passport Office not only controlled the movement of criminals more tightly than "normal" citizens; it also adjudicated their intentions.

After the movement to abolish slavery, at the turn of the twentieth century there arose public anxiety regarding so-called white slavery. White slavery was equated with prostitution, specifically the trafficking of women over international borders.[86] As Judith Walkowitz writes, "During the 1870s and 1880s officials and reformers were able to uncover a small traffic in women between Britain and the continent," which was exaggerated in the public realm as a major threat to the national body of England.[87] In 1904 and 1910, treaties were signed regarding the surveillance and control of trafficking in women.[88] The trafficking of women was expressed as a threat to public health (through sexually transmitted diseases) and as a threat to public morality. Although the records of the Passport Office on this subject remain sealed for another twenty years, we can see how passport officers interpreted their obligations to protect young women travelers. A 1922 Passport Office circular states: "When a passport is applied for by or on behalf of a girl in circumstances which give good reason to suspect White Slave traffic it should be refused."[89] In particular, two women were refused passports on the grounds they were of "bad moral character."[90] The control of female immigration on the grounds of sexuality and vulnerability was an indication of the expansion of the role of the state, especially in the control of the lower classes.[91]

World War I marked with violence the image of a civilized and pacific Europe. Though the event was prefigured in many ways by the U.S. Civil War, Europeans were unprepared for the impact of mass conscription and static trench warfare in France. Unlike the French Revolution, the promise of martial citizenship was belied by class politics. As Brian Bond argues,

> Mass armies provided buttresses for the status quo as year by year young men from the peasantry and working class were "re-educated" to support the conservative establishment. . . . Military service not only improved the townsmen's health and so extended their potential working life; it also accustomed them to minimal pay, regimentation, and unquestioning obedience to orders.[92]

The loyalty of conscript armies was put into question, especially by the French mutinies in 1917 (which were put down by French colonial troops). Part of the governmental response to the mass conscription of working-class men was the introduction of the passport before an official international passport regime was in place. With mass conscription, freedom of travel and commerce became untenable. Anxiety over the presence of spies made control over national borders all the more salient. Whereas racially coded others, such as colonial subjects or Mata Haris, could be identified visually, there was little way to distinguish between a loyal Briton and a German spy from visage alone. Horatio Bottomley, a British writer, suggested that Germans within England be "marked with a distinctive badge."[93] Immigration and border control can be viewed a barometer of national anxiety. As Egidio Reale argues, "during this time of general suspicion, of constant vigilance against military espionage and of food shortage [the passport] seemed the only means of controlling aliens and of assuring the protection of the military and economic interests of the state."[94] The passport was an important way that the government could manage the state's military and economic interests by regulating the movement of its citizens.

World War I and the use of mass conscription made travel and mobility a possible threat to the national interest. This perception of threat was displayed in three ways: the control of military personnel to a great extent through bureaucratic means; the control of nonmilitary personnel in reference to widely held societal beliefs; and the control of domestic space through a system of passes. There is another interesting aspect to the control of movement in Britain during World War I and World War II: the internal control of movement. In a further effort to hinder espionage efforts, and in addition to stricter passport and customs controls, all of the railway signs, town signs, street signs, and other such identifying marks were removed from England. Consequently, the geography of wartime Britain was entirely local—and foreign. National space was made foreign by the removal of all identifying marks. Supplementing this regime was a system of identity documents and passes, which were derived from the passport and influenced it in turn. As Torpey argues,

> The (re)imposition of passport controls by numerous West European countries and the United States during the First World War and their persistence after the war was an essential aspect of that *"revolution identificatoire"* that vastly enhanced the ability of governments to identify their citizens, to distinguish them from noncitizens, and thus to construct themselves as "nation-states."[95]

The institution of wide-scale controls also had the effect of changing the material and geopolitical space of Europe and the world. The world was no longer characterized by freedom of movement within civilized spaces and securitized movement within colonial spaces; instead, World War I augured a regime of restricted movement. In addition to the construction of states, there was the creation of the modern international society. This modern international society was characterized by border and frontier controls that emphasized the production of documents for passing. Customs officials, immigration officials, and border guards were the frontline of the government, and the frontier represented a truly international space. Although the passport played a fundamental role in determining the limits of sovereign power, it could not guarantee the intentions of the traveler and consequently the safety of the nation-state. In the next section, I look at the attempts to document agents of unauthorized violence in the international sphere.

Antipassports

Anxiety about violence, specifically nonstate violence, is a central theme in the development of the passport. The passport can identify a traveler to some degree of success, although often only in relation to other government documents, but it cannot guarantee that his/her intentions are benign. In this section, I take the lead from James Der Derian's analysis of "antidiplomacy" in which he argues that the use of spies and terror is a vital part of international diplomacy. Passports play a central role in the antidiplomacy realm, even when they are false.

Passports had been issued during the French Revolution in the areas of the armies precisely to deter and catch any attempts to infiltrate the French army.[96] Crossing the border is considered the most dangerous part of any espionage mission, and fake passports are a way of facilitating that entry. The issuance of false documents and false identities was a staple of espionage. John Le Carré describes the importance of identities and switching passports, which has added intertextual salience since his admission that he worked for the Secret Service. George Smiley, le Carré's infamous mole-hunter, has a pet theory that closer attention should be paid to the histories that spies invent for themselves on their passports.[97] Alec Leamas, the spy who came in from the cold, describes receiving a false passport for his imminent, and fraudulent, defection as "like getting married again."[98] However, when the document is fraudulent, the spy and sovereign conspire to break the code of sovereign noninterference and subsequently lose any notion of protection that the passport might afford (although, in point of fact, the passport offers little protection). Der Derian argues that the spy is the necessary opposite of the diplomat: "The spy could carry on unrestrained, but only in the shadows of—and, if caught, without—sovereign protection."[99] Although several thousand blank passports go missing from national stocks every year through corruption or bureaucratic error, countries often provide cooperating intelligence services with blank passports in order to run so-called false-flag operations: inserting an operative under an assumed nationality to deflect attention from the actual sending country.[100]

Perhaps the most famous fraudulent use of Canadian passports was in the smuggling of Americans out of Iran after they were hidden by the Canadian embassy staff in Tehran.[101] A recent episode involving the fraudulent use of Canadian passports made explicit the unspoken agreement between the Israeli and Canadian governments.[102] A report in the 1970s stated that in exchange for "safe" Canadian passports, which were blank, the Canadians would gain a share of the information that the espionage might garner the Israeli intelligence services.[103] In fact, there is a long history of the use of Canadian passports in espionage. Peter Worthington reports, "Canada was important if not crucial to Soviet espionage. The Canadian passport was an essential component in the bag of tricks of every Soviet spy worthy of the name. Few KGB agents left home without it."[104] Worthington provides a list of infamous examples:

- Prior to World War II, when working for the Comintern (Communist International), Yugoslavia's Tito carried a forged Canadian passport.
- The killer of Leon Trotsky, in Mexico City in 1940, carried the passport of a Canadian killed in the Spanish Civil War.
- The Richard Sorge ring in Japan, which gave early warning to Moscow of Japan's intent to bomb Pearl Harbor, carried Canadian passports.
- Col. Rudolf Abel, the most successful Soviet spy caught by the U.S. and exchanged for U-2 pilot Gary Powers, shot down over the USSR in 1960, carried a Canadian passport.[105]

The use and abuse of Canadian passports came to the fore with the attempted bombing of the Seattle millennium celebration and the September 11 attacks on the United States.

Terrorist groups, because they lack power-projection capabilities, often rely on passports for entry into the target country or onto their target vehicle. Jean Louis Brugiere argues that "for these groups, passports are as important as weapons."[106] This practice is not confined to the developed world but is global in scope. Terrorists using false passports have been captured in in India, Kuwait, Japan, China, and Lebanon.[107] Since the September 11 attacks, media attention has been directed at the U.S.-Canadian border.[108] This anxiety followed the millennium plot that was foiled on the U.S. Canadian border when Ahmed Ressam was arrested with bomb materials and a false Canadian passport.[109] Ironically, what makes passports vulnerable to falsification in bureaucratic states is that "the American and Canadian passport system has a major problem because its 'breeder' document—the birth certificate—is such a weak document for certifying identity."[110] The case of Ressam brings to light the frailty of the system. He was able to procure the passport he used through "a fraudulent baptismal certificate from a Montreal church, photos forged with a Montreal doctor's signature and a fabricated student card from the Université de Montréal."[111] This case illustrates the weakness inherent in any bureaucratic procedure: no institution can completely or perfectly identify someone without reference to documents or social scripts that cannot be checked. Thus, we see that in the cases of nonstate violence, the passport provides an incomplete tool for protection of borders. The use of fraudulent passports by spies and terrorists illuminates the incompleteness of state control over movement.

False passports can offer protection for terrorists and against terrorists. In some instances, travelers do not want to be associated with a particular state. False passports allow the bearer to be associated with a different state and thus a different set of social scripts in his examination. Then there is the issue of camouflage passports.[112] They are a passport from a country that no longer exists (e.g., Rhodesia, Zanzibar, Dutch Guiana, and the Netherlands East Indies).[113] Although these camouflage passports are not authentic documents, they are "officially recognised by the US Government for use by their armed forces when off duty in 'difficult' countries."[114]

A firm that sells camouflage passports, Finor Associates, advises the construction of a "camouflage history" that the bearer will remember in "stressful situations." Another such firm, Espionage International, offers a regular and diplomatic "completely legal, British Honduras passport" at a premium price: "this incredibly authentic looking, instant new identity system" is available for only $399 or $449, respectively.[115] The reasons provided for the use of a false passport, "for novelty purposes only," include:

> Hijackings: One from a "third world" country isn't as likely to be singled out like a US citizen. After the invasion of Kuwait, one of the hostages gained his freedom thanks to his second passport!
>
> Keeping your real passport safe: In some countries, certain hotels require you to leave your passport in an unprotected cubby space overnight. Unless you plan on vacationing another month with beautiful accommodations at the US embassy, bring your British Honduras Passport!
>
> Keep your real identity a secret: There are many reasons that you may want to keep who you really are a secret. Who wants to go through life as "Charles Manson, Jr."? This is definitely true if you are at all high profile or wealthy. The rich are constantly exploited in many situations that you would never guess. Constantly being overcharged, blackmailed (especially in foreign countries), they are always targets in one way or another.
>
> Permanent Vacation: Almost anywhere, tourists are likely to get better treatment in restaurants and pubs, etc.—because tourists are money! Get faster, friendly service, free drinks and who knows what else! We even have a client who uses his "far away home" to

start conversations with the opposite sex! Wouldn't you like to be a "tourist" all the time?[116]

These fraudulent passports "alone grant you no priveledges [sic]," but this advertisement reflects contemporary anxieties and fantasies about travel. Travelers are subject to blackmail, harassment, and possible violence yet they also possess the allure of the exotic, the unknown, and romance. The position of wealth traveler both "get[s] better treatment . . . faster, friendly service, free drinks and who knows what else?" and is "constantly being overcharged, blackmailed" and in general being a target "in one way or another." Americans, being members of an imperialist power, are represented here as being more likely to be targeted by terrorists from the third world. Hotels in the third world (and hotels in the first world) often require travelers to relinquish their passports, which invokes an anxiety of being unable to invoke sovereign protection.

These camouflage passports have been described by major news outlets such as the *New York Times, Time,* and *U.S. News and World Report* with the headline "AMERICAN? NOT ME." Other companies offer programs to obtain a second citizenship legally, but these are available only with substantial financial commitment.

It is also possible to obtain a passport from a "virtual state" such as the Dominion of Melchizedek, the principality of Sealand, or the islands of Howland and Baker.[117] The Dominion of Melchizedek claims sovereignty over several unoccupied pieces of territory and marks Jerusalem as its historic capital.[118] The principality of Sealand, which lies six nautical miles off the coast of the United Kingdom, has recently been plagued with false reports regarding its own passports, which it insists are not for sale.[119] Although the principality itself has issued only 300 passports, the government suspects that up to 150,000 have been sold through an unofficial website.[120] The issuance of passports, and the implied sovereign protection of its citizens, are hallmarks of the modern state. The ability or propensity of nonsovereign actors to issue passports creates lacunae in international law. Sealand's legal battle with the United Kingdom is emblematic:

> Though Sealand issues its own currency, stamps, and passports, the United Kingdom insists that the upstart platform is still within UK

territory and has no legitimate claim to independence. Sealand argues the contrary, and cites a 1968 court decision in which a British judge ruled that the court had no jurisdiction over Sealand because it was located just outside British territorial waters. The British responded by extending their territorial waters.[121]

However, Sealand is expanding its online presence by offering, through the services of Havenco.ltd, a data haven. Given the move toward biometric information and virtual security, it could be that a virtual state might offer virtual passports that carry some advantages.

By contrast, the republic of Howland and Baker Islands is a "political exercise only."[122] Similar to the Jorge Luis Borges short story about the fictional encyclopedia, Stephen Abbot established the republic of Howland and Baker as an "alternate history" of an "imaginary nation" for the purposes of advertising and displaying his writing, presentation, and creative talents. However, he has since felt the need to post an explanatory page that reads in part, "*This website is in no way an attempt to take over the islands and set up an actual nation in the real world.* Nor is it the intention of its creator to set up offshore accounts under this nation's name, either in the Pacific region or elsewhere."[123] This imaginary nation invokes a reconsideration of the role of sovereign power and territory.

The commodification of passports should come as no surprise. DeLaRue, the world's largest private provider of passports to governments, counts "passports" and "brand protection" as two central programs of its "global services."[124] This company provides passports to seventy countries, develops systems for the reduction of passport fraud (which are proprietary rather than public), and protects global brands such as Wrigley's chewing gum, Halls cough drops, and Microsoft. States have been branding their international identity as places for multinational corporations, travel destinations, and places to live. States have also been in the business of selling immigration status, especially in the globalized marketplace of modern capitalism. Canada requires a $500,000 investment; the United States requires a $1 million investment; Peru and Argentina require only $25,000 and $30,000, respectively.[125] These "backdoors" to immigration caused some interesting public discussion in Canada immediately prior to the reversion of Hong Kong to the People's Republic of China. In an inversion of the rhetoric of the 1920s, when Asian immigration was first restricted on the Pacific Coast in the

United States and Canada, immigrating Chinese were seen to be buying landed immigrant status and even citizenship to ensure they had an "escape route" after the reversion. Rather than being poor laborers, the Chinese in the 1990s in British Columbia were rich entrepreneurs. Canada's immigration policy has long been oriented toward the economic health of the nation.[126] In this instance, however, Canada's branded image as the best place in the world to live (although not for women or members of aboriginal groups) contrasted with the notion that Canadian citizenship was for sale. These examples suffice to indicate that the commodification of passports, and indeed citizenship, is a by-product of the implicit promise of sovereign protection. However, in the cases of camouflage and illegal documents, the promise of sovereign protection is broken. The passport by itself cannot guarantee security to the state.

Conclusion: The Control of Violent Movements

Following Weber, the monopolization of legitimate use of violence is a key factor in the development of the European state.[127] As the histories of the safe-conduct pass and letters of marque indicate, control over the means of legitimate movement was crucial to the development of the state. While the state struggled to consolidate its monopoly of violence, it used the safe-conduct pass to generalize its violence beyond any specific agent. The connection of domestic safety to the sovereign was generalized in the passport. The borders of the king's authority were actualized by the limit of his ability to protect individuals in his territory. In early modern Europe, a sovereign was able to dispose of subjects and foreigners as he wished. As a consequence, safe-conducts were the documentary evidence of tenets of protodiplomacy and domesticated space. The system of diplomacy and safe-conducts was generalized throughout the fifteenth and sixteenth centuries to the extent that by the turn of the eighteenth century the form of the safe-conduct pass and passport was familiar to all European states.

Sovereigns used the letter of marque to bring nonstate violence within the ambit of the state. Privateers were a vital part of every major navy and were a cheap auxiliary force. However, in the absence of letters of marque the problem of piracy presented a technical as well as governmental problem for states. States did not have the technical, military, or governmental power to impose the safety of civil society onto the international anarchy, and all state-based attempts to curb piracy in domestic law were useless. It was only the British, who depended on free trade upon the high seas, who devoted the resources necessary to stop piracy altogether.

Throughout the eighteenth century, passports were generally related to a single border crossing and usually issued solely to diplomats or members of the upper classes who knew the sovereign. Most travelers found that passports were not needed on any rigorous or consistent basis. However, should the travelers go through a war zone, or travel through a colony that was at war with its home country, then a passport was advisable.[128] As we will see in Chapter 3, the biggest limits on travel concerned the cordon sanitaire, which restricted the movement of tourists from North Africa and the Ottoman Empire.[129] However, during the nineteenth century the passport system was generally confined to members of the upper (i.e., traveling) classes and bore little relation to national origin.

The French Revolution's break with tradition echoes in the realm of the passport. First, all citizens were mobilized for the army, which required a system of enlistment, description, and mobilization. Second, "foreigners" (those who were foreign by birth as well as those who were foreign by allegiance) were expelled from the *patrie*. All citizens were controlled through identity documents and passports. The nineteenth-century conservative order, represented by the Congress of Vienna, instituted a new geopolitical regime. "Civilized" space was safe, whereas "barbarian" space was dangerous. As such, travelers within Europe during the nineteenth century were not required to provide passports. Those few countries that retained passport laws on their books did not enforce them at the borders. Travel to or within the colonies required a great deal of governmental control, including passports.

Following a pattern similar to that of the French Revolution, with the mass mobilization of British, French, and German citizens, a more rigorous passport regime was needed during World War I. For the first time, we see passports being issued not in reference to personal recognizance as a member of the foreign or consular service but in reference to other documents issued by the state. The mobility regime took a nascent form, distinguishing between the "zone of the armies" and the rest of the world, which was safe to varying degrees. The British Passport Office also patrolled to some extent the safety of the travelers to whom it would issue passports. Based on prevalent social beliefs regarding criminality, gender, and public health, passports were restricted to those who would endanger the national interest as well as to those who might endanger themselves physically, sexually, or fiscally.

The specter of nonstate and state-sponsored violence seems more present after September 11, 2001. The necessity of passports for espionage and terrorist groups is an indication of the victory of the sovereign state in controlling movement. However, at the moment of that triumph, the terrorist attacks—and precisely the admission of terrorists to the United States by U.S. immigration and customs officials—illustrate that the mobility regime cannot control all violence and cannot deter nonstate violence. What these examples demonstrate is that the passport is the document of choice but that national security still relies on the interrogation of customs and immigration officials at the border. In Chapter 3, I will examine a supplement to this history: the way in which the international system has addressed threats to national health.

Notes

1. Hedley Bull, *The Anarchical Society: A Study of Order in World Politics* (London: Macmillan, 1977), p. 354.

2. Henry Kamen, *Early Modern European Society* (London: Routledge, 2000), p. 5.

3. N. W. Sibley, "The Passport System," *Journal of Comparative Legislation and International Law* 7 (1906): 32.

4. Magna Carta, Section 41 (1215).

5. Sibley, "The Passport System," p. 32.

6. Daniel Norden, "Sauf-conduits et passeports, en France, à la Renaissance," in *Voyager à la Renaissance: Actes du colloque de Tours,* edited by Jean Céard and Jean-Claude Margolin (Paris: Maisonneuve et Larose, 1987), p. 148.

7. Linda S. Frey and Marsha L. Frey, *The History of Diplomatic Immunity* (Columbus: Ohio State University Press, 1999), p. 94.

8. John Gerard Ruggie, "Territoriality and Beyond: Problematizing Modernity in International Relations," *International Organization* 47 (Winter 1993): 150.

9. Norden, "Sauf-conduits et passeports," p. 145.

10. Janet L. Abu-Lughod, *Before European Hegemony: The World System, A.D. 1250–1350* (New York: Oxford University Press, 1989), p. 58.

11. J. M. Blaut, *The Colonizer's Model of the World: Geographical Diffusionism and Eurocentric History* (New York: Guildford Press, 1993), p. 165.

12. Abu-Lughod, *Before European Hegemony*, pp. 70–71.

13. Hendrik Spruyt, *The Sovereign State and Its Competitors* (Princeton, NJ: Princeton University Press, 1994), pp. 88–89.

14. Ruggie, "Territoriality and Beyond," pp. 154–155.

15. Robert I. Burns, "The *Guidaticum* Safe-Conduct in Medieval Arago-Catalonia: A Mini-Institution for Muslims, Christians, and Jews," *Medieval Encounters* 1 (1995): 61.

16. Ibid.

17. Frederick C. Lane, "Economic Consequences of Organized Violence," *Journal of Economic History* 17 (December 1958): 401–417.

18. Sibley, "The Passport System," p. 29.

19. Egidio Reale, "Passport," in *Encyclopaedia of Social Sciences, Vol. 12*, ed. Edwin R.A. Seligman (New York: Macmillan, 1934), p. 14.

20. The function of the police is also important in this regard. Michel Foucault, "Security, Territory, Population," in *Ethics: Subjectivity and Truth* (Essential Works of Michael Foucault, Vol. 1), translated by Robert Hurley et al. and edited by Paul Rabinow (New York: New Press, 1997), p. 71.

21. Georg Schwarzenberger, "International Law," *New Encyclopedia Britannica*, vol. 21, 15th ed., p. 725.

22. Janice E. Thomson, *Mercenaries, Pirates, and Sovereigns: State-Building and Extraterritorial Violence in Early Modern Europe* (Princeton, NJ: Princeton University Press, 1994), p. 22.

23. Barbara Fuchs, "Faithless Empires: Pirates, Renegadoes, and the English Nation," *English Literary History* 67 (2000): 46.

24. Ethan A. Nadelmann, "Global Prohibition Regimes: The Evolution of Norms in International Society," *International Organization* 44 (Autumn 1990): 487.

25. Jens Bartelson, *A Genealogy of Sovereignty* (Cambridge, UK: Cambridge University Press, 1995), p. 89.

26. Fuchs, "Faithless Empires," p. 48.

27. G. Edward White, "The Marshall Court and International Law: The Piracy Cases," *American Journal of International Law* 83 (1989): 732.

28. Hugo Grotius, *De Jure Belli ac Pacis Libri Tres*, vol. 1, translated by Francis W. Kelsey (Buffalo, NY: William S. Hein, 1995), p. 373. Grotius continues to say that oaths and bonds must be kept with pirates as human beings, but not as with a state.

29. Joel Baer, "'The Complicated Plot of Piracy': Aspects of English Criminal Law and the Image of the Pirate in Defoe," *The Eighteenth Century* 23 (1982): 7.

30. Nadelmann, "Global Prohibition Regimes," p. 497.

31. Sibley, "The Passport System," p. 30.

32. Thomson, *Mercenaries, Pirates, and Sovereigns*, p. 111.

33. Ibid.
34. Ibid., p. 107.
35. Marcus Rediker, "Life Under the Jolly Roger," *Wilson Quarterly* 12 (Summer 1988): 166.
36. Ibid., p. 157.
37. Thomson, *Mercenaries, Pirates, and Sovereigns*, p. 72.
38. Janice E. Thomson, "Sovereignty in Historical Perspective: The Evolution of State Control over Extraterritorial Violence," in *The Elusive State: International and Comparative Advantages*, edited by James A. Caporaso (London: Sage, 1989), p. 228.
39. The role of chartered companies is also important here but somewhat outside the scope of this project.
40. Harold Tollefson, *Policing Islam: The British Occupation of Egypt and the Anglo-Egyptian Struggle over the Control of the Police, 1882–1914* (Westport, CT: Greenwood Publishers, 1999), p. 1.
41. Gerrit W. Gong, *The Standard of "Civilization" in International Society* (Oxford, UK: Clarendon, 1984), p. 36.
42. Richard F. Burton, *Personal Narrative of a Pilgrimage to Al-Madinah and Meccah*, edited by Isabel Burton (New York: Dover, 1964), p. 18. Several contemporary writers lament the necessity of passports in the colonies, when they have been dispensed with in Europe, as will be examined in Chapter 5.
43. I will not look at involuntary travels such as people who were transported to the colonies as punishment for a crime.
44. Passport Registers, 1841–1850 (FO 610 3).
45. Tollefson, *Policing Islam*, pp. 122–124.
46. Passport Office, "Passport Office Reorganization" (1922) (FO 612 232)
47. Helen Anne B. Rivlin, *The Agricultural Policy of Mohammed 'Ali in Egypt* (Cambridge, UK: Harvard University Press, 1961), p. 59.
48. Timothy Mitchell, *Colonizing Egypt* (Berkeley: University of California Press, 1988), p. 97.
49. Ibid., p. 34.
50. Radhika Viyas Mongia, "Race, Nationality, Mobility: A History of the Passport," *Public Culture* 11 (1999): 536–538.
51. Amitava Kumar, *Passport Photos* (Berkeley: University of California Press, 2000), p. 32.
52. Lydia Potts, *The World Labour Market: A History of Migration*, translated by Terry Bond (London: Zed Books, 1990), pp. 66–73.
53. John Torpey, "The Great War and the Birth of the Modern Passport System," in *Documenting Individual Identity: The Development of State Practices in the Modern World*, edited by Jane Caplan and John Torpey (Princeton, NJ: Princeton University Press, 2001), pp. 256–270.
54. John Torpey, *The Invention of the Passport: Surveillance, Citizenship, and the State* (Cambridge, UK: Cambridge University Press, 2000), p. 27.

55. Ibid., p. 31.
56. Ibid., p. 28.
57. John Keegan, *A History of Warfare* (London: Pimlico, 1993), p. 233.
58. Ibid., p. 234.
59. Torpey, *The Invention of the Passport*, p. 62.
60. See ibid., chap. 4; and Torpey, "The Great War and the Birth of the Modern Passport System." Torpey glosses the regulations and policies within a number of European countries but does not discuss the formation of the *international* efforts.
61. Passport Application No. 94700, "Applications for Passports," 1916 (FO 737 24). Single-use passport included in 1916 application of Form A.
62. Andreas Fahrmeir, "Governments and Forgers: Passports in Nineteenth-Century Europe," in *Documenting Individual Identity: The Development of State Practices in the Modern World,* edited by Jane Caplan and John Torpey (Princeton, NJ: Princeton University Press, 2001), pp. 221–222.
63. Foreign Office, "Regulations Respecting Passports," 28 March 1892 (FO 612 61).
64. That is, "known to the Secretary of State or recommended to him by some person who is known to him; or upon the application of any banking firm established in London or in any part of the United Kingdom; or upon the production of a Certificate of Identity signed by any Mayor, Magistrate, Justice of the Peace, Minister of Religion, Physician, Surgeon, Solicitor, or Notary, resident in the United Kingdom." Ibid.
65. E. R. Cowly to Mr. Firth, "History of Home Office Documents of Identity," 11 October 1946 (HO 213 777).
66. Ibid.
67. Jon Agar, "Modern Horrors: British Identity and Identity Cards," in *Documenting Individual Identity: The Development of State Practices in the Modern World,* edited by Jane Caplan and John Torpey (Princeton, NJ: Princeton University Press, 2001), pp. 101–120.
68. Passport Office, "Form A," 1915 (FO 737 24); "Applications for Passports," 1916 (FO 737 24).
69. Paul Fussell, *Abroad: British Literary Traveling Between the Wars* (Oxford, UK: Oxford University Press, 1980).
70. Ibid., p. 26.
71. This system was inadequate, and it remains in place today. Further class dynamics were present in several applications made by peers or women of the upper classes. One such lady, enumerating the names of her children, does not name the "2 maidservants" who traveled with them. Passport Office, No. 10687, "Applications for Passports" (FO 737 24).
72. Passport Office, No. 142637, "Applications for Passports" (FO 737 24).
73. Refusal of Passport: see correspondence between Lord Reading and Lord Grantchester (FO 612 319)

74. R. Bloore, Director, Passport Office, to J. Keith, Colonial Office, Welfare Department, 9 April 1947 (FO 612 244).

75. H. S. Martin, "Validity of British Passports," T.3889/21 (FO 612 355).

76. H. S. Martin, "Refusal of British Passports," 1926 (FO 612 355).

77. Passport Office, "Refusal of Passports to British Subjects Going Abroad" (FO 612 273).

78. What I find interesting about this archive of governmental documents—especially the passport applications for December 1916 that are kept in full at the Public Records Office—is that passports are not denied for evidence of criminal behavior. Correspondence between Mr. Swan and Mr. Martin, Chief Passport Officer, regarding prisoners obtaining passports, 3 March 1929 (FO 612 105).

79. Correspondence between J. Keith, Colonial Office, Welfare Department, and R. Bloore, Director, Passport Office, 9 April 1947 (FO 612 244).

80. Ibid.

81. Passport Office, "Refusal of Passports," T 4623 (FO 372 4707).

82. Ann Laura Stoler, *Race and the Education of Desire: Foucault's History of Sexuality and the Colonial Order of Things* (Durham, NC: Duke University Press, 1995), p. 47. Stoler illustrates the same anxiety in Dutch Indonesia.

83. R. Bloore, Minute Sheet, "Refusal of Passports," 12 April 1947 (FO 612 244).

84. R. Bloore, Chief Passport Officer, to Under Secretary of State for the Colonies, "Refusal of Passports," Misc: 14288, 21 April 1947 (FO 612 244).

85. H. L. Martin, "Issuance of Passports to Criminals," 28 March 1929 (FO 612 105).

86. Mary Ann Irwin, "'White Slavery' as Metaphor: Anatomy of Moral Panic," *Ex Post Facto: History Journal* 5 (1996), available online at www.walnet.org/csis/papers/irwin-wslavery.html.

87. Judith R. Walkowitz, *Prostitution and Victorian Society: Women, Class, and the State* (Cambridge, UK: Cambridge University Press, 1980), p. 247.

88. Carol Miller, "The Social Section and Advisory Committee on Social Questions of the League of Nations," in *International Health Organisations and Movements, 1918–1939*, edited by Paul Weindling (Cambridge, UK: Cambridge University Press, 1995), p. 157.

89. "Refusal of Passports," T4623.

90. Martin, "Refusal of British Passports," 1926.

91. Walkowitz, *Prostitution and Victorian Society*, p. 251.

92. Brian Bond, *War and Society in Europe, 1870–1970* (London: McGill-Queens, 1998), pp. 65–66.

93. Cate Haste, *Keep the Home Fires Burning: Propaganda in the First World War* (London: Penguin, 1977), p. 127.

94. Reale, "Passport," p. 15.
95. Torpey, *Invention of the Passport,* p. 121.
96. Leo Lucassen, "A Many-Headed Monster: The Evolution of the Passport System in the Netherlands and Germany in the Long Nineteenth Century," in *Documenting Individual Identity: The Development of State Practices in the Modern World,* edited by Jane Caplan and John Torpey (Princeton, NJ: Princeton University Press, 2001), p. 241.
97. John le Carré, *Tinker, Tailor, Soldier, Spy* (New York: Bantam, 1974), p. 207.
98. John le Carré, *The Spy Who Came in from the Cold* (New York: Coward-McCann, 1963), p. 76.
99. James Der Derian, "Spy Versus Spy: The Intertextual Power of International Intrigue," in *International/Intertextual Relations: Postmodern Readings of World Politics,* edited by James Der Derian and Michael J. Shapiro (New York: Lexington Books, 1989), p. 170.
100. Gregory F. Treverton, *Covert Action: The CIA and the Limits of American Intervention in the Postwar World* (London: I. B. Tauris, 1987), p. 126.
101. Antonio J. Mendez, "CIA Goes Hollywood: A Classic Case of Deception" *Studies in Intelligence* 43 (Winter 1999) (accessed 15 September 2002), www.cia.gov/csi/studies/winter99–00/art1.html.
102. Faisal Kutty, "Canadian Press Calls for Inquiry into Allegations Regarding Mossad Use of Passports," *Washington Report on the Middle East* (January/February 1998) (accessed 19 July 2000), http://www.washington-report.org/backissues/0198/9801026.htm.
103. Howard Schneider, "Canada Pulls Ambassador from Israel," *Washington Post* (3 October 1997): A29.
104. Peter Worthington, "Canadian Shield an Attractive Cover: Criminals and Spies Have Hid Behind Our Passports for Years," *Toronto Sun* (1 February 2001) (accessed 18 December 2001), www.canoe.ca/CNEWS Features0102/01_spies-sun.html.
105. Ibid.
106. Orianne Zill, "Crossing Borders: How Terrorists Use Fake Passports, Visas, and Other Identity Documents," N.d., PBS documentary. *Frontline* (accessed 15 October 2002), http://www.pbs.org/wgbh/pages/frontline/shows/trail/etc/fake.html.
107. Paul J. Smith, "The Terrorists and Crime Bosses Behind the Fake Passport Trade," *Jane's Intelligence Review* (1 July 2002).
108. Sam Howe Verhovek, "Vast U.S.-Canada Border Suddenly Poses a Problem to Patrol Agents," *New York Times* (4 October 2001).
109. James Neff, Duff Wilson, and Hal Bernton, "Few Resources Spent on Guarding Canada Border," *Seattle Times* (23 September 2001): A1.
110. David Simcox, quoted in Zill, "Crossing Borders." n.p.
111. Robert Russo, "Canadian Passports Easily Obtained" (Canadian Press) (14 March 2001) (accessed 2 February 2002), www.canoe.ca/CNEWS Law0103/14_ressam-cp.html.

112. Immigration Services International, "Camouflage Passports," n.d. (accessed 18 December 2001), www.tcfb.com/secondpassport/camouflage_english.htm.; International Solutions Incorporated, "Camouflage Passports," www.ptclub.com/Campassport.html; see also www.camouflagepassports.com.

113. Finor Associates, "Camouflage Passports," n.d. (accessed 18 December 2001), www.finor.com/en/camouflage_passports.htm.

114. Ibid.

115. Espionage Unlimited, "British Honduras Passports," n.d. (accessed 18 December 2001), www.espionage-store.com/passport.html.

116. Ibid.

117. Roy Smith, "Fit to Govern?" *World Today* 56 (October 2000): 14–16.

118. See www.melchizedek.com and www.melchizedek.com/gvmtdocs/citizenship-online.html for online passport applications.

119. Principality Notice: PN 012/01: Forged Sealand passports (3 October 2001), http://www.sealandgov.org/notices/pn01201.html.

120. Smith, "Fit to Govern?" p. 16.

121. "Findings," *Wilson Quarterly* 25 (Autumn 2001): 12.

122. Stephen Abbott, "The Official Government Website of the Republic of Howland and Baker Islands," n.d. (accessed 26 December 2001), users.metro2000.net/~stabbott/Visithowlandbaker.htm.

123. Stephen Abbott, "Too Good to Be True: An Explanation of This Website," n.d. (accessed 26 December 2001), users.metro2000.net/~stabbott/RHBIexplained.html (emphasis in original).

124. DeLaRue, PLC, "Global Services," n.d. (accessed 26 December 2001), www.delarue.com/global.

125. United Nations, Department of Economic and Social Affairs, Population Division, "International Migration Policies" (New York: United Nations, 1998), p. 34 (ST/ESA/Ser.A/161).

126. James D. DeRosa, "The Immigrant Investors Program: Cleaning Up Canada's Act," *Case Western Reserve Journal of International Law* 27 (Spring/Summer 1995): 359–406.

127. Max Weber, "Politics as a Vocation," in *From Max Weber: Essays in Sociology*, edited by H. H. Gerth and C. Wright Mills (London: Routledge, 1991), p. 83.

128. Jeremy Black, *The British Abroad: The Grand Tour in the Eighteenth Century* (New York: St. Martin's, 1992), p. 162.

129. Ibid., p. 160.

3

Health and the Body Politic

> *Behind the disciplinary measures [of population control]
> can be read the haunting memories of contagions, of the plague,
> of rebellions, crimes, vagabondage, desertions, people who
> appear and disappear, live and die in disorder.*
> —Michel Foucault, "Governmentality," 1978

In addition to the threat of violence, early sovereigns faced the threat of communicable diseases within the populations they ruled. Thus, there are two narratives to tell in regard to passports in early modern Europe: the prince and the plague. The first concerns the royal prerogative to decree who may leave and enter his personal territory; the second reflects the government's intention to control the population through bureaucratic means. Having discussed in Chapter 2 the ways in which the history of the sovereign state can be read from the perspective of the passport, I want to now consider a different kind of control. In this chapter, I examine the ways in which the health of the body politic and the physical health of its bodies are related through the lens of disease. I focus here on the state-centered responses to three epidemics: the plague, cholera, and HIV/AIDS. These examples illustrate three different regimes of epidemic and movement control. Governments tried to control the plague through quarantines, enforced by the physical isolation of safe and unsafe space. In the case of cholera, governments did not employ quarantines, and the role of the Health Organization of the League of Nations (HOLN) primarily was to disseminate information about the disease to member nations. HIV/AIDS is controlled by a disjointed regime governing the movement of infected individuals, which shows the importance of passports to indicate to national authorities the purported health of travelers; this regime attempts to facilitate travel as well as limit the infection of the national body. In each of these cases, health passports made travel possible or impossible.

Diseases proliferate through biospheres and populations, taking no notice of arbitrary political boundaries. Armies, treaties, and diplomatic agreements—the traditional tools of high politics—cannot stop the transmission of plagues. Governments can, however, identify the carriers of diseases, against which those traditional instruments may be used. (Not only is the army often mobilized against epidemics in the form of quarantine enforcement; the government defines itself as a protector of the health of the body politic in literal as well as metaphorical ways.) Health concerns are a strong indicator of the importance of population movements and population control for the modern international system.

The Prince and the Plague

Renaissance Italian city-states are particularly important to students of world politics, because they closely resemble the modern international system. This comparison is based on the work of Machiavelli, where we get the notion of raison d'état, and the Italian subsystem of competing city-states, which is considered a precursor of an anarchical international society. Here, however, I am concerned with another history of the Italian Renaissance—a story in which the primary threat that the government faced was not the French or the papal states but rather the plague. This health-oriented history paints a different picture of the origins of states and, indeed, the topography of international society. Focusing on the reaction of Italian city-states to the plague, we can see the advantages and limitations of using documents such as the health passport to safeguard populations.

Faced with a threat to the bodies of the state, Renaissance states tried new governmental mechanisms to control the plague. Their modes of control were based on miasma theories of disease propagation.[1] Based on the notion that bad air causes illness, miasma theory was related to specific, often poor, locales. Because this theory was prevalent, the methods used by Italian city-states most often involved the control of space and movement between spaces. Governments used a variety of methods to control the effects of the plague: passports, social regulations, police, armies, and plague-houses.

When faced with the plague, Florence and Milan were the first city-states to institute quarantine regulations in a systematic way.[2] During the mid–fourteenth century, similar forms of plague control sprang up all over Europe: armed guards to protect the city from pest-carriers, boards of health to monitor the disposal of waste, and legislation to regularize or minimize the bad air that was thought to cause the plague.[3] However, by the end of the fifteenth century to the beginning of the sixteenth century, new governmental devices had come into common use. Plague victims were centralized in publicly funded hospitals. New legislation was passed regarding the circulation of potential plague-bearers (the poor, the morally corrupt, etc.). Two state-centered methods of plague control were: quarantine, in which movement was restricted for the entire population; and mobility regimes, which targeted specific categories of the population. Over the course of the early modern period, we see the coexistence of these two modes of control.

In Italy, a number of sovereigns convened boards of health to administer only those laws that related to the plague, as well as to issue passes to and from the city.[4] The boards of health in the Italian city-states were staffed not by agents of the sovereign per se but by a board of "doctors, humanists, and jurists."[5] These boards were not mere agents of the prince, because they operated even when no prince was in power. As Sheldon Watts points out, during times of transition, these boards of health continued to administer the laws regarding the containment of the plague.[6] The republican system of Florentine government might explain the operation of these boards in the absence of a sovereign, but governmental structure does not explain similar boards of health in more autocratic places like Venice, Siena, and Milan. Michel Foucault points to the use of experts in the configuration of systems of power that are not simply repressive but productive of specific relationships.[7] In this case, the panel of experts restricted movement to control the population unevenly and produced and reproduced particular social relations. Movement was easy for the rich and influential, whereas movement was increasingly difficult for the poor and marginalized.

In Renaissance Italy, bodily disease was associated with social ills, and governments moved to control the disease through the control of the social body. Through these boards of health, the marginalized were controlled to a much greater extent than the rich. The primary role of many boards was to vet potential travelers wishing to flee from the city and the examination of potential entrants to the city.[8] Ann Carmichael comments that "control of some individuals—poor, wanderers, beggars, 'ruffians'—and not others (cardinals and ambassadors, for example) was seen as integral to the control of plague."[9] Plague controls in Venice also included prevention of immigration from the Adriatic.[10] The death in Venice seemed to be originating from the "East," and consequently immigrants were barred from entering the city or were confined once arrived. Of course, such confinement often had the effect of worsening the epidemic among the imprisoned immigrants, which in turn justified the measures.

Among other marginal groups, prostitutes in Siena, Perugia, and Venice were controlled using a similar logic.[11] Prostitutes were seen as a double threat to the social order and the bodily health of citizens. Because the plague's mode of transmission was unknown, experts assumed that the plague was associated with sinful activities. Prostitutes were often restricted to poorer areas: government regulations often targeted prostitutes for confinement, surveillance, or expulsion. Suzanne and James Hatty argue that this control of prostitutes is not aberrant but rather an indication of a general discourse of control over the sexualized female body.[12] The boards of health controlled the marginal in society from leaving the infected areas, often increasing the effects of the disease, which in turn reaffirmed their prejudices. In sum, those who could flee the city—the rich—did so; the poor were disproportionately left to the ravages of the disease.[13] As a consequence, a discourse of disease and public safety was invoked to control the "dangerous" elements of society: the poor, the indigent, criminals, prostitutes, and "unofficial" immigrants.

The notion of sovereignty during the Renaissance period changes from one based on an ecclesiastical foundation to one based on a secular notion of virtue. As Machiavelli illustrates, the secularization of authority was not an immediate process. The Catholic Church held substantial terrestrial power, and in addition there were political actors on the scene who attempted to retain the connection of the sovereign to a heavenly mandate.[14] Girolamo Savonarola was a populist preacher who criticized the Florentine government and instigated the so-called bonfire of the vanities. He "saw the origins of the plague in divine punishment for the sins of the city, and for him, these were principally bodily sins."[15] Thus, Savonarola linked the bodily plague affecting Florence to the moral illness of the ruling classes. Machiavelli describes his downfall as a result of lacking violence (i.e., arms): "Girolamo Savonarola . . . came to grief with his new institutions when the crowd started to lose faith in him, and he had no way of holding fast those who had believed or of forcing the incredulous to believe."[16] Although the lack of terrestrial power may be the structural cause of Savonarola's weakness, the government of Florence silenced him in a more immediate way. Rather than risk a popular revolt if Savonarola was suppressed using direct political means, legislators prohibited public sermons on account of the plague. Thus, threats to the public order were construed as threats to the public health and were also controlled using plague legislation.[17] Savonarola's sermons were a threat to the political health of Florence, and the government controlled that threat by taking away the bodily crowd that supported him. Carmichael concludes that "by the end of the fifteenth century [control of the poor, the itinerate, and prostitutes] was expressly linked to the spread of plague rather than to pleasing God."[18] This connection of the plague to political control, rather than divine punishment, reflects a secularization of the Italian city-state, which Savonarola's story of decline corroborates.

Plague legislation was a part of a larger set of social and governmental controls of the dangerous elements. Richard Trexler highlights the ambivalence of the legislators in their regard of the poor:

> Citizens were uncertain if the lower class was susceptible to plague or possessed some cunning immunity to it, preserving its solidarity while citizens broke and ran; they were unsure as well if plague struck the plebs because of their lowly sins, or as an ominous prelude to the meek inheriting the earth if "good men" did not reform.[19]

This fear was well-founded as riots had broken out in northern Europe as a result of the plague.[20] Precisely, the area where the plague first became visible in 1522 in Florence was immediately isolated: "the 'impure' bodies of the poor were to be segregated from the 'pure' bodies of the rest of the community."[21] This notion of purity helped distinguish safe citizens from unsafe outsiders, whether that security was written in terms of labor, capital, docility, or health.

In medieval and Renaissance culture, there was a prevalent anxiety about the "identity" of individuals. Valentin Groebner argues that before literacy and the transcription of names onto official documents, it was difficult if not impossible to be certain of the identity of travelers.[22] This anxiety was accompanied by the notion that liminal groups—the poor, the itinerate, the criminal—were experts in dissimulation. Consequently, the Venetian board of health assigned visible labels or colors to be worn by various marginal groups: prostitutes, self-identified ruffians, lepers, and Jews.[23] Governments in early modern Europe often assigned individuals or groups visible markers for invisible characteristics. As above, prostitutes were often prescribed (or proscribed) colors or clothing that helped distinguish them from honest women.[24] And whereas wearing the Star of David signified Jews, wearing yellow clothing, a man's hat, or a cord belt differentiated elegant and well-dressed prostitutes from honest citizens. The fact that the poor were marginalized more so than the rich is, of course, true of travel generally in early modern Europe (and perhaps most of European history). However, in this instance travel was restricted not because of access to wealth alone but because of general access to a civilian bureaucracy of enforcement.[25]

All travelers who wanted to leave the city had to obtain a health passport (*billeta de sanità*) that certified the bearer did not carry the plague. The health passport did not certify identity or citizenship or request another sovereign to afford the bearer protection and assistance—the traditional functions of the modern passport. The health passport assured other states and sovereign rulers that the bearer was safe. Medical geographers today argue that quarantine regulations had the effect of lessening the incidence of plague in Europe.[26] Furthermore, the health passport served a dual function—assuring both bearer and other sovereigns that he/she was free of the plague. European governments took to issuing similar quarantine regulations fifty years later. It became common practice to isolate a state from international society when the latter was seen as a source of plague within fifty years of the Italian experiment.[27]

At the same time, Florence used its army in a novel way: to intercept all that would break the quarantine—that is, those escaping as well as those attempting to enter Florence. "It became standard Florentine practice to employ squads of soldiers to deal with subordinate towns in the *contado;* people who slipped away from a plague-ridden town were tracked down and shot."[28] The army was also used as a kind of police force as the rich fled their homes in pest-ridden cities to the countryside.[29] These two aspects reflect the internal and external faces of early statecraft. In the first instance, the use of the army to limit transmission of the plague indicates a concern with health among the domestic and international communities. Preventing plague-bearers from fleeing the city and spreading the disease indicates an ethic of care for other members of the international community. When a government protects other states from becoming infected with disease by preventing the exit of potential carriers, we see an acute sensitivity toward the health of the international community that cannot be explained fully in terms of national interest. In the second instance, the state had to consolidate control over its own territory and population. Naturally, this consolidation of power and authority involves caring for the wealthy and influential within the state.

Renaissance citizens and states (at least those in Italy) recognized themselves as international actors whose actions had an impact on the international realm or other national realms. The city-states thus served a domestic-national interest in protecting their reputations by preventing the exiting of plague-bearing travelers. However, this restriction also indicates a more immediate concern for the health of other state populations. In conclusion, the health passport and the quarantine regulations illustrate an important supplement to the origin of the state as simply a successful protection racket. Health passports indicate that control of legitimate movement is central to the health of the body politic, in addition to the political bodies in the polis. Dangerous individuals were disproportionately governed through sanitation and mobility regulations as sources of political and physical contagion. As we will see, this theme recurs in the colonial scene.

Colonialism, Cholera, and Passports

Traditional histories of the modern nation-state often ignore the evolution of state practices in the colonial scene. The colony presented a problem to liberal colonizers, and the development of the postcolonial state presents several problems to historians of European statecraft. The colony is not a state per se but has quasisovereign status in international law. John Torpey's landmark survey on the passport in Europe makes a methodological distinction between passports used for international travel and internal passes used for population control. However, as we will see in Chapter 4, the distinction between colonial space and international space had very pragmatic effects on the mobility and passport regimes. Just as passports were being discouraged in Europe, those same European powers were using the internal pass or identity card to control colonized populations.

Colonies as international actors complicate the simplistic dichotomy between domestic and international space. Although there is merit in making a methodological distinction, Torpey accepts the distinction between national and international space. As I have argued, however, the colonial scene complicates that distinction.[30] The colonial government controlled colonial space juridically but was never actually in complete control of that space. The colonies were never entirely safe for Europeans or for the colonists. The colonies were neither the anarchy of the truly international—such as the realm of the pirate on the high seas—nor the domesticated safety of the state. The colonies were a semicivilized state, an anxious zone of half-belonging marginally controlled by international law, not domestic law. By this logic, then, the passes used in the colonies were neither true passports nor internal passes. Among many possible colonial examples, I will focus on the documents and laws used by the British in their control of India.

An important governmental shift that started in the eighteenth century becomes clear during the nineteenth and twentieth centuries. There was an evolution in the government's perception toward persons in the realm of the state. Writings on government cease to discuss the well-being of the people and start to discuss the control of the population.[31] In particular, Foucault asks how these ideational changes were made possible. He situates this governmental change within a larger societal change, whereby individuals were increasingly constituted by experts and institutions outside of their body. He locates changes in the discourse regarding health, madness, criminality, and sexuality. In relation to health, this change was reflected in the shift from a strategy of quarantine to a strategy of surveillance.

The East had been viewed as a place of contagion, the source of the paths of plague during the Middle Ages.[32] Mohamed Said argues that "cholera was endemic to the South Asian region for at least 2,000 years."[33] These diseases followed trade routes, and cholera brought to the fore the tension between trade and quarantine. Cholera is transmitted through waste-contaminated drinking water. C. P. Snow's landmark analysis of cholera through the Broad Street pump helped propagate the germ theory of contagion. Ironically, it was the British who brought cholera out of India. Following Italian responses to the plague, Watts reports the attitudes of the British on the causes of cholera. It was a variant of an English fever that could be expected to target those who were predisposed to it by their immoral living, poverty, neglect of family values, holding of opinions about political matters, and heavy drinking.[34]

As with the plague in the fifteenth century, dangerous individuals in society were assumed to have and to transmit cholera. British boards of health were an important governmental aspect in controlling diseased populations. Colonial medical boards were composed of doctors and surgeons rather than jurists and other notables.[35] Influenced by Thomas Malthus, prevailing wisdom at the time of the first outbreak of cholera in 1817 was that "it is probable that the consequences [of the epidemic] may in the present instance have been beneficial, correcting the influence of an overcrowded population."[36] This Malthusian logic was applied to the colonial situation and revealed an imperial anxiety over the fertility of the colonized populations.

The 1817 cholera outbreak in Calcutta did not result in the traditional transmission problems, which in precolonial India prevented an epidemic. Part of the natural isolation of cholera came from the nomadic nature of many villages. In precolonial India, changing the village's location (and thus the location of its wells) limited the extent of the disease. As William McNeill explains, "An old and well-established pattern for spreading cholera across the Indian landscape intersected new British imposed patterns of trade and military movement. The result was [that] cholera overleaped its familiar bounds."[37]

The relationship between imperial rule and cholera was also important: "In an environment in which epidemiology and empire repeatedly intersected, cholera was a highly political disease, one that seemed to threaten the slender basis of British power in India and to stand at the critical point of interaction between colonial state and indigenous society."[38] The British acutely felt the precariousness of colonial power in India.[39] The bureaucracy of colonial government did not exhibit the same kind of care for the colonial other that epitomized the Italian city-states' use of armies to protect towns from plague. One could argue that the British government was more concerned with the welfare of Britain than that of the colony. At best, the British were more concerned with the control of the colonial population, because order was a precursor to civilization. However, the effects of the civilizing mission were often perversely violent. The British colonial government "coerced people to settle permanently in fixed village sites so that they could be regularly taxed and regularly governed."[40] This policy of fixed settlements had the effect of worsening epidemics when they occurred, because the government would not allow the village to move away from the source of the disease. Cholera was also transmitted by the British army in its movements about the country (especially the troop movements to quell the mutiny of 1857–1858).[41] Indeed, as David Arnold argues,

> On the march or fighting campaigns, soldiers were one of the main vectors of the disease and might carry it with them across vast tracts of rural India. The large-scale movements of troops through northern India from Bengal, cholera's homeland, in 1817–18 facilitated the epidemic invasion of the rest of India. . . . To speak of the "invasion" of cholera as if it were an army on the march was thus more than a casual analogy.[42]

One of the central arguments in this book is that the passport illustrates the contradictory desires of governments to control movement and to encourage international mobility. The transmission of cholera from India to the rest of the world demonstrates the ill effects of this tension. Colonial trade was central to the international dominance and wealth of the British imperial state. Thus, even when cholera threatened Great Britain, the United States, and Europe generally, the British maintained heavy trade with the subcontinent and refused to institute quarantine regulations.

By the twentieth century, writers in the United States and Europe were warning of the "rising tide of color." Lothrop Stoddard links this rise in colonial populations to the success of the "white race" in bringing the benefits of civilization, which prevented the "natural" checks of population control.[43] This general anxiety about the fertility and number of nonwhites is reflected in the beginnings of immigration legislation.[44] The British, however, could not and did not control the subjected Indian population through documentation and laws. Britain, therefore, put in place a kind of racial cordon sanitaire around India. Indians could not migrate in light of their contagion—although the goods they produced were free to flow. Thus, the nineteenth century evidences a shift in governmental strategy: from quarantine to surveillance.

In the late nineteenth century, a system of international conferences attempted to coordinate pressing international problems such as health, sanitation, communications, trade, and similar matters. One of the international conferences held in the late nineteenth century, the International Congress on Hygiene, believed "that Indian-based cholera was a standing threat to the West."[45] The British insisted on the continuation of free trade, as well as the rejection of absolute quarantines, at the International Sanitary Conference in Constantinople. Quarantines were "an instrument of continental despotism, inimical to free commerce, a source of hardship and oppression to travelers, traders, and residents alike, and, not least, ineffective in preventing the spread of the disease."[46] However, it was not until eighty years after the first international epidemic, in 1903, that a cordon sanitaire was put in place (albeit unsuccessfully) around the United States and Europe against cholera.[47]

Because the administration of colonies was a domestic matter under the purview of British sovereignty, there was little legal opportunity for *international* regulation in the colonies. However, selective quarantining and isolation did exist. Anticholera measures were disproportionately imposed on immigrants, who were coded in racial and colonial terms. Radhika Mongia traces the ways that Canadian and British authorities used the secondary racial characteristics of Indian migrants to prevent immigration to Canada. She argues that Indian immigration to British Columbia, despite a labor shortage there, was discouraged and prevented on the grounds of climate and disease.[48] The passport came to be used as a mechanism to prevent immigration; it was a marker of origin and suitability. Thus, European immigrants were accepted into Canada, whereas Indian immigrants were rejected.

Alan Kraut charts similar reactions in the United States to cholera, although the immigrant group that was identified as the vector of contagion was Irish immigrants.[49] During the 1832 cholera epidemic in New York city, "the poor—often immigrants—were the primary victims both of the disease and the blame."[50] Wide-scale quarantines and restrictions were not feasible. According to U.S. authorities, quarantines were a "useless embarrassment to commerce."[51] This tension between the desire to protect the national economy and the desire to protect the national body was present throughout the nineteenth and twentieth centuries. Racially coded restrictions were not only feasible but also supported by the social beliefs of the time.[52]

As a consequence, in the United States, Britain, and Canada, officials attempted to restrict the entry of infected immigrants. The U.S. government required all ships to have an international certificate of health. Individuals also had to have an international certificate of heath following an examination before their departure to the United States.[53] However, the examinations, and thus the certificates, were singularly unsuccessful—the inspectors were overworked and the examinations cursory. British officials encouraged emigration of the poor and sick, and so doctors were pressured to restrict exit as little as possible. As a consequence, U.S. immigration officials at Ellis Island instituted their own medical inspections. The U.S. government attempted to require certificates of health from the immigrants' point of departure, but the lack of a robust international regime necessitated that the U.S. Public Health Service take on the responsibility itself. The investigation of potential immigrants by customs and immigration officials expressed anxieties about identity and health similar to those seen in Italy during the Renaissance. Because the medical examination at the point of departure was not sufficiently rigorous and immigrants were understandably reluctant to disclose medical conditions that they knew would restrict their entry into the United States, great stress was placed on a visual medical examination of potential immigrants. As one U.S. Public Health Service surgeon described it,

> "facial signs" could reveal "with considerable regularity" such "conditions" as "nationality, temperament, occupation, sexual relations and habits, sensuality, drug addictions . . . and such disease as brain tumor . . . melancholia, manic depressive insanity, chorea . . . renal disease, appendicitis . . . and impending death."[54]

Fueled by the cholera epidemics of the late nineteenth century, medical examinations—and medical exclusions based on potential costs to the state and potential for productive work—became an integral part of U.S. immigration law.

As the structure of the immigration examination at Ellis Island suggests, governments in the nineteenth century shifted from policies that attempted quarantine and exclusion to policies that monitored and reported the vectors of disease. In short, there was a move from a quarantine regime to a surveillance regime. This was part of a general shift in government strategies corresponding to the growth of the modern bureaucratic welfare state; it was also part of a recognition that international travel was necessary and, in many ways, unstoppable. Following this move, there was a different reaction from international bodies (as opposed to national policies). Whereas national policies were prompted by the concern for the nation's health against foreign diseases, international conferences on the cholera epidemic recommended ways that travel could be facilitated through monitoring and the dissemination of information about disease and its prevention. Thus, between 1860 and the late 1930s, except during times of war, the desire to increase trade and travel trumped the desire for security.

One of the key, and often overlooked, successes of the League of Nations was the control of several epidemics. The Health Organization of the League of Nations had three essential functions: the centralization and standardization of information; education in proper methods for quarantine and treatment; and the coordination of national members of the League in preventing the spread of diseases. Several scholars have remarked on the rise of statistics as a method of population control in the nineteenth and early twentieth centuries.[55] The HOLN took one of its central tasks to be the standardization, collection, and dissemination of information regarding diseases. The statistical association of vectors of contagion and the East was persistent, following what Arjun Appadurai has called the process of "exoticization and enumeration."[56] The relationship was reinforced by the HOLN in its public pamphlet:

> In Europe, plague and cholera are rare diseases, and in Russia they have only gained ground as a result of war and revolution, but they are always prevalent in an endemic state in certain Eastern countries—*e.g.* in India and China—and make these regions dangerous sources of contagion to their neighbours.[57]

In fact, a special Eastern Bureau was established to publicize the presence of cholera at different Eastern ports. British India did not encourage this international effort, seeing it as an unnecessary repetition of imperial modes of data collection.[58] The Eastern Bureau, as a nexus in the collection of information, was emblematic of the belief that epidemics could be controlled through statistics. As Lenore Manderson argues,

> Whilst the primary enemy in epidemiological surveillance was disease—especially plague, smallpox, and cholera—the implicit enemy was the outside, and tensions of authority, empire, and territory were played out literally and metaphorically in the work of the Bureau. In pursuing the metaphor, epidemiological information was represented as the mechanism of reconciliation.[59]

Quarantine and vaccination were the primary methods for controlling the international spread of disease. However, quarantine was an ineffective strategy because the control of international mobility was always incomplete. As such, quarantine could not stop the transmission of cholera and other epidemics, and therefore it only inconvenienced trade and travel. The Epidemic Commission (which became the HOLN in 1922) coordinated a zone sanitaire along the Russian-Polish border in 1920 because "railway traffic and persons passing through frontier stations could be controlled, but thousands of others were thought to be crossing the border undetected."[60] Soldiers returning from Russia brought with them typhus, which threatened Poland. Because of new borders, the lack of frontier controls, and the lack of an international mobility regime, epidemics spread quickly in post–World War I Europe.[61] The Spanish influenza epidemic, in fact, caused more deaths than World War I—the epidemic caused twenty-five million dead between 1918 and 1919, while World War I caused just under seventeen million dead between 1914 and 1919. After the Epidemic Commission became the HOLN, its members attempted to institutionalize and internationalize the organization, which had been created specifically to meet the threat represented by returning soldiers. The Russian-Polish zone sanitaire was only marginally successful and required a great deal of international support and governmental resources. Because of the HOLN's experiences in eastern Europe, an international scientific consensus emerged that quarantine was no longer an effective strategy.[62] The HOLN attempted to improve the health systems of states, and international epidemic treatment became a matter of coordinating state policies as much as independent action by the organization. The roles of the HOLN, and its successor, the World Health Organization (WHO), were thus limited to coordinating, recommending, advising, and assisting—but only at the behest of states.

These tactics bear some similarity to the control of plague in Renaissance Italy. The government and international society were mobilized to control the vectors of contagion through increasingly bureaucratic measures. What is important to note is that frontier controls like the zone sanitaire alone could not prevent contagion, either from Russia or from the Far East. Consequently, the HOLN had to extend its mandate beyond borders and frontiers to protect a zone between Europe and disease. By 1944, it became clear that the control of populations along with specific controls at the borders were the best defenses against disease.[63] An examination of the modern international epidemic regime reveals the degree to which quarantine has largely been abandoned in favor of surveillance.

New Plagues, the New World Order, and the World Health Organization

When moving among countries in the undeveloped third world, the modern traveler often needs proof of vaccinations in order to prove that she is not a threat to the sending or receiving country. Such proofs are contained in the WHO's International Certificate of Vaccination—a modern-day equivalent of the health passport. Following Robert Kaplan's fearful description of the post–Cold War world in his 1994 article "The Coming Anarchy," disease has been described as a primary threat to the Western world.[64] Disease in the post–Cold War era is figured as originating from the global South rather than the East in a relocation of the "diseased" periphery. Quarantine is seen as largely unacceptable, whereas surveillance is seen as the key to international epidemic control. Because the WHO is not an independent agency, its role is one of surveillance and the dissemination of information so that national health services can act accordingly. Today, WHO health passports are used to patrol new vectors of contagion. The U.S. Department of State frames its version of the WHO vaccination certificate in terms of national security and inconvenience. That document, which acts as a supplement to the government-issued passport, "is an official statement verifying that proper procedures have been followed to immunize you against a quarantinable disease which could be a threat to the United States and other countries. The Certificate is essential in permitting uninterrupted international travel."[65]

This supplement to the modern passport of citizenship illustrates yet another aspect of the safe international traveler, that is, his/her freedom from disease. The modern health passport also illustrates the shift from the inspection of the individual, as was done at Ellis Island, to the inspection of the documents.

The dangers of disease transmission (including the disease of poverty), which had previously been confined to the global South, has increased during the era of globalization. Writing in 1997, Albert Paolini usefully summarized the practices and trends that are understood by the term *globalization:* "these transformations in communications, technologies, capital, labour, markets, trade, the production and distribution of goods and services, and the mass movement of peoples have been seen as embodying a 'global character.'"[66] The anxieties expressed by critics of globalization can be classified into three groups: economic nationalists; cultural analysts; and human rights and labor activists. Each of these groups is critical of the dynamics of sovereignty and globalization—either in sovereignty's absence of control, or in the persistence of unjust sovereign control. However, another anxiety of globalization is not expressed as frequently. As articulated by the WHO: "Epidemics and newly-emerging infections are on the move as never before, threatening the health of people around the world and affecting travel and trade in the global village."[67] As the Joint United Nations Programme on HIV/AIDS (UNAIDS) warns, "Studies of certain highly mobile groups (e.g., truck drivers, itinerant traders of both sexes, military, seafarers) have identified travel or migration as a factor related to infection."[68] While open borders and free travel is considered a positive benefit of globalization, disease also travels across these open borders. A geography of disease and vaccination is laid over the supposedly open space of globalization.

The WHO is committed to maintaining freedom of international travel. The International Health Regulations, passed in 1969, are the primary international legal instrument in this issue area. The regulations articulate the freedom-of-mobility regime:

> Art. 76: Bills of health, with or without consular visa, or any certificate, however designated, concerning health conditions of a port or an airport, shall not be required from any ship or aircraft.
> Art. 81: No health document, other than those provided for in these Regulations, shall be required in international traffic.[69]

This is prima facie evidence that the freedom-of-mobility regime has overcome the health-passport regime. However, international certificates of vaccination are afforded a place in the International Health Regulations and thus stand in place of health passports. And yet such health passports do not consider HIV/AIDS to be grounds for exclusion or restriction in light of the limited ways that the disease can be transmitted. HIV/AIDS has been described as a modern plague, and the ways that the international and national communities have reacted to the threat illustrate several important points.

Although Kaplan laments the expense of vaccinations, he seems entirely unconscious that vaccination against and testing for tropical diseases is a privilege shared by few in the West African countries he visits.[70] This bifurcated regime is especially apparent in the HIV/AIDS epidemic. Many developing countries require a certificate of health before a traveler is allowed entry. Belarus, China, Hungary, Saudi Arabia, and Egypt have connected these discourses of disease and national security by refusing any immigrant who fails a domestic HIV test.[71] Since the late 1980s, the number of countries that require an HIV/AIDS test has increased. In 1989, when Margaret Duckett and Andrew Orkin conducted their first survey, only 41 percent of all countries restricted entrants in some way.[72] Today, 53 percent restrict entry or settlement.[73]

The facts of the global HIV/AIDS epidemic are stark indeed. From a total of 36.1 million people infected with HIV/AIDS in 2001, 25.3 million are in sub-Saharan Africa, 5.8 million in Southeast Asia, and 1.4 million in South America. In short, 90 percent of all HIV/AIDS-positive cases are from the global South.[74] It is hard to overstate the effect of the epidemic on the future of Africa. In terms of overall demographic health, poverty, urbanization, and development, the HIV/AIDS epidemic is radically changing the shape of African politics.[75] The global response to HIV/AIDS has been slow. Allan Brandt argues that the slow response is a function of the relatively plague-free environment of the late twentieth century: "AIDS appeared at a historical moment in which there was little social or political experience in confronting a public health crisis of this dimension. The epidemic fractured a widely held belief in medical security."[76] Since, popular sensitivity toward other tropical diseases, such as the Ebola virus, has increased dramatically.[77] However, governments quickly resurrected methods for coping with this new threat. Upon the recommendation of the U.S. Centers for Disease Control and Prevention, "since 1987, the United States has banned non-citizens with HIV from entering the country without a special waiver."[78] These entry restrictions were relaxed with the Immigration Act of 1990, but the immigration ban remains in effect.[79] Similar restrictions were enacted in Canada in 2001.[80] U.S. restrictions on HIV-positive immigrants are also striking, but they are justified by a different logic, that is, with reference to the spread of infection from migrants and the cost of treatment. As Sarah Qureshi points out, this argument is made despite the fact that "ironically, the United States appears to be a net exporter of AIDS."[81]

The HIV/AIDS epidemic is described by experts as originating from Africa, but the history of the disease reflects anxieties similar to those displayed in the plague and cholera epidemics. AIDS first came to light in North America among practicing homosexual men in Los

Angeles.[82] In its early days, it was termed the "gay plague" and vilified in similar religious and moralistic terms as the plague.[83] This domestic dynamic is clearly connected to the international dynamic. As the extent of the disease was discovered, AIDS gained several origin narratives. Paul Farmer describes the reaction of the U.S. public to Haitian AIDS patients in terms of a "geography of blame."[84] Haitian AIDS patients provided a puzzle: "Unlike other North American patients meeting diagnostic criteria for AIDS, the Haitian immigrants denied that they had engaged in homosexual activity or intravenous drug use. Most had never had a blood transfusion."[85] Consequently, the press speculated that there was some predisposition to the new disease among the Haitian population. The pattern is familiar: Haitians and Haitian Americans "present preexisting characteristics of an already non-normative character. They are black, tend to be poor, are recent immigrants, and the association of Haiti with cult-religious practices fuels the current tendency to see deviance in groups at risk with AIDS."[86] The result of this myth of origin was that tourism to Haiti evaporated and immigration regulations for Haitians became imbricated with fear of HIV/AIDS transmission and health.

The second myth of origin regarding the HIV/AIDS epidemic is Africa.[87] Early attempts to trace the disease to Africa were considered based on racist presuppositions rather than hard science.[88] Recent investigation of the origins of HIV/AIDS has led experts to pin the blame on Central African bushmeat.[89] States in sub-Saharan Africa face a grave future. In several states, large percentages of the populations are infected with HIV. These include Botswana (35 percent), Zimbabwe (25 percent), Zambia (20 percent), South Africa (20 percent), Kenya (14 percent), and Mozambique (13 percent). Although a few demographers argue that mortality rates have had a perversely positive effect on sustainability, one could hardly praise the situation. The main vector of transmission in sub-Saharan Africa is heterosexual intercourse; the problem is exacerbated by grinding poverty, extended family structures, and increasing urbanization. At the UNAIDS conference, President Thaba Mbeki of South Africa questioned whether HIV and AIDS were related.[90] In most countries in sub-Saharan Africa, foreigners are required to show proof of an HIV/AIDS test for entry, in addition to the WHO's vaccination certificate for yellow fever. Governments make the argument that they also have a duty to protect their citizens from infection from foreign disease-carriers (using the same argument as the United States). The rise of passport unions in sub-Saharan Africa among the East African Community and the Economic Community of West African States (ECOWAS) may contribute to rates of regional infection. UNAIDS has already undertaken programs within West African states to reduce the transmission of HIV/AIDS along transportation routes.[91] A further complication in Africa is the number and routes of refugees, who often exist along the margins of marginal societies. As a consequence of their liminal position, refugees are often stigmatized and unable to receive government attention. Also, some HIV/AIDS prevention and treatment strategies are based on governmental policies or those of nongovernmental organizations, which by their nature are national in focus. In short, underdevelopment, political instability, and mobility combine to make the geography of HIV/AIDS an international and largely unregulated issue.

The transmission of HIV/AIDS gives new anxiety to the increased travel and trade brought about by globalization. As before, much of the governmental reaction to this anxiety has been the control of international movement. As with previous attempts at quarantine during the plague and cholera epidemics, travelers in some places today are required to show a health passport that certifies their benign health. Leonard Nelson notes that in the administration of the WHO "emphasis on quarantine—i.e., the erection of entry barriers by each nation—has been diminishing in favor of increased reliance on epidemiological surveillance and the improvement of basic health services in member nations."[92] As indicated above, however, a number of countries in the global North and global South have taken on interdiction of HIV/AIDS patients themselves.[93]

There are two groups of countries—representing the core and periphery of international society—that have excluded or restricted the travel and/or settlement of HIV/AIDS-positive immigrants.[94] Two developing regions in the world stand out for their restrictions on the entry of HIV-positive travelers: Southeast Asia, and sub-Saharan Africa. Although the countries in sub-Saharan Africa and Southeast Asia face a very high percentage of infected populations, and have enacted governmental policies to restrict infection within the national populations, one of the main vectors of HIV/AIDS transmission in Southeast Asia has been tourism from the global North. UNAIDS and the Centers for Disease Control and Prevention describe three patterns of transmission for HIV/AIDS, which are related to three "zones":

Pattern I includes North America, Western Europe, Australia, New Zealand, and many urban centers in Latin America. In these industrial, highly developed areas, transmission has been predominantly among homosexual and bisexual men.[95]

In Pattern II countries, comprised of sub-Saharan Africa, and increasingly, Latin America, transmission of HIV occurs predominantly through heterosexual contact.[96]

Pattern III countries, which include North Africa, the Middle East, Eastern Europe and Asia, and the Pacific, have thus far experienced less morbidity and mortality from the pandemic.[97]

These zones and corresponding patterns of transmission are related to mobility and control. In particular, those in Pattern I countries attempt to regulate entry through testing, either for the provision of targeted care (in the case of Sweden, France, and the United Kingdom) or exclusion (in the case of the United States). In Pattern II countries, regulation is becoming increasingly stringent.

Southeast Asia presents an unusual case for the transmission of HIV/AIDS. Sex tourism in Southeast Asia, and the ability of infected travelers from developed countries to access sex workers, has caused an explosion of the number of HIV-positive persons in this region. Ryan Bishop and Lillian Robinson argue, "In these international interactions, including the sexual ones, the flow from center to periphery, from here to there, is virtually unidirectional."[98] Sex tourism in the region is a legacy of Japanese and U.S. imperialism and the extension of military base prostitution to a wider sex trade industry.[99] The dynamics of sex tourism in Thailand are particularly illustrative of the impact of mobility on disease transmission. Girls and women from the rural north of Thailand are often sold into prostitution or migrate themselves to the lucrative sex trade. As Chris C. Ryan and Michael Hall contend, describing sex work as "voluntary" or "exploitative" constructs a false dichotomy in which the economic and social conditions of rural women are oversimplified: "sex work is the means by which single women provide food, a home and clothes for their families . . . for others it may be a passport to safety, avoiding a lot of other rape and violence in [their] life generally."[100] As the women return home, they often bring with them not only social stigma but also the HIV/AIDS virus.[101] As tourism is a central source of foreign exchange and development for Thailand, the sex trade was encouraged in the past by Southeast Asian governments through various public policies and legislation. Although Thailand, South Korea, and the Philippines consciously fostered the sex tourism industry to aid economic development, the governments and their populations are now reaping the fruits of this policy.[102] However, the epidemiological impact of HIV/AIDS is dire, and the Thai government is now taking steps to restrict the transmission of the disease. China, Vietnam, Japan, the Philippines, and Indonesia specifically prohibit the entry of all HIV-positive foreigners.[103] Although public programs attempt to stem the spread through safe-sex education and by subsidizing the distribution of contraceptives, Thailand has also implemented restrictions on travelers.

The requirement of certificates of health, specifically certifying the lack of HIV/AIDS infection, has roots in the geopolitics of the Cold War. In 1988, because of HIV/AIDS transmission from U.S. service personnel stationed at Subic Bay and Clark Air Force Bases, "US military personnel and all foreign sailors arriving in the Philippines would be required to present certificates showing that they are free from AIDS."[104] These countries are caught between the desire to protect their citizens and the need for economic development through sex tourism. Since the mid-1990s, Thailand and the Philippines have both relaxed their initially restrictive policies to HIV-positive tourists.[105]

The modern geopolitics of contagious diseases illustrates how the vectors of mobility have an impact on infection. The WHO vaccination certificate acts as a modern-day health passport, but it does not treat the modern plague of HIV/AIDS. While professing an international regime that is concerned more with surveillance than quarantine, two sets of states have put into place restrictions based on HIV/AIDS: the United States, with its relatively low infection rates, and poor countries, with high infection rates. A broader division exists between rich, healthy nations of the North and poor, diseased nations of the South. Thus, it is fair to say that the disease of poverty leads to other diseases such as cholera, tuberculosis, and HIV/AIDS. In the meantime, states in the North inoculate and certify their travelers into the South, whereas citizens and refugees from the South are denied entry into the North.

Conclusion:
Health and the Citizen—Disease and the Stranger

The health of the body politic is a central concern of governments. At root is a tension between the cosmopolitan aim of international society, which is the necessity for freedom of mobility, and the national aim of governments, which is to protect populations from disease. This chapter has illustrated three kinds of international regimes: an early modern regime, a colonial regime, and a core-periphery regime. In each case, the danger of disease was projected onto the marginalized segments of society. Also in each case, documents issued by governmental institutions, which were not necessarily linked directly to the sovereign ruler, certified the health of a citizen often by figuring the individual as part of the larger social structure of the nation. As students of Foucault would expect, we have seen the regime transform from one of explicit population control to one of surveillance and self-discipline.

This chapter has demonstrated that when a society is faced with an epidemiological threat, the marginalized in society are disproportionately governed. This governing, though perhaps well-intentioned, reflects the social attitudes towards "others." As Geunter Risse argues:

> The stereotypical responses of anxious and frightened individuals and groups confronted by the ravages of disease [are] . . . flight and denial, followed by the scapegoating of those who are judged to be different by virtue of religious beliefs, cultural practices, or economic status. These social reactions reveal our ambiguities about the meaning of such disease while furnishing convenient targets for projecting responsibilities and blame. The stranger, the Jew, the poor, the immigrant—all were victims of discrimination.[106]

The ways in which the stranger, the Jew, the poor person, the immigrant, and the prostitute are controlled often involve restriction of movement. In each case, trade and travel are seen as vital aspects of international society. International organizations such as the International Committee of the Red Cross, the Health Organization of the League of Nations, and the World Health Organization shifted their focus over time from a strategy of quarantine to a strategy of surveillance and prevention. An important example is found in the text of the International Certificate of Vaccination issued by the World Health Organization. Rather than the governmental examination of immigrant arrivals as was seen in the time of cholera, immigration officials now examine the vaccination certificate, which is filled out by the traveler and his national physician. National actors, however, retain a single-minded focus on protecting the health of the body politic. Similar governmental procedures are established in each of the epidemics we have examined: regulations that aim to restrict the infection of the national populace from a foreign disease; attempts to quarantine the most affected groups within the polis; association of the disease with nonnormative characteristics, be they religious, class, moral, racial, or sexual; documentation, surveillance, and control of the affected groups. Over the course of the eighteenth and nineteenth centuries, quarantine ceased to be a desirable solution because of the restrictions on trade it imposed. As a consequence, governmental mechanisms of surveillance and subsequently information became central to the international efforts to control disease. Because disease and identity are often not written on the body, other means of authentication were necessary—and the health passport serves this function. Thus, the health passport stands in for the body of the traveler. This reflects a general trend toward the examination of documentation rather than the examination of individuals, an issue I explore in Chapter 4.

Notes

1. Ann G. Carmichael, "Plague Legislation in the Italian Renaissance," *Bulletin of the History of Medicine* 57(1983): 508.

2. Sheldon Watts, *Epidemics and History: Disease, Power, and Imperialism* (New Haven, CT: Yale University Press, 1997), p. 16.

3. Ann G. Carmichael, *Plague and the Poor in Renaissance Florence* (Cambridge, UK: Cambridge University Press, 1986), p. 99.

4. Ibid., p. 104.

5. Watts, *Epidemics and History,* p. 17.

6. Ibid., p. 18.

7. Michel Foucault, "Truth and Power," in *Power/Knowledge: Selected Interviews and Other Writings, 1972–1977,* edited by Colin Gordon and translated by Colin Gordon, Leo Marshall, John Mepham, and Kate Soper (New York: Pantheon, 1980), p. 119.

8. Carmichael, *Plague and the Poor,* p. 121.

9. Ibid., p. 107.

10. Ibid., p. 117.

11. Ibid., p. 123.

12. Suzanne E. Hatty and James Hatty, *The Disordered Body: Epidemic Disease and Cultural Transformation* (Albany: State University of New York Press, 1999), pp. 140–141.

13. Ibid., p. 88.

14. Niccolo Machiavelli, *The Prince,* translated by George Bull (New York: Penguin Books, 1981), chaps. 7 and 11.

15. Hatty and Hatty, *The Disordered Body,* p. 123.

16. Ibid., p. 52.
17. Carmichael, *Plague and the Poor*, p. 106.
18. Ibid., p. 107.
19. Richard C. Trexler, *Public Life in Renaissance Florence* (New York: Academic, 1980), p. 363.
20. William H. McNeill, *Plagues and Peoples* (Toronto: Anchor, 1976), p. 182.
21. Hatty and Hatty, *The Disordered Body*, p. 144.
22. Valentin Groebner, "Describing the Person, Reading the Signs: Identity Papers, Vested Figures, and the Limits of Identification, 1400–1600," in *Documenting Individual Identity: The Development of State Practices in the Modern World*, edited by Jane Caplan and John Torpey (Princeton, NJ: Princeton University Press, 2001), p. 22.
23. Carmichael, *Plague and the Poor*, p. 124.
24. Leah Lydia Otis, *Prostitution in Medieval Society: The History of an Urban Institution in Languedoc* (Chicago: University of Chicago Press, 1985), pp. 80–81.
25. Henry Kamen, *Early Modern European Society* (London: Routledge, 2000), pp. 40–42.
26. Ann G. Carmichael, "Diseases of the Renaissance and Early Modern Europe," in *The Cambridge World History of Human Disease*, edited by Kenneth F. Kiple (Cambridge, UK: Cambridge University Press, 1993), p. 281.
27. McNeill, *Plagues and Peoples*, pp. 181–182.
28. Watts, *Epidemics and History*, p. 23.
29. Carmichael, *Plague and the Poor*, p. 116.
30. Mark B. Salter, *Barbarians and Civilisation in International Relations* (London: Pluto, 2002).
31. Michel Foucault, "Security, Territory, Population," in *Ethics: Subjectivity and Truth*, edited by Paul Rabinow (New York: New Press, 1997), p. 71.
32. David Arnold, "Inventing Tropicality," in *The Problem of Nature: Environment, Culture and European Expansion*, edited by David Arnold (Oxford, UK: Blackwell, 1996), pp. 141–168.
33. Mohamed Said, "Premodern Period in South Asia," in *The Cambridge World History of Human Disease*, edited by Kenneth F. Kiple (Cambridge, UK: Cambridge University Press, 1993), p. 414.
34. Watts, *Epidemics and History*, p. 193.
35. McNeill, *Plagues and Peoples*, pp. 241–242. Boards of health were established in England also in response to cholera.
36. Watts, *Epidemics and History*, p. 185.
37. McNeill, *Plagues and Peoples*, p. 232.
38. David Arnold, *Colonizing the Body: State Medicine and Epidemic Disease in Nineteenth-Century India* (Berkeley: University of California Press, 1993), p. 156.
39. T. O. Lloyd, *The British Empire, 1558–1995*, 2nd ed. (Oxford, UK: Oxford University Press, 1996), p. 178.

40. Watts, *Epidemics and History*, p. 182.

41. David Arnold, "Modern Period in South Asia," in *The Cambridge World History of Human Disease*, edited by Kenneth F. Kiple (Cambridge, UK: Cambridge University Press, 1993), p. 421.

42. Arnold, *Colonizing the Body*, p. 169.

43. Lothrop Stoddard, *The Rising Tide of Color Against White World-Supremacy* (New York: Charles Scribner's Sons, 1920), p. 8.

44. Michael S. Teitelbaum and Jay Winter, *A Question of Numbers: High Migration, Low Fertility, and the Politics of National Identity* (New York: Hill and Wang, 1998), p. 138.

45. Watts, *Epidemics and History*, p. 174.

46. Arnold, *Colonizing the Body*, p. 191.

47. Martin David Dubin, "The League of Nations Health Organization," in *International Health Organizations and Movements, 1918–1939*, edited by Paul Weindling (New York: Cambridge University Press, 1995), p. 56.

48. Radhika Viyas Mongia, "Race, Nationality, Mobility: A History of the Passport," *Public Culture* 11 (1999): 534.

49. Alan M. Kraut, *Silent Travellers: Germs, Genes, and the "Immigrant Menace"* (New York: Basic Books, 1994), pp. 31–36.

50. Geunter B. Risse, "Epidemics and History: Ecological Perspectives and Social Responses," in *AIDS: The Burdens of History*, edited by Elizabeth Fee and Daniel M. Fox (Berkeley: University of California Press, 1988), p. 48.

51. David F. Musto, "Quarantine and the Problem of AIDS," in *AIDS: The Burdens of History*, edited by Elizabeth Fee and Daniel M. Fox (London: University of California Press, 1988), p. 73.

52. Risse, "Epidemics and History," p. 46.

53. Kraut, *Silent Travellers*, pp. 51–59.

54. Ibid., p. 62.

55. Ian Hacking, *The Emergence of Probability: A Philosophical Study of Early Ideas About Probability, Induction, and Statistical Inference* (New York: Cambridge University Press, 1975).

56. Arjun Appadurai, *Modernity at Large: Cultural Dimensions of Globalization* (Minneapolis: University of Minnesota Press, 1996), p. 115.

57. League of Nations, Health Organization, *Health* (Geneva: League of Nations, Information Section, 1931), p. 8.

58. Lenore Manderson, "Wireless Wars in the Eastern Arena: Epidemiological Surveillance, Disease Prevention, and the Work of the Eastern Bureau of the League of Nations Health Organization, 1925–1942," in *International Health Organizations and Movements, 1918–1939*, edited by Paul Weindling (New York: Cambridge University Press, 1995), p. 11.

59. Ibid., p. 116.

60. Marta Aleksandra Balińska, "Assistance and Not Mere Relief: The Epidemic Commission of the League of Nations, 1920–1923," in *International Health Organizations and Movements, 1918–1939*, edited by Paul Weindling (New York: Cambridge University Press, 1995), p. 92.

61. F. G. Boudreau, "International Health Work," in *Proceedings of Academy of Political Science* 12 (1926): 381.

62. Frank Gutteridge, "The World Health Organization: Its Scope and Achievements," *Temple Law Quarterly* 37 (Fall 1963): 1–14, 2.

63. Frank G. Boudreau, "International Health Work," in *Pioneers in World Order: An American Appraisal of the League of Nations*, edited by Harriet Eager Davis (New York: Columbia University Press, 1944), p. 195.

64. I have argued in *Barbarians and Civilisation* that this position constitutes a reinvestment in the civilized/barbarian discourse of the nineteenth century.

65. U.S. Department of Health and Human Services, "International Certificate of Vaccination," PHS-731 (Rev. 11-91) (Washington, DC: U.S. Government Printing Office, 1997).

66. Albert Paolini, "Globalization," in *At the Edge of International Relations: Postcolonialism, Gender and Dependency*, edited by Phillip Darby (London: Continuum, 1997), p. 35.

67. World Health Organization, "The Global Risk of Infectious Diseases" (WHO, Department of Communicable Disease, Surveillance and Response), available online at http://www.who.int/emc/pdfs/GlobalhealthsecurityE.pdf.

68. UNAIDS, *Population Mobility and AIDS* (UNAIDS: Technical Update, February 2001, p. 4, available online at www.unaids.org.

69. World Health Organization, "International Health Regulations (1969)" (Geneva: WHO, 1983), available online at http://www.who.int/emc/IHR/int_regs.html.

70. Robert D. Kaplan, *The Ends of the Earth: From Togo to Turkmenistan, From Iran to Camodia—A Journey to the Frontiers of Anarchy* (New York: Vintage, 1996), pp. 18–19.

71. Suzanne B. Goldberg, "Immigration Issues and Travel Restrictions," in *Encyclopedia of AIDS: A Social, Political, Cultural and Science Record of the HIV Epidemic*, edited by Raymond A. Smith (New York: Fitzroy Dearborn Publishers, 1998), available online at www.thebody.com/encyclo.immigration.html.

72. Margaret Duckett and Andrew J. Orkin, "AIDS-Related Migration and Travel Policies and Restrictions: A Global Survey," *AIDS* 3 (1989): S251.

73. UNAIDS, "Technical Update: Population Mobility and AIDS" (February 2001), p. 4.

74. UNAIDS/WHO, "AIDS Epidemic Update," UNAIDS (UNAIDS/00.44E—WHO/CDS/CSR/EDC/2000.9), available online at http://www.unaids.org/wac/2000/wad00/files/WAD_epidemic_report.htm.

75. April A. Gordon, "Population, Urbanization, and AIDS," in *Understanding Contemporary Africa*, 3rd ed., edited by April A. Gordon and Donald L. Gordon (Boulder: Lynne Rienner Publishers, 2001), pp. 207–212.

76. Allan M. Brandt, "Acquired Immune Deficiency Syndrome (AIDS)," in *The Cambridge World History of Human Disease*, edited by Kenneth F. Kiple (Cambridge, UK: Cambridge University Press, 1993), p. 549.

77. Shirley Lindenbaum, "AIDS: Body, Mind, History," *AIDS in Africa and the Caribbean*, edited by George C. Bond, John Kreniske, Ida Susser, and Joan Vincent (Boulder: Westview, 1997), p. 191.

78. Goldberg, "Immigration Issues and Travel Restrictions."

79. Ibid.

80. G. Pendleton, "Immigration: Canada Joins US in Limiting Admission of People with AIDS," *AIDS Policy and Law* 16 (20 July 2001): 3.

81. Sarah N. Qureshi, "Global Ostracism of HIV-Positive Aliens: International Restrictions Barring HIV-Positive Aliens," *Maryland Journal of International Law Trade* 18 (1995): 9.

82. Brandt, "Acquired Immune Deficiency Syndrome," p. 547.

83. Susan Sontag, *AIDS and Its Metaphors* (New York: Farrar, Strauss, Giroux, 1988).

84. Paul Farmer, *AIDS and Accusation: Haiti and the Geography of Blame* (London: University of California Press, 1992), p. 16.

85. Ibid., p. 211.

86. Edward Albert, quoted in ibid., p. 221.

87. Jon Cohen, "The Hunt for the Origins of AIDS," *Atlantic Monthly* 286 (October 2000).

88. Richard Chirimuuta and Rosalind Chirimuuta, *AIDS, Africa and Racism*, 2nd ed. (London: Free Association Books, 1989), p. 104; Richard C. Chirimuuta and Rosalind J. Harrison-Chirimuuta, "AIDS from Africa: A Case of Racisms vs. Science?" in *AIDS in Africa and the Caribbean*, edited by George C. Bond, John Kreniske, Ida Susser, and Joan Vincent (Boulder: Westview, 1997), p. 180.

89. SIV cpz, or Simian Immunodeficiency Virus, Chimpanzee. Jon Cohen, "AIDS Debate Declared Dead," *Science Now* (25 April 2001): 1.

90. David Brown and Jon Jeter, "Hundreds Walk out on Mbeki," *Washington Post* (10 July 2000), n.p.

91. UNAIDS, "Population Mobility and AIDS," p. 8.

92. Leonard J. Nelson III, "International Travel Restrictions and AIDS Epidemic," *American Journal of International Law* 81 (January 1987): 234.

93. Duckett and Orkin, "AIDS-Related Migration," pp. S231–S252.

94. Qureshi, "Global Ostracism of HIV-Positive Aliens."

95. Brandt, "Acquired Immune Deficiency Syndrome," p. 547.

96. Ibid., p. 548.

97. Ibid.

98. Ryan Bishop and Lillian S. Robinson, *Night Market: Sexual Cultures and the Thai Economic Miracle* (New York: Routledge, 1998), p. 61.

99. Cynthia Enloe, *Bananas, Beaches, and Bases: Making Feminist Sense of International Politics* (Berkeley: University of California Press, 1990), pp. 82–83.

100. Chris Ryan and C. Michael Hall, *Sex Tourism: Marginal People and Liminalities* (New York: Routledge, 2001), p. 51.

101. Ibid., pp. 48–49.

102. Ibid., p. 141.
103. Qureshi, "Global Ostracism of HIV-Positive Aliens."
104. Enloe, *Bananas, Beaches, and Bases*, p. 89.
105. Qureshi, "Global Ostracism of HIV-Positive Aliens," pp. 7–8.
106. Risse, "Epidemics and History," pp. 57–58.

4

Passports and International Society

A small piece of tattered paper, marked August 5, 1914, [is] brought in every year. It reek[s] of barbed wire and machine-guns. Why could we not begin to tear it up, and take little corners off it every year?
—Viscount Hinchinbrooke, quoted in "Control of Aliens: Permanent Legislation Demanded," *The Times*, 25 November 1955

The modern international passport system arose in the aftermath of World War I, prompted by the British Passport Office's institutional innovations and the League of Nation's control of refugees by the Nansen passport regime (which allowed refugees temporary residence after alienation from their homeland). The modern mobility regime takes its lead from the liberal desire for travel and trade, as well as the postwar skepticism displayed toward foreigners, spies, and the fifth column. The regime was codified by the League of Nations at a conference of the Provisional Committee on Communications and Transit Conference on Passports, Customs Formalities, and Through Tickets held in 1920 in Paris. One of the most notable aspects of the early international passport regime is that many of its architects thought that the passport as a tool of domestic and international population control would be unnecessary after world politics returned to normal. At the moment of its inception, the international passport regime illustrates the twin desires of porous borders and security. Delegates at the conference also expressed their belief that the passport could guarantee security to states and that only the economic prosperity and international exchange that travel facilitates would provide security. I will explore these issues by examining the promise of the passport as a document of international travel, citizenship, and identification.

Formation of the Modern International System

With the outbreak of World War I, there came a bureaucratic-governmental need to track combatants and verify deserters. Just as World War I was a shock to European culture, it also represented a break in the nineteenth-century European mobility regime. However, once the passport regime was instituted, it seemed indispensable to security and stability. At the first League of Nations Conference on Passports and Frontier Formalities, held in 1920, several justifications for the passport regime were offered.[1] First, the passport regime was seen as a necessary security measure to prevent the influx of spies and malcontents. As Edigio Reale argues, "During this time of general suspicion, of constant vigilance against military espionage and of food shortage it seemed the only means of controlling aliens and assuring the protection of the military and economic interests of the state."[2] Second, passports were seen as a way to control the refugee problem—an extension of the refugee regime described so well by Nevzat Soguk.[3] Third, passports and visas were seen as a way to regulate the size of the labor market and thus to regulate wages. Fourth, passports and border formalities helped regulate the spread of epidemics.

Before discussing the ways in which European countries formalized the passport regime, I would like to highlight the reluctance of the international community to issue passports. In preparatory meetings for the 1920 and 1926 League of Nations conferences, the delegates and experts expressed their desire to do away with the passport regime. Despite the clear governmental imperative to protect the nation in its post–World War I form, and especially given some of the treatment of foreign nationals during the war, the statement from the 1920 conference is clear:

> The International Conference on Passports, Customs Formalities and Through Tickets
> . . .
> Convinced that many difficulties affecting personal relations between the peoples of various countries constitute a serious obstacle to the resumption of normal intercourse and to the economic recovery of the world;
> Being of the opinion, further, that the legitimate concern of every Government for the safeguarding of its security and rights, prohibits, for the time being, the total abolition of restrictions and that complete return to pre-war conditions which the Conference

hopes, nevertheless, to see gradually re-established in the near future;

Proposes that the League of Nations should forthwith invite the Governments to adopt the following measures with as little delay as possible.[4]

As Craig Murphy argues in regard to the early attempts at international organization, this conference and the international movement regime were promoted by the interests of capital (railways and travel) and reflected the idealist belief that personal interactions and economic recovery were aided by travel.[5] The legal basis for this attempt to dismantle borders was drawn from the Covenant of the League of Nations, which charged the League with the "provision[s] to secure and maintain freedom of communications and transit and equitable treatment for commerce."[6] This statement reflects the liberal mood that was prevalent in the immediate interwar period, which sought free movement and national security through economic integration. The attempted removal of passport and border controls is found throughout the League's history until the early 1930s. The nineteenth-century freedom-of-movement regime was applauded at the beginning of every League meeting until 1926 but was never deemed possible. During this time, the League encouraged the removal of passport, visa, and border controls by member countries. In its first recommendation, the League committee on passports suggested that countries that were contiguous should do away with visa and passport controls. However, the removal of visa and passport controls was seen to be a bilateral, rather than a multilateral, issue. Thus, contiguous borders could be made safe by mutual agreement, but no amount of agreement could make international space safe. By the same token, the League subcommittee on the passport regime recommended that passports be made valid for all countries, contrary to the practice of many countries, including Britain, at the time.[7] Bilateral relations could be made safe, but multilateral space was deemed to be equally unsafe.

Because two bureaucratic rationalities, or norms, were competing at this juncture, we can see how one explanation, one regime, comes to triumph over another way of configuring international politics. In the post–World War I international community, states chose a securitized regime of population movement over an ethic of freedom of movement. The British delegate to the League of Nations conference in 1926 argues precisely that, although many countries wished to dispose of the passport, because a few countries would not give up the passport—in fact, no country could afford to give up the passport. It would be impossible for a state to require a passport from a traveler whose government did not issue them. So, if one country required passports, all countries would be obliged to issue passports. At a British meeting, however, other considerations were aired. First, the passport was considered a primary mechanism for immigration officials to monitor and track foreigners and aliens in Britain. Second, the passport allowed the British Passport Office to control the international movements of its nationals. This control was exercised most assiduously against those wanting to emigrate to "certain South American countries where climate and other conditions are known to be unsuitable"; those who might be taking advantage of their British passport to act against British interests (through criminality, anti-colonial protest, or communism); and those who might be taken advantage of (such as women emigrating against their parents' wishes or women of "poor moral character").[8] Consequently, there were two faces, internal and external, that the passport provided in controlling population movement: It certified the nationality and identity of foreigners; and it certified the destination of nationals. Were passports to be abolished, foreigners could not be identified (and nationalized), and nationals might travel without control.

This ambivalence toward the passport and freedom of movement can also be seen in the specifics of the international passport regime. The 1920 League of Nations conference followed the British model in recommending that all passports be valid for a single journey (or at most for a period of two years). By 1922, the League Assembly made an important change. Rather than emphasize the single journey, the assembly emphasized the two-year duration idea. By 1925, the League recommended a duration of five years. What accounts for this change? A meeting of the subcommittee on the passport regime provided the answer. A delegate reported that in 1920 "it was not supposed that the regime of passports would last five years longer."[9] Each of the conferences from 1920 through 1926 contained an unresolved tension: the League urged a decrease in border and passport controls, and states moved to increase the security of the passport regime. For both sets of policies, governments expressed the need to resurrect a European trade and tourism sector.[10]

A central aspect of the modern international system was determined at this time as a result of the competing desires for freedom of movement and national security. States chose to follow the wartime mobility regime rather than the peaceful mobility regime of the nineteenth century. The security of individual states was placed above the integration of the world: state control of movement trumped individual freedom of movement. For example, the League committee recommended that facilities for foreigners who have been legally admitted into the country be

> compatible with their health regulations, their economic situation and with the interests of national security, and that, with this end in view, States should simplify as far as possible the regulations and procedure in force with respect to the sojourn of foreigners admitted into their respective territories.[11]

This anxiety was reflected in all subsequent passport agreements. For example, the exceptions to the freedom of movement described in the European Convention on Establishment (1955) and the International Covenant on Civil and Political Rights (1966) were "national security, public order, [and] public health or morality."[12] There is the persistence of a host ethic, yet there remained a priority on national interests in terms of health, economics (labor), and national security.

For citizens and governments alike, the passport regime was a necessary inconvenience to control the marginal and dangerous elements of society: criminals, prostitutes, colonial subjects, working women, and spies. Within European culture during the interwar period, we see a great deal of anxiety about the internal other—which some have argued is a necessary part of the construction of a national identity.[13] Because the national passport guaranteed entry into the country as a right of the individual over the right of the nation-states (primarily to exclude nonnationals), the passport became a way to counter the exclusionary power of the nation-state. It was a fundamental right of an individual to demand entry into his or her native state; it was the fundamental responsibility of the nation-state to admit all nationals. Thus, the passport became a central document of nationality: "British passports are only issued to British subjects and to British-protected persons. . . . *It is therefore of the utmost importance that before a passport is issued that the national status of the applicant should be established beyond all reasonable doubt.*"[14] The British passport would ensure entry for its bearer—and so the security function of the passport for nationals was displaced from the border to the Passport Office. Because the refusal of a passport was a matter of parliamentary concern, the Passport Office wanted to be sure that it ascertained the nationality of the bearer.[15]

British hegemony depended in part on the freedom of entry and exit for foreign and British merchants. However, as anxiety about foreigners grew, the British government implemented a series of increasingly tighter controls on entry into Britain. This modern regime can be traced to the 1905 Aliens Act, which expanded the government's ability to restrict entry and expel aliens. The 1914 Aliens Restriction Act was part of the wartime legislation. As an internal history of the Aliens Department of the Home Office contends, "Although legislation was used chiefly for war time purposes advantage was taken to build up side-by-side methods for dealing with economic and social problems in connection with aliens e.g. white slave traffic, international criminals and control of foreign labour."[16] In this description of institutional politics, we see the creep of legislation affecting national aliens extending to a number of marginal or antisocial groups. After the war, in the 1920 Aliens Act, the Parliament extended these "emergency powers." This legislation normalized emergency conditions and put in place a system of restriction of movement rather than freedom of movement.

The passport regime was created in pursuit of economic aims. After World War I and World War II, two economic imperatives shaped the continental mobility regime. First, countries wanted to reintegrate European economies in pursuit of the liberal belief that integrated markets reduced the potential for armed conflict. Second, passports and visas were seen as macroeconomic tools of the government—a way to regulate the size of the labor market and, consequently, wages.[17] One of the main arguments against the passport regime was that passport and frontier formalities inhibited business and tourist travel. As a consequence, the League of Nations committee of experts recommended bilateral agreements that would eliminate border and passport formalities between countries. The countries that took advantage of this opening were those that were economically secure or depended on economic interchange with their neighbors.[18] This selective elimination of border controls presaged the contemporary bifurcation of the international mobility regime. In each case, countries that were economically secure took different immigration precautions compared to those that were economically insecure.

The movement of labor was not viewed with the same degree of optimism. Given the example of the communist revolution, the British government was extremely concerned with labor unrest and low wages. As a consequence, immigration was tied closely to the Ministry of Labour. The statement of the Home Office is important in this regard:

> Every alien who enters this country for the purpose of seeking employment must be in possession of a permit issued to his prospective employer by the Minister of Labour. . . . By means (of coordination between the Ministry of Labour and the Aliens Dept.) a very strict control has been maintained over the employment of aliens in every kind of occupation in this country since the end of the war. The principle which has been followed in granting permits for aliens to take employment here is that no British subject is available for the job in question or that the alien has such special knowledge or skill that the interests of this country demand he should be allowed to take the employment offered.[19]

This legislation shows a remarkable similarity to contemporary immigration requirements. The demobilization of the armies after World War I threatened to flood the labor markets. This national dynamic of labor, wages, and skills came to be even more salient during the Depression. Also interesting is the way in which this class dynamic was gendered:

> The shortage of resident domestic servants in this country has created a demand for foreign domestic labour. A great part of the work of the Aliens Department of the Ministry of Labour has been to deal with applications to bring in foreign female domestics. Another large group which has occupied the attention of the Ministry has been aliens in the theatrical, musical and variety professions.[20]

During World War I, jobs opened up for women and immigrants in Britain because a large segment of the working male population was mobilized for the war. Thus, both women and men from the lower classes had the possibility of greater class mobility. However, this was also seen as a threat to the stable, conservative order, and these upwardly mobile people were controlled, at least in part, through the workings of the passport regime and its corollary, the labor permit regime.

Another tension between the freedom-of-movement regime and the securitized passport regime is seen in Britain's control of criminals. The League's technical subcommittee on the passport regime recommended in 1925 that the issuance of passports be bureaucratized and decentralized in order to minimize inconvenience and delay. However, in an attempt to restrict the movement of criminals, it was suggested that police stations, rather than post offices, be the subregional office that issued passports. A subcommittee delegate argued that using the police in this way was necessary because "the state which issued the passports took, to a certain extent, the responsibility of allowing one of its nationals to cross its frontier and proceed to a foreign country. In many cases, the police record of the person would have to be consulted."[21] Few delegates found this argument compelling. Furthermore, suggestions to implement fingerprints as identifying marks, to use two separate photographs rather than one, and to use security perforations were soundly rejected.[22] In the early passport regime, then, we see an attempt to balance the ethic of care in restricting the emigration of criminals and the ethic of freedom of movement in limiting inconvenience and delays.

Passports were also seen as a way to control the refugee problem.[23] This topic has been covered by Nevzat Soguk in *States and Strangers,* so I will not dwell on it except to give an indication of the value of his excellent work. Soguk argues that the presence of refugees, and the regime through which the international community dealt with refugees, helped to normalize the operation of the sovereign state. Refugees were the excluded, the dispossessed, the supplemental category that was not included in the universal categories of "citizen" and "nation."[24] The sovereign state and the international community both framed laws for the management of refugees. Refugees were constructed as a problem; the sovereign state was the solution. The Nansen passport—which allowed refugees temporary residence after alienation from their homeland—is one of the primary ways that this abnormality-normality, refugee-citizen matrix was constructed.[25] The British government issued "emergency certificates" that acted in many ways like the Nansen passport.[26] Many developed nations, such as Canada, Britain, and the United States, still have refugee passports, that is, emergency travel documents that confer no rights of citizenship, residence, or even repatriation.

The League of Nations passport regime was reaffirmed by the United Nations Organization in 1947, when the Meeting of Experts recommended the continued use of the "international" model of passports based on the British form. As in the earlier League meetings, the first item discussed was the feasibility of abolishing the passport, which was again dismissed as being impossible due to security issues.[27] Provisions were made for international certificates of vaccination. The experts also urged the removal of restrictions for travel and the lessening of inconvenient examinations at frontiers. The passport regime remained largely unchanged until the introduction of machine-readable passports in 1985 (see below).

One of the interesting facts about the modern passport regime is that despite calls for one in 1947 there was never an international passport conference (as there was with the law of the sea and other issues). The standards promulgated for the current international passport regime were formulated and promulgated by the International Civil Aviation Organization (ICAO). The management of passports by the ICAO would seem to support the functionalist theory of technical cooperation. However, functionalist theory cannot explain why the regime continues to be governed by the ICAO rather than by a purpose-built organization. The primary aspects of the contemporary passport regime are:

1. One person per passport;
2. Biometric information (face, eyes, voice, hand, fingers, signature) allows the identification of the bearer; and
3. Similar global format (e.g., for name, nationality, date of birth, place of birth, signature, security features, space for visas, permits, etc.).[28]

The passport's primary function is to "[denote] a person's identity and citizenship and provides an assurance for the State of transit or destination that the bearer can return to the State which issued the passport."[29] Security features of the passport include the encoded information at the bottom of the first page of the passport, holograms, and digitized photos.

In conclusion, at its inception the European passport regime served several important governmental needs: nationalist, security, and economic. The control of persons shifts from personal to documentary examination, and marginal groups, which were already subject to greater state control in everyday practice, were subject to greater controls at the border. Working and unmarried women, colonial subjects, criminals, prostitutes, and members of the lower classes were constrained far more than were middle-class envoys of business (whether merchants or consumers) and the upper-class envoys of the state. The construction of the nation during the interwar period shifted and became increasingly documentary. As postcolonial scholars have shown, this move is best illustrated at the margins of the national project: the colonies.

Citizenship, Immigration, and the Return of the Repressed

Some scholars argue that one of the hallmarks of modern national identity is a common narrative of founding and of sacrifice.[30] Canadian nationalism certainly notes its sacrifices in World War I and marks its first recognition as an international actor in being a signatory to the Versailles Treaty and the Covenant of the League of Nations. However, after World War I, Canadians needed a passport to travel to the United Kingdom. This requirement was questioned in the Canadian Parliament on the grounds of convenience and national prestige. If Canada was a full member of the empire and the international community, then its citizens should not be required to produce a passport to travel within the empire. Canadians felt that the requirement of the passport was embarrassing. The response from the British secretary of state for foreign affairs to the governor-general of Canada indicated that passports were necessary for Canadians because of the absolute need to control all entries into Britain. Though inconvenient and perhaps embarrassing, passports provided the most convenient instrument to prove national identity.[31]

The Canadian objection forced the issue of the new restriction of mobility regime. During the nineteenth century and prewar twentieth century, British subjects (but not colonial subjects) did not need passports to travel within the empire. However, with the Aliens Act of 1920, "it [was] necessary for all persons, whether British subjects or not, to be in possession of passports when traveling to any part of the British Empire and it [was] found that the passport system [was] a necessary and satisfactory safeguard."[32] In fact, because India did not have specific immigration legislation, the Aliens Act was the only legal instrument that could be applied to entry.[33] Though juridically under the control of one sovereign, British subjects needed a passport to travel between and within the different territories of the empire. This reflected the new movement regime and provided a powerful counterargument to John Torpey's distinction between "internal" passes and "external" passports.[34]

The British passport system had largely solidified by World War II. The application form had been standardized.[35] And the Passport Office had undergone two reorganizations to accommodate the large demand for travel documents. In 1938, the British passport had acquired its blue cardboard cover with the gold coat of arms and resembled almost precisely the passport issued in Britain until the appearance of European Union passports at the end of the twentieth century.[36]

British nationality was codified in a number of acts of Parliament (the British Nationality Acts of 1895, 1870, 1772, 1730, and 1708) that had ramifications for the application and granting of passports. The British Nationality and Status of Aliens Act (1914) made clear the distinction between colonial and national citizenship. In brief, second-generation British colonial subjects could no longer claim British nationality.[37] With revisions to this legislation, it became necessary to print on the back of the passport applications the different ways that the applicant might obtain British citizenship. Thus, the legal differentiation between Britain, dominions, colonies, and protected states came to be embodied in the citizenship and passport legislation. Naturalization for aliens was possible according to the following conditions:

> (a) that he has either resided in HM dominions for a period of not less than five years in the manner required by this section, or been in the service of the Crown for not less than five years within the last eight years before the application; and
> (b) *that he is of good character and has an adequate knowledge of the English language;* and
> (c) that he intends . . . to reside in HM dominions or to enter or to continue in the service to the Crown.[38]

English fluency thus was a marker of cultural assimilation. Wives derived their status entirely from their husbands, and children derived their status through their fathers (this act was repealed in 1948). The legislation also prohibited the naturalization of any "person under disability. . . . [For the purposes of this Act] 'disability' means the status of being a married woman, or a minor, lunatic, or idiot."[39] This definition spelled out the marginalized groups that were subject to control based on notions of rationality, gender, and madness. Colonial and racial discourses were also implicated in these regulations. Radhika Mongia illustrates the ways in which these regulations restricted entry based on the secondary characteristics of race (like fluency in English or suitability of climate) rather than race per se.[40] Although the origins of British citizenship stem from the territory of birth (jus soli), as the British dispersed across the globe the doctrine of citizenship by descent (jus sanguinis) came to predominate. In the first instance, citizenship was conferred if a subject's paternal grandfather possessed British citizenship. This right of jus sanguinis (the right of citizenship based on the citizenship status of one's parents) changed in 1914 to the first generation born outside the territories of Britain. As above, the Canadian nationality problem arose as a specific instance of dominion citizenship, and British citizenship was split. Though it had long been illegal to hold two citizenships or allegiances, dominions offered their nationals distinct citizenship; they were also entitled to hold British citizenship as members of the empire. The dominions, except Canada, passed citizenship legislation in accordance with the British Nationality and Status of Aliens Acts of 1914 and 1948. However, Canada reverted to the doctrine of jus soli and based citizenship on domicile. As a consequence, Canadian passports were issued with two colors of pages (pink for Canadians, blue for Britons).[41] Should a Canadian lose his/her Canadian citizenship through absence from the territory, his/her British citizenship would not be affected. Canadians were lucky to be living in a dominion: British-protected persons had no such protection. Unlike the case of British citizens and dominion citizens, "there is no exhaustive definition for British-protected persons," and this lack of juridical status was reflected in their lacking the right to citizenship.[42] Because the Passport Office is the de facto policing agency of the state in regard to citizenship, it published a memorandum about the British Nationality and Status of Aliens Act, which summarized the new law for its passport officers:

> British nationality is acquired at birth by any person born within HM dominions and allegiance but birth within a state over which the British Protectorate is exercised is not sufficient to confer British status upon the individual concerned. Thus, *although the Crown has complete authority over these territories, persons born therein are not regarded as British subjects, but as British-Protected Persons.*[43]

This illustrates a distinction between natural sovereignty and colonial control. Herein the imperial doctrine of trusteeship is connected to the doctrine of nationality. Whereas the French and British felt a duty to undertake civilizing missions, the French and British governments framed imperial expansion within a clear racial and political discourse in which colonies did not merit full independence and colonial subjects did not merit full citizenship.

The importance of this issue is evidenced by a report written by R. C. Cox, the chief passport officer in 1950.[44] Although Cox ends with a memorandum summarizing the important legislative changes for the Passport Office, he starts with a history of nationality and citizenship in law that reaches back to British common law in the twelfth century. We must ask what effect this long excursus on national identity and national law had on the Passport Office. Because the passport has no statutory basis, this report established the passport as a pragmatic solution to the problems of nationality. This report also makes explicit the implicit role of the Passport Office, which was to police nationality and national status. Whereas the role of the wartime Passport Office was to regulate movement, the role of the postwar Passport Office was (as it is today) to regulate nationality.

In discussing this history, Cox argues that the notion of citizenship is a modern invention and that the common law root of the concept was the feudal relationship of allegiance. This feudal period is described as a "pure" time when identity was understood as a relationship of allegiance and responsibility. This tradition carried "right down to the Naturalisation Act of 1870, [when] British nationality was indelible; it could neither be taken away nor renounced. Nor could it be conferred except by statute."[45] This unambiguous, indelible nationality-cum-allegiance was made possible by the largely contiguous nature of British space (though the cases of Ireland, Gibraltar, and the colonies are unexamined). However, with the expansion of the empire and extraterritorial sovereignty, British subjects who were born to British fathers, or British grandfathers, were considered citizens. This assignation of citizenship to grandchildren was considered to have gone too far. Thus, the colonies presented the first problem of citizenship.

The second problem of legal citizenship comes from what Cox describes as the "nationality" problem: "the rapid development of intercourse between nations and . . . the flood of emigration from the United Kingdom [led to the recognition that] nationality was now becoming an international problem."⁴⁶ This increased intercourse often led to the "evils of dual nationality." Cox characterizes the nineteenth century:

> Improved communications, increased wealth, expanding trade and industry had all contributed to this result. Movements of population resulting from the wars were still in progress; emigration was beginning to create anxieties and perplexities; nations were intermarrying and children were being born in foreign countries, bringing the world with them a crop of nationality problems. . . .
> Intercourse between nations was, in short, beginning to cause friction and to call for the same sort of regulation as intercourse between individuals.⁴⁷

Thus, because of greater travel, commerce, and intercourse, international society itself posed a threat to the old model of allegiance, and "nationality" came to be figured as a problem of citizenship. Citizens were figured as the marrying, fecund envoys of the sovereign, who in their dalliances produced children of dual nationality or no nationality. Dual nationality was negotiated between states so that the dual citizen could not call on the protection of one sovereign against the other sovereign. Statelessness remained unresolved, however. Cox argued that parliamentarians unfamiliar with the common law poorly drafted the British Nationality and Status of Aliens Act of 1914 and did not clarify sufficiently a subject born "within the allegiance of the Crown." The result was an imprecise citizenship regime. In 1946, Canada was the first dominion to pass its own, distinct, separate citizenship law, which divided Canadian citizenship from British citizenship. This move was received with some surprise within the Commonwealth, but dominion governments found separate legislation appealing from a pragmatic point of view, and all the dominions (except Pakistan) followed suit. This colonial legislation had the effect of shifting "the focal point of nationality, or allegiance, . . . from the centre [Britain] to the perimeter [the colonies]."⁴⁸ This Canadian act set the precedent, and was the model, for the other Commonwealth countries to align their nationality policies with Britain (but stemming from their national parliaments). Cox hails the revisions of 1948 for reconnecting place of birth, parentage, and citizenship.

Finally, Cox concludes by summarizing the British Nationality Act of 1948 for passport officers. After a section-by-section summary, the report concludes that in the new act "conciseness and clarity of diction has thus been achieved together with economy of phrase, but not without making some demand on the readers of the text who have to make themselves acquainted with the exact meaning of an unusual number of such terms of art."[49] Thus, the passport officer should supplement his reading of Cox's own summary with the original legal document.[50] The history must then serve some other purpose than a summary or introduction, because the officer is instructed to read the full act in the original. I would argue that this circular, which was distributed to all examining officers, served the function of creating an ideational, historical, and governmental "origin" of the passport—a myth of origin for citizenship and the passport itself. In this narrative, the Passport Office occupied a place at the vanguard of the battle for British citizenship, newly and precisely defined. Within the framework of this document, examiners were not merely enforcing rules but defending the nation.

The right of abode in the United Kingdom connected the passport-bearer's racial and national identities. Faced with the threat of the postcolonial returnees, Britain controlled the specter of immigration through passport and immigration legislation. In this configuration, we see that the two worlds of movement were not geographical but rather reflected two populations. There were two components to this system: passport controls that illustrate controls on citizenship, and immigration controls.

As argued above, the defense of the nation was figured in terms of threats, often from those at the margins of mainstream society. In the postimperial state, a danger came from the "return of the repressed" (i.e., the immigration of postcolonial subjects). The Commonwealth Immigration Act of 1968, the Immigration Act of 1971, and the British Nationality Act of 1981 each represented the contested obligations of the British government to its former imperial subjects and its "natural" citizens.[51] The Commonwealth Immigration Act of 1968 restricted entry to those with "close ancestral ties to the United Kingdom." This legislation was prompted by racial tensions in England and the expulsion of Asians from Uganda by dictator Idi Amin.[52] These Asians were neither Ugandan citizens, nor Indian citizens by virtue of their birth, nor British citizens.[53] These were peoples, displaced in the first instance or later in diasporas, who were alienated from their country of origin, their country of birth, and/or their country of past colonial control. Hong Kong Chinese also fell into this category, as they were granted UK passports that also restricted rights of immigration.

Decolonization represented a direct assault on the narrative of imperialist nationalism. Non-Europeans were secondary members of the British, French, and Belgian Empires and were rarely afforded the same rights as true citizens. In the British case, as decolonization meant independence for the majority of the British Empire in the 1960s, new legislation was introduced to create citizenship requirements for entry into and residence within the United Kingdom. Passports are markers of citizenship, and as with the dominions, there were different categories of citizens. There were natural-born British citizens, British citizens by right of birth or parentage, and, finally, "citizens of the United Kingdom and Colonies" who had no right to enter, live, or work in Britain.[54] The British relied on policies in use during the interwar period, namely, employment vouchers from the Ministry of Labour.[55] Meanwhile, the Passport Office acted as the guardian of citizenship. During the process of decolonization, it was easier to determine who was *not* a citizen than who *was* a citizen. Thus, the discourses of family linkages, suitability, and culture (secondary characteristics of "race") came into play in the drafting of immigration legislation.

The widespread acceptance of the passport as a travel document and as proof of citizenship is striking in the British case because the passport itself had no statutory authority. The Passport Office and the passport itself were temporary, pragmatic solutions to a governmental problem of movement. Once institutionalized, the "emergency" was normalized, and passports became "necessary" even in peacetime. The director of the Passport Office in 1945 argues, "Although our present system of organisation leaves much to be desired especially from a security angle, it is in my view the best that can be done under any system of Treasury Control and in the absence of settled policy as to the continuance of the Passport system."[56] By 1947, identity was certified with reference to other government documents, such as the National Registration Identity Card and birth certificate.[57] This system of documentation was facilitated by wartime legislation that required all persons in Britain to possess and be able to present some kind of identity document when requested. It was recognized by the Home Office that "the card constitutes evidence of bodily identity of the strictest kind. It provides, however, no evidence of character or loyalty."[58] As a consequence, these cards were solely "a physical means of attaching to a person a number through which particulars of that person can be traced in other records."[59] Although the marginalized were still controlled to a greater extent than the mainstream, this legislation was a step toward the governmentalization of the process, wherein the document must be consistent only with itself and not the body it claims to represent. Thus, the modern passport does not certify the "security" or even "identity" of the bearer: the passport certifies only that the document of the passport is identical to other documents. The accumulation of papers and documents creates the identity.

Indeed, the process had been regularized to the extent that the recommendation of a member of the upper classes (although chartered accountants had been removed from the potential list of recommenders) was pro forma rather than substantive. A treasury auditor even argued that the directories and lists by which recommmenders were checked were incomplete and that no examination of the recommender was undertaken. Consequently, "only fools are caught and knaves escape"; investigation into the name of a *real* doctor, lawyer, or bank officer was enough to recommend a passport.[60] Thus, the auditor suggested that apart from a consultation with the "suspect recommenders' list," only the formal examination of the form was necessary. In short, because the recommendation of a member of the upper classes could be forged (i.e., the source of the passport was "leaky"), the Passport Office confined itself to an examination of the form of the application rather than its content.

Machine-Readable Identity

In aiding movement, passports must be consistent throughout international society to facilitate inspection at borders and to minimize the potential for forgery. In 1920, the League of Nations committee recommended a single, ideal passport form: the international form of passport following the British model. This included a photograph, a limited physical description, employment, and destination. Following the trend toward racial taxonomy in the early anthropology and photographic discourse, photographs were initially corroborated by written physical descriptions of facial features.[61] This stress on visuality was also present in the hiring and training of Canadian border guards.

Visuality and technology remained a central concern of the Canadian Passport Office, which intended "to introduce a new passport document . . . to permit the use of digitized photographs, signatures and other biometric information and to begin collecting biometric data."[62] This completed the transition from reading the person to reading the document and suggested a movement toward reading the body. In the post–September 11 world, a great deal of faith is being placed in biometric technologies.

Biometric information is at the core of the passport document: it certifies some physical connection of the documented identity to the body possessing it. Before the widespread use of photography, applicants were obliged to describe their facial features, hair color, eye color, height, and "any visible distinguishing marks or peculiarities." These descriptions were supplemented by the photograph, and as photographs became more reliable as a technology, biometric information that was visible on the photograph ceased to be duplicated.

The first modern reintroduction of biometric information was the use of fingerprints to identify "illiterates," as opposed the "ordinary Britisher."[63] This particular anxiety of reading the written identity, understood as the unique signature, is linked to those applicants of Indo-Pakistani origin who "can only print his signature labouriously, or can only sign in oriental script."[64] The Indo-Pakistani immigrant group was treated differently for its supposed propensity for passport fraud as well as for writing in a different language. The use of fingerprints and other biometric information used for identification has been a well-established technology in a number of institutions such as "prisons, benefits systems, border-control operations and driver's license bureaus."[65]

In 1985, the first machine-readable passports were introduced.[66] The information of the bearer was encoded so that immigration officials could verify that the passport was identical *to itself*. This inspection regime represents a further progression in the transition from the examination of the person to the examination of the document. The inclusion of biometrics shifts the inspection from the document to the body itself.[67]

The U.S. government is testing several technologies, including handprints and iris scans.[68] Before September 11, use of these technologies was voluntary. However, increased anxiety about terrorists may lead to the widespread integration of these biometric scans into everyday travel. The International Air Transportation Association has argued that "increased use of biometrics for everyone who comes in contact with an aircraft . . . or the outside of an airport" is the best way to increase intelligence and subsequently safety.[69] The U.S. Senate Judiciary Subcommittee on Technology, Terrorism, and Government Information heard from experts on the use of "facial recognition, fingerprints, iris scans, or hand geometry" in new travel documents.[70] Testing is currently being done in the Netherlands at Schiphol Airport to associate iris scans with the passport.[71] Canada will run a similar program, in which a card will store one's documentary and biometric data so that no physical examination of the traveler or his/her passport will take place.[72]

Conclusion: Protecting Whom from What?

Passports have been understood as the solution to several problems in modern government, and the modern movement regime illustrates the increasing promulgation of governmental technology.

The formation of today's movement regime provides more evidence of the move from examining the body to examining the document. Although governments first attempted to assess the intentions and the safety of the traveler, this security function was impossible to fulfill. Consequently, governments contented themselves with certifying that the document was identical to itself and to other documents. The intentions and the body of the traveler were represented by the document. This examination becomes further removed from the individual as machine-readable passports and other biometric travel documents come to the fore.

A nation's passport office thus comes to function as an institution that naturalizes and polices citizenship. Dual nationality is described as a problem that citizenship solves, and the primary indicator of citizenship is the passport. Cox's report on the British Nationality Act of 1948 connects the passport and the British Passport Office to the sovereign through law. The examiner's inherently interpretive role is presented as being steeped in the defense of the British nation. As with many institutions, the Passport Office as well as immigration legislation control different groups in different ways. High-risk groups such as women, criminals, prostitutes, and entertainers are controlled much more restrictively than low-risk groups such as businesspersons.[73] As late as 1969, the British Passport Office retained on the passport application a space to evaluate the "intention" of the traveler. Categories that were specifically noted for administrative attention were: children; female theatrical and variety artistes (who were in natural danger of the white slave trade, prostitution, or generally being taken advantage of); globetrotters ("the increasing number of youngsters proposing to make unusual or hazardous transcontinental journeys or expeditions to remoter parts of the world"); marriage abroad ("British women traveling abroad to marry Hindus, Moslems, etc."); those who traveled behind the Iron Curtain; and business travelers. The Passport Office provided business travelers with extra information about their destination, assistance, and "in exceptional cases [the] grant of second passports."[74] This suggests the two functions of the passport: to facilitate international movement, and to control international movement.

Modern passports thus serve a number of functions: Passports certify identity; they certify nationality; they facilitate commerce; and they provide a way for the nation to define and protect its community. In the current era of globalization, international society remains concerned with the very same anxieties that fueled the formation of the passport regime in the early twentieth century. Governments have a desire to foster travel, trade, and international "intercourse." Following liberal and neoliberal beliefs, states want to be integrated into the world economy and international society. However, states are also charged with being the protector of the nation. As such, they must define and then protect a supposedly homogeneous community from dangers—including the danger of heterogeneity. The constant interruption of national economic, demographic, and cultural borders not only reveals the limits of the nation as an idea of a complete society but also reminds us of the danger of the stranger. The passport becomes a solution to the problem of nationality and the problem of porous borders. In Chapter 5, I will examine historical and current cases in which governments have attempted to eliminate the passport.

Notes

1. League of Nations, *Conference on Passports, Customs Formalities, and Through Tickets* (Geneva: League of Nations, Provisional Committee on Communications and Transit, 1920).

2. Edigio Reale, "Passport," in *Encyclopaedia of the Social Sciences*, vol. 12, edited by Edwin R.A. Seligman (New York: Macmillan, 1934), p. 15.

3. Nevzat Soguk, *States and Strangers: Refugees and Displacements of Statecraft* (Minneapolis: University of Minnesota Press, 1999).

4. League of Nations, *Conference on Passports*, p. 1.

5. Craig N. Murphy, *International Organization and Industrial Change: Global Governance Since 1850* (Cambridge, UK: Polity, 1994).

6. Art. 23, para. e, from League of Nations, Advisory and Technical Committee for Communications and Transit, Subcommittee on the Passport Regime, "Minutes of the 3rd Session, Held in Paris, October 2nd to 5th, 1925" (C.699.M.252. 1925 8), p. 2.

7. Ibid., p. 3.

8. H. S. Martin, "Refusal of Passports" (1926) (FO 612 355).

9. League of Nations, *Conference on Passports*, p. 4.

10. This directly contradicts the argument of Darren J. O'Byrne, "On Passports and Border Controls," *Annals of Tourism Research* 28 (2001): 399–416.

11. League of Nations, *Conference on Passports*, section 1.e.

12. Daniel C. Turack, *The Passport in International Law* (London: Lexington Books, 1972), pp. 3–4.

13. Roxanne Lynn Doty, "Sovereignty and the Nation: Constructing the Boundaries of National Identity," in *State Sovereignty as Social Construct*, edited by Thomas J. Biersteker and Cynthia Weber (Cambridge, UK: Cambridge University Press, 1996), p. 122.

14. Passport Office, Consular Instructions, "Passports and Visas" (October 1921), p. 2 (FO 612 265) (emphasis in original).

15. Martin, "Refusal of Passports."

16. Britain, Aliens Department, Home Office, "General System of Alien Control" (7 July 1939) (HO213 331).

17. League of Nations, "Minutes," October 1925, p. 6.

18. League of Nations, "Action Taken by Governments on the Recommendations Adopted by the Second Conference on the International Regime of Passports" (Geneva: League of Nations, Advisory and Technical Committee for Communications and Transit, June 1929) (C.133.M.48.1929 8) (HO213 331).

19. Ibid.

20. Ibid.

21. League of Nations, " Minutes," October 1925, p. 5.

22. H. S. Martin, "Technical Sub-Committee on the Passport Regime" (14 May 1926) (FO 612 355).

23. Aliens Department, Home Office "General System of Alien Control" (July 7, 1939) (HO 213 331).

24. Soguk, *States and Strangers*, pp. 15–18.

25. Isabel Kaprielian-Churchill, "Rejecting 'Misfits': Canada and the Nansen Passport," *International Migration Review* 28 (1994): 283.

26. Passport Office, Consular Instructions (1921), p. 15 (FO 612 265).

27. United Nations, Economic and Social Council Official Records, "Report of the Meeting of Experts to Prepare for a World Conference on Passports and Frontier Formalities" (Geneva: UNESCO, April 1947), pp. 2–3.

28. International Civil Aviation Organization, "Report by the Council on the Progress of Implementation of Resolution A32–18: International Cooperation in Protecting the Security and Integrity of Passports" (June 2001) (A33-WP/12 EC/7).

29. International Civil Aviation Organization, "Proposed New Section III to Appendix D of the Consolidated State of Continuing ICAO Policies in the Air Transport Field" (June 2001) (A33-WP/12 EC/7).

30. Benedict Anderson, *Imagined Communities: Reflections on the Origin and Spread of Nationalism*, 2nd ed. (London: Verso, 1991), pp. 9–10.

31. Duke of Devonshire, Secretary of State for the Colonies, to Lord Byng, the Governor-General of Canada, "Telegram: Personal" (25 July 1924) (32812/24) (FO 612 129).

32. Foreign Office, "Passports Within the Empire" (6 August 1926) (Cor. 6826.HSM) (FO 612 129).

33. Ibid. (FO 612 129).

34. John Torpey, *The Invention of the Passport: Surveillance, Citizenship, and the State* (Cambridge, UK: Cambridge University Press, 2000), pp. 164–167.

35. Passport Office, *Revision of Form A* (1934/5) (FO 612 181).

36. Passport Office, "Specimens of Passports" (15 September 1938) (FO 612 198).

37. Passport Office, "Revision of Passport Application Forms: Minute Sheet" (1946) (FO 612 246).

38. Passport Office, *British Nationality and Status of Aliens Act, 1933*, 4&5 Geo. 5, Ch. 17, Sec. 2 (I) (26 November 1946) (emphasis added).

39. Ibid., secs. 5(3) and 27(1).

40. Radhika Viyas Mongia, "Race, Nationality, Mobility: A History of the Passport," *Public Culture* 11 (1999): 541.

41. Canada Customs and Revenue Agency, Passport Office, *The History of Passports* (2001), available online at http://www.dfait-maeci.gc.ca/passport/history_e.asp.

42. British Passport Office, "Memo: British Nationality and Status of Aliens Acts 1914 to 1943" (1943) (T. 10741/75/378) (FO 612 258).

43. Ibid. (emphasis added).

44. R. C. Cox, *Notes on United Kingdom Nationality Law*, Examiners Circular No. 470 (1950) (FO 612 275).

45. Ibid.

46. Ibid.

47. Ibid.

48. Ibid.

49. Ibid.

50. Jacques Derrida, *Of Grammatology,* translated by Gayatri Chakravorty Spivak (Baltimore: Johns Hopkins University Press, 1976), p. 144.

51. Katherine Manzo, *Creating Boundaries: The Politics of Race and Nation* (Boulder: Lynne Rienner Publishers, 1996).

52. Derek Humphry, *Passports and Politics* (London: Penguin, 1974).

53. Ibid.

54. "Classes of Passports," *The Times* (2 June 1967) (FO 612 320).

55. Foreign Office, "Circular No. 052" (14 June 1962) (TNN 3542/1) (FO 612 320).

56. J. W. Stafford, Chief Passport Officer, to J. C. Crombie, Treasury Office, "Passport Office Reorganisation" (19 February 1945) (FO 612 231).

57. L. H. Blunker, "Reports on Passport Office Organisation and Procedures by Treasury Organisations and Methods Division" (1947) (9233/35) (FO 612 267).

58. Britain, Home Office, "Draft Booklet for Issuance to Police Consolidating All H.O. Circulars on National Registration Identity Cards" (September 1944), p. 2 (H.O. Circular 700,600/17) (HO 213 754).

59. Ibid., p. 4.

60. Britain, Treasury Office, "Passport Office Reorganisation" (4933/54/505) (FO 612 230).

61. Paul Fussell, *Abroad: British Literary Traveling Between the Wars* (New York: Oxford University Press, 1980), pp. 28–29.

62. Canada, Passport Office, "Strategic Plan 1992–93 to 1996–97" (Ottawa: Department of Foreign Affairs and International Trade, 1993), p. 9.

63. From M. G. Dixon, Chief Passport Officer, to G. L. Angel, Home Office, "Order Book Amendments: P/Misc. 16348" (9 April 1968) (FO 612 349).

64. Ibid.

65. Maryfran Johnson, "The Biometrics Age," *Computerworld* 35 (8 October 2001): 24.

66. R.I.R. Abeyratne, "The Development of the Machine Readable Passport and Visa and the Legal Rights of the Data Subject," *Annals of Air and Space Law* 17, no. 2 (1992): 1–31.

67. David Lyon, "Under My Skin: From Identification Papers to Body Surveillance," in *Documenting Individual Identity: The Development of State Practices in the Modern World,* edited by Jane Caplan and John Torpey (Princeton, NJ: Princeton University Press, 2001), p. 299.

68. Michael Meehan, "Iris Scans Take Off at Airports," *Computerworld* 34 (1 July 2000): 1.

69. Pierre Sparaco, "IATA Advocates Biometric Security," *Aviation Week and Space Technology* 155 (12 November 2001): 50.

70. Dianne Feinstein, "Demonstrations of Biometric Technologies Senate Panel to Examine How Biometric Data Can Be Used to Help Prevent Terrorism," Federal Document Clearing House (FDCH) Press Releases (13 November 2001).

71. Brandon Mitchener, "Dutch Airport Experiments in Trading Privacy for Speed," *Wall Street Journal* (30 October 2001): A20.

72. Michael Meehan, "Canada to Use Iris Scans for Customs IDs," *Computerworld* 34 (4 December 2000): 7.

73. M. G. Dixon, Chief Passport Officer, "Revision of Form A 1969" (12 October 1969) (FO 612 346).

74. Ibid.

5

The Disappearance of Passports

A civilized society does not leave its borders totally open to those who would harm its citizens.
—Office of National Drug Control Policy, in Peter Andreas, *Border Games: Policing the U.S.-Mexico Divide*, 2000

The modern state has mobilized many of its bureaucratic and institutional capabilities toward the surveillance of its population. The passport is one such tool, giving the government precise information about the individual citizen, including her entry into and exit from the national territory. Thus, passport controls act as regulators of immigration and repatriation, balancing freedom of travel against national security.

Given that the passport plays a unique and useful institutional role in the surveillance of national and foreign populations, how can we account for the disappearance of passports in different parts of the globe? Is this simply the product of wealth and security, or does it represent a transformation in the international mobility regime? The passport has always played a limited role in the identification of individual travelers and given an incomplete promise of security to its citizens and other sovereigns. Are we hearing the death knell of the passport?

There are five passport unions currently in effect: the Schengen Agreement, which covers the European Union; the Nordic Council, including Sweden, Norway, Denmark, and Iceland; the Gulf Cooperation Council (GCC), encompassing Saudi Arabia, Bahrain, the United Arab Emirates, Kuwait, Oman, and Qatar; the Economic Community of West African States, which includes Benin, Burkina Faso, Cape Verde, Côte d'Ivoire, Ghana, Guinea, Guinea-Bissau, Liberia, Mali, Mauritania, Niger, Nigeria, Senegal, Sierra Leone, Gambia, and Togo; and the East African Community, consisting of Kenya, Tanzania, and Uganda. This chapter examines the similarities among these passport unions, making comparisons to the situation in the nineteenth century—the only other time in modern history when international travel was unrestricted within Europe.

Bothers, Nuisances, and Passports

Scholars of the nineteenth century, which was notable for the absence of wars among the Great Powers, credit international cooperation and the Concert of Europe for the unprecedented period of international peace.[1] Yet the colonial scene would see a great deal of violence and several major wars. During the eighteenth and nineteenth centuries, it was a social rite of the upper classes to conduct a "grand tour" of the major European cultural sites. Grand tours served the function of introducing eligible nobility to other nobles, as well as fostering a sense of a European culture and identity. These travels were fostered by expatriate nationals and familial or class connections. After the French Revolution, and during the nineteenth century, passports were considered largely obsolete within most of Europe. Several technical innovations also made travel increasingly accessible, namely, the railroad, the steamboat, and the telegraph. The world shrank, and the elimination of passport and border formalities was seen as a by-product. Passports were eliminated between 1843 and 1889 in France, Belgium, Spain, Germany, and Italy. If they were not obsolete, then passports were a function of the petty tyranny of border officials and not a necessary part of international travel.[2] As one traveler at the time stated: "the frontiers were nothing but symbolic lines which one crossed with as little thought as when one crosses the Meridian of Greenwich."[3] Indeed, passports were often issued to nationals but also to foreign travelers of good standing, that is, the upper class. One would obtain a British passport to go from Cairo to Istanbul across Ottoman territories; a French passport to travel to Venice; an Italian passport to enter Switzerland, and so on.[4] Cultivated Europeans saw the elimination of the passport as a sign of the maturity of European civilization.

Furthermore, in the nineteenth century, with the rise of Thomas Cook, we see the growth of mass tourism, which enabled the middle class to travel in Europe and its near-abroad. Thomas Cook in particular and travel agents in general began to procure passports on behalf of their customers directly from the British Passport Office. Over the course of the nineteenth century, middle-class women also gained some independent mobility. In the early part of the century, women "above a certain class" either disguised themselves as men or boys or required an escort to travel to avoid ruining their reputation.[5] However, with the rise of Thomas Cook, unchaperoned women could venture on group tours with little fear of having their virtue questioned.[6] Thus, travel became open to wide segments of the population: the growing middle class, the lower class, and unmarried or widower middle-class women.

Yet how much of the world was *actually* free to travel? Colonial subjects were limited through direct forced migration or through national immigration restrictions. John Torpey cites the elimination of passport regulations in the German states during the nineteenth century as evidence of the new regime. However, even when general passport requirements had been eliminated, "not all *'Inländer'* escaped the requirement of carrying a passport for internal movement; these non-exempt groups included certain types of journeymen, those traveling in postal conveyances, and non-citizen Jews."[7] Andreas Fahrmeir agrees: "An inherent problem of the nineteenth-century passport system [was] its explicit or implicit focus on social status."[8] His analysis indicates that lower-class, peripheral, and dangerous groups were controlled to a greater extent than the upper and middle classes. Outside the northern European core, countries at the edge of Europe persisted in the use of passports. For example, Italy became an example of a peripheral area in Europe in which a documentation regime grew in the nineteenth century and was maintained until 1889. The regulations in Lombardy-Veneto, provinces within the Austro-Hungarian Empire, illustrate the tensions between commerce and security. Andrea Geselle argues, "The passport regulations of 1801 [facilitated] the influx of foreign businesspeople and other unsuspicious travelers, and [prevented] 'shady' and 'work-shy' foreigners from entering or remaining."[9] The passport regime in the Austro-Hungarian Empire at this time was designed to "[constrain] the departure of inhabitants and the entry of foreigners."[10] By the mid-nineteenth century, new travel regulations had been put into place to make passports unnecessary for all journeys within the Austro-Hungarian Empire and to make passports necessary for all external travel.[11] At the height of the freedom-of-movement regime, European governments were so concerned about forgeries that the first security designs came to be applied to the passport.[12] Leo Lucassen is more precise in his refutation of the narrative of free movement:

> The era of free international migration only began around 1860, and even then state controls on movement did not vanish entirely. Moreover, not everybody was able to take advantage of this liberal wind. Some categories of aliens suffered discrimination . . . and the migrant poor in general were regarded with suspicion, increasingly hindered in their movements, and often expelled.[13]

Even in nineteenth-century Europe, the paragon of the freedom-of-mobility regime, the peripheral countries for nationalistic and governmental reasons tracked and controlled movement more carefully than those areas of the core, which could afford freedom of movement. Thus, even in the first era of globalization, there is a bifurcation of the international mobility regime.

Whereas France and Belgium had eliminated their passport controls early in the nineteenth century, Britain never even had passport controls, and Spain and Italy were late in relinquishing the passport. In the majority of European states, passport controls were imposed only during international conflicts between the nationals of warring states or during epidemics.[14] During the Franco-Prussian War and the Crimean War, travelers were advised to carry passports so that they could prove they were not spies. Complete freedom of movement did not occur until the middle-late nineteenth century. This parallels greater international cooperation on a number of functional and technological fronts and follows the conception of Europe as a self-contained safe space for Europeans. This continental geopolitics made movement possible, and travel easier, within the territorial bounds of Europe. However, the persistence of the freedom-of-movement regime did not deter governments from attempting to control their population and especially dangerous groups. At the height of the nineteenth century, when Dutch passport controls were almost nonexistent, there remained "surveillance systems . . . not so much to curb immigration, but to detect [politically] unwanted aliens."[15] Similar anxieties about labor, foreigners, criminality, and political undesirables are at play in the implementation of the freedom-of-movement regime under the Schengen Agreement.

Schengen Again and Again

Freedom of movement for populations, goods, and capital had been the intention of the European states since the League of Nations. This desire was elucidated in the Treaty of Rome and the Single European Act. The Schengen Agreement was implemented in 1995. The Schengen Agreement provides for the elimination of all frontier and border checks within the European Union. This is coincident with the rise of the "European passport," by which EU countries indicate their affiliation on the front cover of the passport. Although the EU passports abide by the international standard format of the passport set by the ICAO, they also include the title "European Union" on the front cover. The remainder of the passport is the same in form and function. As there are no new legal implications in holding the European passport (i.e., compared to earlier national passports), we may infer that the true innovation of the European passport is political in nature. The European passport indicates to a greater or lesser degree the attempt to forge a European identity, which in some way coexists with EU members' national identities. Although this reversion to a nineteenth-century model of freedom of movement within Europe is lauded as transcending the problem of nationality, the new problems that this freedom of movement creates are problems of the margins: crime, illegal immigrants, and unskilled or unregulated labor. Because all movement within the Schengen zone is free and without checks, illicit and undocumented movement cannot be controlled within the zone. Thus, the Schengen Agreement requires members to have extremely proficient and tight control over external borders. The border of the weakest member state comes to be the border of all "Schengenland."

Before examining the Schengen Agreement in depth, two precursors to the agreement should be mentioned: the Council of Europe, and the Nordic Council. The Council of Europe proposed a European passport in the immediate post–World War II period, with little support. However, the Nordic Council has made freedom of movement an essential part of its regional integration since its inception.

The Council of Europe was created in 1949 to forward regional integration and stemmed from the Soviet threat and U.S. sponsorship.[16] It was Europe's first postwar political organization, and for most of the 1950s it was the "most important forum for discussions of integration."[17] The Assembly of the Council of Europe attempted to eliminate or standardize a European passport. The precedents cited for the abolition of passports were the Nordic Council as well as the lack of passport requirements for travel between Ireland and Britain.[18] A questionnaire was distributed to member nations to assess governmental policies. The British foreign ministry, which rightly saw itself as a leader in the development of the contemporary passport (and of the Council of Europe itself), took the questionnaire very seriously. Member countries were asked whether the front cover should be reformed, in addition to including the national coat of arms and the name of the country. The foreign ministry committee saw no real objection to a European passport but thought it hardly necessary.[19] The Council of Europe moved toward the integration of European passports because the intended world conference on the passport was never convened. After the United Nations technical meeting in 1947, no other major intergovernmental conference was ever held. The initial proposals by the Council of Europe consisted of a European passport that would afford consular assistance and visa-free travel throughout the Council of Europe zone. However, these proposals were rejected, in part because the new documents would conflict with national passports. The British expressed the opinion that a duplication of the passport would lead to "problems." The British concluded:

> While there might be some symbolic value in the institution of a common form of "European Passport" it is not at present practicable to contemplate the establishment of a document which would afford its holder any greater facilities than those given by a national passport; and there would be little advantage and some danger in creating a document which would merely duplicate a national passport.[20]

In addition to the problem of overlapping sovereign rights, the Foreign Office argued that one of the main functions of the passport was to indicate the state that must accept a repatriated national. Where would repatriated Europeans be accepted? Furthermore, following R. C. Cox's history of the passport (see Chapter 4), the passport was considered to be a solution to the problems of nationality and immigration. The Foreign Office reported that a European passport could only come after a European *nationality,* as in the Nordic case. As the brief to the minister details, "Such a [European] passport can only be considered at the moment as an abstract possibility whose realisation depends more on the progress made towards a common European nationality."[21] The British rejection of the European passport occurred for reasons familiar to the previous history: regulation of the labor force; control of illegal migration and nationality questions; and, finally, security concerns. In particular, the brief cites the function of the immigration officer. During the examination at the border, the British immigration official is required by law to reject any immigrant who cannot support himself and his dependents (thus being a labor threat); is under extradition for a crime (a security threat); or is "mentally unbalanced or suffering from certain illnesses" (a public health threat).[22] This restatement of the securitized passport regime illustrates that the Council of Europe's decision to replace national passports in the region was premature.

However, after the proposed new passport was rejected, two other measures were adopted: the abolition of visas, and the standardization of passports. Harkening to the interwar period, the Assembly of the Council of Europe heard that the transportation of cars, the twentieth-century equivalent to nineteenth-century railroads, across national borders involved a great deal of bother and inconvenience. Consequently, following the Nordic model, individual states passed separate but corresponding legislation that made the transportation of motor vehicles across borders possible without passports and visas for cars.[23] However, such a tactic would not work in the context of intergovernmental coordination of passports. In 1957, passports ceased to be a requirement for those member nations on a multilateral basis. Thus, the European Agreement on Regulations Governing the Movement of Persons Between Member States of the Council of Europe "[allowed] the nationals of the other Contracting Parties to enter or leave their territory for visits of up to three months on the production of any documents listed in an appendix."[24] This freedom of movement was possible as long as the travelers had other forms of government-issued identification. Thus, the freedom was not to cross German or French borders without examination; rather, it was that the passport ceased to be the crucial and necessary document. Any government-issued document would certify identity.[25] This system did not mean the disappearance of the passport in the same way as in the nineteenth century or the Nordic Council. Passage over the frontier still required governmental documentation—a government-issued indication of identity—but the passport was no longer the primary document. Other documents have since been authorized by governments to stand in for the passport. Put another way, European space was becoming a kind of domesticated space, which is not quite the internal safe space of the nation but still close.

The Nordic Council, founded in 1952, was based on a strong regional identity and historical precedents.[26] The Nordic Council was not initially based in international law but rather an interparliamentary council and a set of corresponding laws passed in the respective national legislatures.[27] One of its first acts was to create a passport union. The passport union was facilitated by the high degree of coordination and cohesion among the Nordic countries. Public policy, in fact, is coordinated to the extent that "a Scandinavian who resides in another Nordic country than that of which he is a citizen enjoys, on the whole, the same social benefits as the citizens of his country of residence. One may actually speak of a Nordic social citizenship."[28] Pensions, unemployment benefits, health insurance, and even easily transferred citizenship all made the elimination of internal borders gain the public's approval. Travelers today need to show only their passport at the external borders of the Nordic Council rather than at the international boundaries within the union. This system was a success and a precedent for the Schengen Agreement. The Nordic Council also suggests the degree to which national and regional identities are linked to international documentation.

The history of the Schengen Agreement illustrates the extent to which rich, secure, trading countries are at the forefront of freedom of movement. During the 1980s, countries of the European Community attempted to reinstate the freedom-of-movement regime. However, there was much dissent, and so the original Schengen countries (France, Germany, Belgium, Luxemburg, France, and the Netherlands) formulated their own treaty in 1985. In June 1991, the European Council passed the External Frontiers Convention (EFC), which prefigured the Schengen Agreement in many ways. The EFC is the mirror of the Schengen Agreement in European law, before the accession of the latter in the European Union. The provisions of the EFC mirror the anxieties displayed in the Schengen process. The EFC guarantees states a "visual inspection" of all entrants to the European zone.[29] The EFC also delimits the "reasons for refusing entry . . . the lack of the necessary documents or a threat to the public policy or national security of member states."[30] In 1997, the Treaty of Amsterdam increased membership to the Schengen Agreement and made it part of EU law, which came into effect in 1999.[31]

Since March 25, 2001, Schengen Agreement has been extended to the countries of the Nordic Council.[32] This in itself poses problems. When Schengen was a companion but separate international regime, states could be admitted to the agreement without being admitted to the European Union, and vice versa. However, the European Union faces two problems: Schengen countries that are not Schengen-capable (Hungary is an example); and Schengen countries that are not EU members.

The definition of "Schengenland" presents an interesting geographical problem: although national legislatures are described as having ratified and acceded to the Schengen Agreement, the meaning ascribed to borders radically shifts. Internal borders are those shared by adjacent Schengen states; external borders are those between Schengen states and adjacent non-Schengen states.[33] Each external national border becomes an entrance for all Schengen states, whereas internal national borders come to be policed less vigorously. This shift represents a radical reformulation of the notion of the territorial state that has traditionally accompanied the doctrine of sovereignty, and several problems are created by this new regime. Just as the passport was seen to be a solution to the problem of nationalities in the interwar period, solutions had to be found to the problems of free movement. The solutions were increased police cooperation, the Schengen Information System, and increased checks at the external borders of the Schengen zone.

Free, uncontrolled movement runs counter to the notion of discipline that characterizes the modern welfare state. Michel Foucault traces the ways that a number of different societal institutions were designed precisely to render the criminal visible and control his movements.[34] The greatest anxieties that the Schengen Agreement have fostered are of transborder crime and immigration. The solution to both problems is increased surveillance. Police cooperation entails the sharing of information as well as the sharing of jurisdiction. Schengen police authorities are allowed the right of hot pursuit to cross borders to capture a criminal. Ethan Nadelmann argues that the general norm that one must either "extradite or prosecute" is one of the primary rules of international society.[35] The Schengen Agreement seems to extend this international legal custom into substantive public policy. Accompanying the right to hot pursuit are efforts to ensure that Schengen police forces can share information. The Schengen Information System involves the transmission of information electronically.

Data entered in one country become available to police forces throughout the Schengen zone. As John Benyon argues, "The [Schengen Information System] is regarded by the . . . Schengen countries as a critical compensatory measure for the removal of all frontier checks."[36]

The international surveillance system not only stands in for national border examinations; it acts as a kind of self-surveillance tool within Schengen countries. As a consequence of the elimination of passport controls, all Schengen nationals are required (at all times in all Schengen territories) to carry some form of identification that contains their national address. Thus, even though passports are no longer required to *cross* borders, they may be necessary to identify oneself *within* Schengenland. In addition to individuals self-policing their identity papers, companies and firms are also subject to sanctions if they hire illegal workers.[37] As Dita Vogel argues, "The employer . . . is thus made to fulfill an immigration gatekeeper function in the labour market."[38] Surveillance has been generalized and dispersed. In the guise of eliminating border controls, the entire space of Schengenland comes to be seen as populated by potentially unsurveillable, and thus dangerous, individuals. There are thus two populations: safe nationals, and unsafe foreigners. Each represents a different possible mobility regime and institutional response. The international mobility regime is bifurcated not with respect to geography but to populations. Some populations have been identified as dangerous, unsurveillable, and illegal—and individuals who fit the profile of these populations face a far less porous border than do safe individuals.

In the Nordic Council, all the external borders are policed with equal vigilance. However, Schengenland leaks from the north and the east.[39] The integration of the Nordic Council countries into the Schengen Agreement is in part a solution to the Norwegian rejection of membership in the European Union itself. When Sweden entered and Norway rejected the European Union in 1994, legal obligations to the other Nordic Council countries posed a problem for the European mobility regime. The European Union, via the Schengen Agreement, insisted that Sweden's external borders—even those with Nordic Council countries—be patrolled and policed as tightly as any other external border. Norwegians, however, did not need an entry visa or passport. Norway could then become a "backdoor" to the European Union, which made European countries very anxious. Thus, the European Union made a temporary exemption for Norwegian nationals.[40] However, a long-term solution was needed. The integration of Norway into the Schengen Agreement in 1996, despite the fact that it is not a member of the European Union, solved this problem. The mobility regime was saved by integrating Norway into the movement regime without any concomitant Europeanization.

But Schengenland also leaks from the east, namely, those countries that are applying for entry to the European Union but do not yet possess the governmental capacity to assuage Schengen members. The elimination of internal borders displaces all frontier anxiety onto the external borders of Schengen states, particularly states possessing a weaker governance capability as compared to the original group. Heather Grabbe points to the dynamic between the requirements and incentives for entry into the European Union and the Schengen Agreement:

> Borders with Schengen countries become more porous as [Central and Eastern European] countries become part of the common frontier zone, but these concessions on their western borders are made only if they apply harder controls on their eastern borders. Extending Schengen eastwards thus implies a bargain: freer movement westwards at the price of not allowing free movement from the east.[41]

Grabbe points to Hungary and Poland, which are both on track for membership in the European Union. Schengen members, especially Germany, link their fears of immigration, crime, and refugees to the eastern border zones and point to the lack of border controls. This fear of the "East" as a place of contagion, refugees, and crime is a long-standing trope in European political discourse.[42] As the president of the Ukraine stated: "The EU is replacing the Iron Curtain with a paper curtain across Europe."[43] Eberhard Bort details the specific rise in document fraud: "Passport and visa cases increased from 221 in 1991 to 620 in 1993, and have since remained at that high level."[44] To stop the leaks in Eastern Europe, which the EU integrated for economic and political reasons, Schengen member states must be assuaged that their external borders are secure. In many ways, this shift in attention marks the reorientation of Europe and European regional organizations away from the southern flank toward the east, although this new threat is figured in precisely the same language as before.[45]

The Schengen zone reflects the complete extension of the surveillance-of-movement regime. The Schengen Agreement follows from the multilateral agreement attempted by the Council of Europe and institutes a regional geography similar to the Nordic passport regime. The role of the government in the regulation of movement can be seen as an extension of the power to exclude or protect; as the bureaucratization of that power; and as a shift from quarantine (exclusion) to surveillance. One of the primary mechanisms of the surveillance regime is the definition and description of populations that are deemed safe or dangerous. The dynamics of Schengen illustrate the triumph of the surveillance regime. Those safe populations may move freely within and into Schengenland, but individuals from the dangerous populations find more stringent controls on their mobility. This condition has been exacerbated since the September attacks on the United States and the subsequent U.S. war on terrorism. As one expert has argued, the failure of the government was not in suspecting Richard Reid (the alleged shoe bomber) as an individual but rather in not classifying British Muslims as a target group. "Profiling has not been invalidated by the Reid case; it simply needs to be updated to take into account British Muslims of this militant stripe."[46] Furthermore, the European example reaffirms the previous argument that the movements of marginalized and peripheral groups are far more stringent than the movements of core groups. Freedom of movement is not equally accessible to all, and the groups that are targeted for control are defined by national and political discourses already in play.

Passports in the Periphery

After this consideration of passports and surveillance at the core, it is necessary to consider the postcolonial or peripheral scene. This section examines efforts in the global South to develop freedom-of-movement regimes. In particular, there are three passport unions outside of Europe: the Gulf Cooperation Council, the East African Community (EAC), and the Economic Community of West African States. In each case, national governments have agreed to implement a passport union within member countries. Although the GCC is something of an outlier, comprising relatively rich and small national populations, there is a great degree of similarity between the EAC and ECOWAS.

The GCC was formed in 1981 and comprises the governments of Saudi Arabia, Bahrain, the United Arab Emirates, Kuwait, Oman, and Qatar. It was formed due to regional security concerns but now considers other issues. Economic cooperation is an important part of the work of the GCC, and it has moved steadily to create a common market, reducing internal trade and tariff barriers.[47] Following a general commitment to economic integration in 1997, a simplified system was put in place in which governmental identity cards could substitute for a passport in travels to other GCC countries.[48] These was also a move to provide machine-readable passports that would substitute for the required entry and exit forms.[49] Attempts to form a customs union have been frustrated by member states, with implementation postponed until 2005. The GCC is also investigating the use of electronic passports to further facilitate travel.[50] Despite these efforts, the passport union has been put into practice on a bilateral basis, emulating the League of Nations regime more than the Nordic regime.[51] In GCC countries, women are largely unable to obtain passports or even leave the country without their husband's permission.[52] Although the GCC does not represent the type of passport union seen in the Nordic states and Schengen, it is an example of states in the global semiperiphery that see frontier and passport controls as impeding trade. One possible explanation for this move, in the absence of any comparable regional grouping, is the relative geographical isolation of the Gulf states and their relative wealth, which make crossing their borders secretly almost impossible. Regardless, the GCC is using a Council of Europe model in that other governmental documents come to stand in for the passport, but checks and examinations of documents remain in place.

ECOWAS is a regional organization that also aims for economic union, in part as a path to development. Robert Kaplan indicates the difficulties crossing the borders of West Africa: "The more fictitious the actual sovereignty, the more severe border authorities seem to be in trying to prove otherwise. Getting visas for these states can be as hard as crossing their borders."[53] Reports indicate that numerous blockades, roadblocks, and customs stations exist throughout border regions, not simply at the actual legal border. Although Kaplan had a relatively trouble-free journey, "women who could not read or write . . . were singled out and subjected to inhuman harassment by these unscrupulous public officials."[54] Even those with correct and true papers have problems crossing the many official and unofficial borders. Anthony Asiwaju, the former commissioner of the National Boundary Commission for Nigeria, describes the attempt at liberalization in the early 1990s as "continuing to be rendered ineffective by the border-enforcement agencies of member states, staffed for the most part by poorly trained, ill-motivated, inadequately paid and corrupt officials."[55] ECOWAS governments have long promoted the free movement of persons within member states, with some important recent successes. Benin and Niger have attempted an open-border policy, and Nigeria has engaged in bilateral negotiations with its neighbors.[56] Current plans include a uniform Schengenlike visa that would be valid for all ECOWAS members; a common ECOWAS passport; an ECOWAS travel document used by nationals for travel within the region; the removal of security checks, roadblocks, and other impediments to travel; and joint border patrols.[57] The first ECOWAS passports were issued on November 6, 2001.[58] However, unclear reports from the region make analysis of the actual use of the passport on the ground difficult. Although Nigeria and Benin have begun to issue ECOWAS passports, Paul Ejime argues that the regional passport has failed to garner "the much-anticipated enthusiasm."[59] It is simply too early to tell. At this point, however, we may conclude from press releases and official statements that the ECOWAS member states hope that the free movement of peoples will aid the integration of their economies and lead to economic development. Yet little West African identity seems prevalent. In some respects, the ECOWAS passport is as much a reflection of the practice of actual transborder mobility as it is a desired public policy.

The East African Community was first inaugurated in 1967 by Tanzania, Kenya, and Uganda but quickly collapsed under the uneven weight of its participants.[60] The EAC was resurrected in 1999, with a passport union being high among government expectations.[61] The EAC passport appears to be running into the same problems as the ECOWAS passport. Recent reports indicate that although the passport is honored at regional border posts, it does not significantly facilitate border crossings as was hoped.[62] Furthermore, businesspersons and government officials alike have complained that the EAC passport is useless because it is not internationally recognized.[63] One may point to a similar lack of East African identity as in the case of ECOWAS. The EAC's secretary-general has decried the squabbling and the regionalist rhetoric: "Actors from member states—Tanzania, Kenya and Uganda—must behave like soldiers by overcoming self interests."[64]

ECOWAS and EAC passports each take their inspiration from the Schengen Agreement and the European zone of free movement.[65] However, both regional organizations lack the economic prosperity or the sense of regional identity that made the Nordic and Schengen regimes acceptable by politicians. Furthermore, EAC passports are not accepted in the international community (although we are led to believe that camouflage passports from Rhodesia, Tanganyika, and Nyassaland are accepted by some immigration officials).

Conclusion: Integration, Not Freedom

The disappearance of the passport reflects the persistence of regimes to retain power as well as the reluctance of states to relinquish power. Several conclusions can be drawn from the examples above. First, even though passports have a nation-building or community-building function, passport unions are embraced when a regional identity already exists. As in the cases of ECOWAS and the EAC, formal passport unions are a reflection of practices attending border crossings. Second, freedom of movement within regimes is not equally enjoyed by all travelers. As in the nineteenth century, anxieties about labor, criminality, and politically unreliable foreigners affect the practice of border controls today. In the case of the Schengen Agreement, the elimination of internal borders within Europe was possible only with the creation of a security infrastructure that would substitute for border examinations. Furthermore, even as border controls are largely eliminated, citizens in Schengenland are now subject to examination anywhere in the territory and must carry official identity documents at all times. Thus, the freedom-of-movement regime internalizes the surveillance that used to take place at the borders of Europe. Third, passport unions are impelled by the desire to integrate economies rather than polities. In the formal passport accords, nowhere is political integration mentioned; rather, economic benefits were touted as the primary motive. This desire for economic integration was tempered by the desire for national integrity and territorial security. These motives became clear in the processes that existed at the frontier borders, the issue I examine in Chapter 6.

Notes

1. K. J. Holsti, "Governance Without Government: Polyarchy in Nineteenth-Century European International Politics," in *Governance Without Government: Order and Change in World Politics,* edited by James N. Rosenau and Ernst-Otto Czempiel (Cambridge, UK: Cambridge University Press, 1992), p. 38.

2. Jeremy Black, *The British Abroad: The Grand Tour in the Eighteenth Century* (New York: St. Martin's, 1992), p. 88.

3. Stephen Kern, *The Culture of Time and Space, 1880–1918* (Cambridge, MA: Harvard University Press, 1983), p. 195.

4. Black, *The British Abroad,* p. 160.

5. Ibid., p. 173.

6. Cynthia Enloe, *Bananas, Beaches, and Bases: Making Feminist Sense of International Politics* (Berkeley: University of California Press, 1990), p. 29.

7. John Torpey, *The Invention of the Passport: Surveillance, Citizenship, and the State* (Cambridge, UK: Cambridge University Press, 2000), p. 63.

8. Andreas Fahrmeir, "Governments and Forgers: Passports in Nineteenth-Century Europe," in *Documenting Individual Identity: The Development of State Practices in the Modern World,* edited by Jane Caplan and John Torpey (Princeton, NJ: Princeton University Press, 2001), p. 228.

9. Andrea Geselle, "Domenica Saba Takes to the Road: Origins and Development of a Modern Passport System in Lombardy-Veneto," in *Documenting Individual Identity: The Development of State Practices in the Modern World,* edited by Jane Caplan and John Torpey (Princeton, NJ: Princeton University Press, 2001), p. 204.

10. Ibid., p. 204.

11. Ibid., p. 217.

12. Fahrmeir, "Governments and Forgers," p. 225.

13. Leo Lucassen, "A Many-Headed Monster: The Evolution of the Passport System in the Netherlands and Germany in the Long Nineteenth Century," in *Documenting Individual Identity: The Development of State Practices in the Modern World,* edited by Jane Caplan and John Torpey (Princeton, NJ: Princeton University Press, 2001), p. 236.

14. Fahrmeir, "Governments and Forgers," p. 220.

15. Lucassen, "A Many-Headed Monster," p. 253.

16. Frederick L. Schuman, "The Council of Europe," *American Political Science Review* 45 (September 1951): 726–727.

17. Derek W. Urwin, *Historical Dictionary of European Organizations* (London: Scarecrow, 1994), p. 85.

18. A. H. Robertson, *The Council of Europe: Its Structures, Functions, and Achievements* (New York: Praeger, 1961), p. 206.

19. "Minutes of Meeting in Foreign Ministry to Discuss Council of Europe Questionnaire" (WU 10713/11) (FO 612 290).

20. W. Conway, Home Office, to Downing, Foreign Office, "Council of Europe European Passport" (13 March 1951) (WU 10713/13/6) (F0 612 290).

21. "Brief for the Committee of Ministers on the Establishment of a European Passport" (15 October 1949) (IOC [49] 255) (FO 612 290).

22. Annex A, "Brief for the Committee of Ministers on the Establishment of a European Passport" (15 October 1949) (IOC [49] 255) (FO 612 290).

23. Robertson, *The Council of Europe*, p. 208.

24. Ibid., p. 209.

25. "Passport-Free Trips to Germany: Council of Europe Citizens," *Manchester Guardian* (9 September 1955).

26. Frantz Wendt, "Nordic Cooperation," in *Nordic Democracy: Ideas, Issues, and Institutions in Politics, Economy, Education, Social, and Cultural Affairs of Denmark, Finland, Iceland, Norway, and Sweden* (Copenhagen: Det Danske Selskab, 1981), pp. 653–657.

27. Urwin, *Historical Dictionary of European Organizations*, p. 237.

28. Wendt, "Nordic Cooperation," p. 666.

29. Malcolm Anderson, *Frontiers: Territory and State Formation in the Modern World* (Cambridge, UK: Polity, 1996), p. 185.

30. Ibid.

31. European Union (Justice and Home Affairs), "Incorporating the Schengen *Acquis* into the European Union," 10 January 2002 (accessed 14 December 2001), europa.eu.int/scadplus/leg/en/lvb/l33020.htm.

32. Ibid.

33. See, for example, "Norway and Schengen: How Will This Affect You?" Government of Norway, Ministry of Justice and the Police (G-0303 B) (Oslo: Algard Offset, 2001).

34. Michel Foucault, *Discipline and Punish: The Birth of the Prison*, translated by Alan Sheridan (New York: Vintage, 1977), p. 281.

35. Ethan A. Nadelmann, "Global Prohibition Regimes: The Evolution of Norms in International Society," *International Organization* 44 (Autumn 1990): 499.

36. John Benyon, "The Politics of Police Co-operation in the European Union," *International Journal of the Sociology of Law* 24 (1996): 360.

37. Makbool Javaid, "Passport Control," *People Management* 5 (6 March 1999): 28.

38. Dita Vogel, "Identifying Unauthorized Foreign Workers in the German Labour Market," in *Documenting Individual Identity: The Development of State Practices in the Modern World*, edited by Jane Caplan and John Torpey (Princeton, NJ: Princeton University Press, 2001), pp. 328–329.

39. Schengenland also leaks from the middle. For an examination of the Swiss case, see Malcolm Anderson and Eberhard Bort, *Frontiers of the European Union* (London: Palgrave, 2001), pp. 126–128.

40. Nicholas Emmett, "Norway's Rejection of the European Union," *Contemporary Review* 268 (June 1996): 287.

41. Heather Grabbe, "The Sharp Edges of Europe: Extending Schengen Eastwards," *International Affairs* 76 (July 2000): 525.

42. Iver B. Neumann, *Uses of the Other: "The East" in European Identity Formation* (Minneapolis: University of Minnesota Press, 1999), chap. 5.

43. Leonid Kuchma, quoted in Grabbe, "The Sharp Edges of Europe," p. 536.

44. Eberhard Bort, "200km Eastern Frontier of the EU," in *Boundaries and Identities: The Eastern Frontier of the European Union,* edited by Malcolm Anderson and Eberhard Bort (Edinburgh: University of Edinburgh, International Social Sciences Institute, 1996), p. 72.

45. Rajendra K. Jain, "Fortifying the 'Fortress': Immigration and Politics in the European Union," *International Affairs* 34 (1997): 169.

46. Gail Russell Chaddock and Francine Kiefer, "Lessons of Shoe-Bomb Incident," *Christian Science Monitor* 93 (28 December 2001): 1.

47. Melani Cammett, "Defensive Integration and Late Developers: The Gulf Cooperation Council and the Arab Maghreb Union," *Global Governance* 5 (July–September 1999): 387.

48. "Sultan Qaboos of Oman on Private Visit to UAE" (Deutsche Presse-Agentur), Lexus-Nexus (accessed 12 January 2002) (6 May 1996); "Gulf Interior Ministers' Meeting Discusses Freedom of Travel, Iran, Women" (British Broadcasting Corporation), Lexus-Nexus (accessed 12 January 2002) (27 October 2000).

49. "GCC Leaders Welcome Iranian President's Offer of Talks About Islands" (British Broadcasting Company), Lexus-Nexus (accessed 8 January 2002) (24 December 1997).

50. Ahmad Mardini, "Iran Turns Towards U.S., Gulf States" (Inter Press Service), Lexus-Nexus (accessed 9 January 2002) (26 December 1997).

51. "First Bahraini Enters UAE Using ID Card" (Financial Times Information), Lexus-Nexus (accessed 3 January 2002) (4 July 2000).

52. U.S. Department of State, "Human Rights Report 2000: Oman" (Human Rights Watch) (accessed 8 January 2002) (February 2001), www.humanrights-usa.net/reports/oman.html.

53. Robert D. Kaplan, "The Coming Anarchy," *Atlantic Monthly* 360 (February 1994): 44–76, 52.

54. Accra Mail, "Extortion at Border" (Africa News), 27 November 2001 (1 October 2001).

55. Anthony Asiwaju, "Public Policy or Overcoming Marginalization: Borderlands in Africa, North America, and Western Europe," in *Margins of Insecurity: Minorities and International Security,* edited by Sam C. Nolutshungu (Rochester, NY: University of Rochester Press, 1996), p. 263.

56. Ibid., p. 265.

57. Economic Community of West African States, "Mini Summit of Heads of State and Government on the Creation of a Borderless ECOWAS: Final Communiqué" (March 2000).

58. "ECOWAS Passport Ready" 8 November 2001 (6 November 2001), allafrica.com/stories/printable/200111060180.html.

59. Paul Ejime, "ECOWAS: Appraising Sub-Regional Integration Process," *Financial Times* (2 December 2001).

60. Peter J. Schraeder, "African International Relations," *Understanding Contemporary Africa,* 3rd ed., edited by April A. Gordon and Donald L. Gordon (Boulder: Lynne Rienner Publishers, 2001), p. 157.

61. "Afrabet Soup," *The Economist* (2 October 2001): 77.

62. *The East African,* "Build Business Consensus for Region," *Africa News Service* (10 December 2001).

63. *The Monitor,* "Mushega Tells Investors to Go into Politics," *Africa News Service* (21 December 2001); *The Monitor,* "Regional Passport Useless, Say MPs," *Africa News Service* (20 November 2001).

64. "East African Community Secretary-General Decries Regional Polarization" (British Broadcasting Corporation) (30 November 2001).

65. *The Nation,* "Precedent Set as Woman Is Picked for Regional Assembly," *Africa News Service* (30 October 2001).

6

Borders, Frontiers, and Formalities

I have nothing to declare but my genius.
—Playwright Oscar Wilde, in 1882, upon arriving at New York Customs

In this chapter, I focus on the actual, lived experience of the passport at the international border.[1] Given the international mobility regime, how are passports and people examined and admitted or expelled? One of the key arguments I make in this book is that passports play a limited role in the identification and classification of travelers. But that role was essential to the institutional procedures of separating safe from dangerous persons, who often are classified according to their membership, or assumed membership, within a particular population. A look at passport control areas and procedures illustrates this state function, as well as the fact that the passport cannot guarantee security for states. Although the passport plays a central role in the process of border defense, it cannot operate perfectly.

The Frontiers of Sovereignty

Before examining the activities at the border, below I sketch a brief history of the emergence of borders. Political communities in early modern Europe were divided by frontiers, or borderlands. With the consolidation of the sovereign state as a territorial entity, borders became paramount. A growing number of researchers have studied the nexus between sovereignty, nationality, and territoriality—the grouping of legal authority, identity, and place. The primary aim of these theorists is to historicize the "sovereignty territorial ideal."[2] The modern state system, which is being undermined by technology, communications, transportation, and critical theory, must be examined as a specific, historically constructed geopolitical order; the organization of communities into sovereign and equal states is neither historically necessary nor functionally efficient. These theorists emphasize the transition from medieval spatial arrangements with overlapping spheres of authority to the sovereignty territorial ideal, in which a single sovereign commands the allegiance of the contiguous and coterminous community within his territory. This transition is reified by the postcolonial acceptance of colonial territorial boundaries. The universality of the sovereignty territorial ideal is corroborated by recent historical research by Robert Jackson and Mark Zacher, who argue that there is a "territorial covenant" within international society in which

> only existing interstate borders are legitimate and legal; if borders are to be changed, all states affected by the change must give their consent; change of borders by force is illegitimate and illegal; the only recognized nation-state is the political nationality defined by state juridical boundaries; and colonialism is illegitimate and illegal.[3]

In other words, one should not dismiss the importance of physical borders. In addition to the discursive and cultural boundaries that each state requires, governments must also construct physical boundaries and marshal bureaucratic, administrative, and military assets to police them.

There are two prevalent theories about the state of borders. First, the notion promulgated by Jackson and Zacher, among others, is that frontiers and borders have never been more stable. Second, the notion promulgated by Arjun Appadurai and James Rosenau, among others, is that frontiers and borders have never been more irrelevant and are increasingly distanced from the lines seen on the map. At this juncture, I want to take seriously the persistence of formal borders (I address the second contention in another section of this chapter).

Friedrich Kratochwil differentiates two ways of analyzing borders: according to function or to location.[4] He argues that international society has shifted from holding the function of borders as sacrosanct toward holding the location of borders as inviolable. Kratochwil distinguishes borders between the unit and its environment (referred to in anthropological writings as the "frontier," borders between core and periphery, and borders between similar units). He insists that in the formation of the modern state system the location of borders became fixed, whereas the function of borders became fluid and contested. This argument inverts the integrationist argument that strong states may reduce the specific power at the their borders while weak states jealously guard their frontiers.

There is a consensus among critical scholars that the particular form of the sovereignty territorial ideal represents an attempt to naturalize the cultural borders of a "nation." Henri Lefebvre describes the spatial impact of sovereignty: "each state claims to produce a space wherein something is accomplished—a space, even, where something is brought to perfection: namely, a unified and hence homogenous society."[5] Other scholars have examined the various processes by which nationality is reified and made natural. Such arguments focus on the bureaucratic manner that immigration is policed according to national and racial characteristics.

Critical as well as traditional scholars take for granted the very boundaries and borders that they are attempting to historicize and problematize. What is missing from each account is the micropolitics of the borders and boundaries that constitute different geopolitical orders. The way that the sovereignty territoriality ideal came to triumph over other possible territorial orders is not merely a question of the sovereign's intention, the increasing capacity of the state, and the proclivity of the international system to formulate a stable system of sovereign states. There must also be a popular acceptance and bureaucratic rationale for controlling populations. This control takes place in the assignation and policing of nationality, in addition to the description and maintenance of physical, juridical borders.

Design, Space, and Interrogation

As one waits in line for passport control, one anticipates the moment of examination, which is always fraught with anxiety.[6] As reported by one observer, "To be a [border] guard is to know all power and control."[7] Recent architecture and design writings reveal that the space of passport control is "usually tense."[8] Legitimate frontier crossings occur in two basic ways: by foot or by vehicle. Air carriers and ships disembark their passengers, but automobile and railroad traffic is often accommodated in situ. As such, most border crossings echo those of the nineteenth century (if not earlier). A uniformed officer examines the passport, examines the face it represents, and then proceeds to ask questions that determine the traveler's fate. The ways in which border posts, passport control areas, and entrance interrogations are framed reveal important aspects of the state sovereignty regime, as well as the international mobility regime.

The Berlin Wall—"the most inhumane border in the world"— was an emblem for the always incomplete attempt of the state to seal its boundaries.[9] The Berlin Wall was created by and destroyed by extreme mobility restrictions, made evident in the form of the passport. "Checkpoint Charlie" and the edifice of the Berlin Wall itself signified the geopolitical division of Europe. The fact that the border was continually jumped, tunneled under, and evaded speaks to the inability of the state to present a real obstacle to a previously unified community, such as Berliners or Germans. The division between East Berlin and West Berlin was created not only by the Berlin Wall but also by a host of geopolitical practices and ideological arguments (not the least of which was miles of electrified fence). Without investigating the Cold War's spheres of influence, which are clearly implicated in this division of Europe, Germany, and Berlin, I want only to insist that this border in particular was a crucial point of state control on the life-world of Berliners and Germans. Although the border did not succeed in cauterizing the separated Berlin populations, it created new meanings for crossing the border. Within the geopolitical discourse of the Cold War, to cross the border from East to West was indicative of changing ideological allegiance, escaping oppression, or infiltrating the enemy bastion. The raising of the Berlin Wall in 1961 by the East Germans and Soviets was indicative of wider problems. As Ernest May contends, "The Wall prevented more people from leaving for the West and shuttered the Berlin showcase of Western capitalism [but] it also served as an open confession that the GDR [German Democratic Republic, or East Germany] could hold its population only behind a prison barricade."[10] The frontier control at Friedrichstrasse (Checkpoint Charlie) became a stage for the larger geopolitical struggle. R. L. Garthoff describes how the initial standoff between U.S. and Soviet tanks stemmed from a passport incident:

> The senior American diplomat in Berlin, Deputy Commandant Allan Lightner, and his wife were about to enter East Berlin. . . . The East German police (Volkspolizei) asked to see their diplomatic passports. While the request may seem reasonable, compliance would have implied recognition of East German (rather than

Soviet) authority in East Berlin—a concession the United States was determined not to offer.[11]

Three days later, U.S. tanks came to support the attempted entry of U.S. citizens recognized by Germans (but not Soviets), which prompted a Soviet response; the crisis escalated. In this example, the diplomat and the passport officer stand in as representatives of the sovereign state at its limits. Relinquishing a U.S. passport to an East German border guard was seen by U.S. policymakers as acceptance of East German control over East Berlin. I will return to the implicit contract that the border represents whereby travelers relinquish their rights with the implicit promise of return once inside. At this point, I want to emphasize that the East German border guard was seen as a representative of a sovereign at the frontier and that recognition of that envoy at the frontier would be similar to accepting the legitimacy of sovereign control over the entire territory.

Another important reason to include this particular border is because the fall of the Berlin Wall in 1989 was taken as a sign of the collapse of the Eastern bloc and the end of the Cold War.[12] U.S. President Ronald Reagan's public challenge to Mikhail Gorbachev's policy of perestroika—"Tear down this wall!"—no doubt hastened the downfall.[13] The opening of the border foreshadowed the end of closed society and the victory of the West's doctrine of openness. However, it should be noted that the border was opened not as the result of a high political gesture but rather through a bureaucratic error compounded by the immediacy of television in broadcasting this mistaken message. John Borneman describes how the "collapse" of the Berlin Wall actually derived from the misinterpretation of a new visa policy by an East German official and the subsequent broadcast of his error. Border guards were thus faced with large groups who felt they had been authorized to travel. Stopping such a group was not feasible without a massacre, and the Berlin Wall ceased to be a barrier.[14] As interpreted by Berliners, "foreign policy was being made not by the Politburo at the center of power but by the border guards on the periphery."[15] This display of power by the state and "the people" illustrates the degree to which the border must be reinforced by the police as well as the policed to retain any relevance. The fall of the Berlin Wall—or rather its penetration by mistakenly authorized travelers—also indicates the fragility of state mobility policies. As Malcolm Anderson summarizes, "When the

German Democratic Republic could no longer control its borders, it collapsed."[16]

This leads us to the design of Checkpoint Charlie and passport control spaces generally, something that has not been considered in depth previously. Critics have focused on recent attempts by architects to design airport passport controls that "diffuse the natural anxiety felt in these places." At the newly designed Inchon Airport near Seoul,

> The Korean granite, which wraps three sides of the security area, serves to enclose sensitive spaces, but it also makes symbolic reference to the traditional stone gates of the city of Seoul. Wood paneling and soothing colors, designed to lower stress levels, line the walls of the security and customs areas. After passing through them, departing passengers emerge into the bright expanse of the concourse itself.[17]

Thus, the anxiety is diffused by the materials on the floor and reinscribed by the granite walls of the state. This design of the space of the passport control area parallels the legal and psychic journey from being controlled and contained at the border to the comparative freedom of the safe domestic space. The airport is a much understudied site of international relations, and few scholars are working in this area.

There is a common structure to passport controls (facilitated by design companies and architects) in which an entry hall is divided into lines (often drawn onto the floor) that lead to inspection booths.[18] Although there is often an armed presence, the degree to which passport control relies on the assumptions of self-discipline is remarkable. There is no evidence that any passport control space physically restrains illegal entry—there are no gates, no doors, and no barriers other than those that authority presents. What is striking about the particular structure of the passport control spaces is that the default spatial assumption is that most travelers will enter the territory with a minimum of delay.[19]

The authority of the passport officer as the gatekeeper of the nation is embedded in the structure of the space of interrogation. The officer, protected by a booth and a uniform, takes each traveler individually and compares the individual to the document presented. This examination generally lasts between two and three minutes.[20] The language of examination is often the national language or English. As Jacques Derrida warns,

Among the serious problems we are dealing with here is that of the foreigner who, inept at speaking the language, always risks being without defense before the law of the country that welcomes or expels him: the foreigner is first of all foreign to the legal language in which the duty of hospitality is formulated, the right to asylum, its limits, norms, policing, etc.[21]

The interrogation is then continued as the traveler declares goods for customs inspection by her movement into the customs area. In many modern airports, the customs inspection is panoptic, with mirrored glass lining the path toward the exit, leading to self-discipline among passengers. Thus, the sovereign, taxing power of the state and the docile, self-policing nature of the citizen are reinforced immediately. What is particularly interesting about the border as a site of sovereign statehood is that in many countries the passport control area represents a special case of national laws, often exempt from traditional protective rights. For instance, in a U.S. passport control and immigration area, U.S. Immigration and Naturalization Service (INS) agents "hold significantly unchecked rights to detain, search, and interrogate all persons, citizens or not, who must surrender themselves for inspection before they acquire permission to enter the country—and more complete rights there."[22] Foreign nationals and citizens alike must subjugate themselves to the complete sovereign power of the state to enter it. The passport represents the act of submission and recognition of new legal authority.

This construction of the literal border as a state-space where sovereign laws, but not state rights, are applied is reminiscent of the Middle Ages. Depriving travelers of their rights demonstrates the absolute authority of the sovereign state, the dangerous nature of international society, and the reliance of the citizen and foreign national on the state. At the border, travelers are subject to the unlimited power of the state. Giving one's passport to the border guard is symbolic of a dialogue between two sovereign states in which one foreign secretary asks another foreign secretary for entry on the bearer's behalf. Malcolm Anderson describes how in pre-Schengen Europe "search and seizure powers were absolute and there was a virtual absence of judicial review of executive actions."[23] Once the traveler is within the territorial jurisdiction of the state, however, the state then grants the traveler rights.[24] U.S. Attorney General John Ashcroft's statement regarding alleged "dirty bomber" Jose Padilla is particularly misleading on this point. Padilla's U.S. passport would not have facilitated travel within the United States any more than would a suspect passport. What might have happened is that Padilla's U.S. passport would shorten his initial entry into the country. Padilla is also important because he was declared an "enemy combatant" precisely so that he could be denied his rights as a U.S. citizen.[25] At the time of publication, public demands for an independent inquiry into the failure of intelligence with regard to the terrorist attacks had resulted in the formation of a commission headed by former New Jersey governor Thomas Kean. The prime question may be why domestic authorities such as the Department of Justice, the Federal Bureau of Investigation, and the Central Intelligence Agency failed to track the movements of foreign nationals previously identified as dangerous.

I would argue that the space of interrogation, which is constituted by the laws, practices, and discourse of the border, functions as a "technology of the self" whereby individuals recognize themselves as subjects of the state. This phrase (borrowed from Michel Foucault) suggests "the way by which . . . we have been led to recognize ourselves as a society, as part of a social entity, as part of a nation or of a state."[26] When travelers enter the state, they illustrate that the nation is not a homogeneous or stable community. The transit of citizens and foreigners presents a clear interruption of the nation as a continuous, complete community. As such, the process of crossing the border, which is predicated on the existence of the international (i.e., nonnational) realm attempts to reify the presence and centrality of the sovereign state. Derrida explains this moment of interrogation:

> This foreigner, then, is someone with whom, to receive him, you begin by asking his name; you enjoin him to state and to guarantee his identity, as you would a witness before a court. This is someone to whom you put a question and address a demand, the first demand, the minimal demand being, "what is your name?" or then "In telling me what your name is, in responding to this request, you are responding on your own behalf, you are responsible before the law and before your hosts, you are a subject in law."[27]

Even as a national citizen, the traveler must relinquish the rights that her home country grants when she petitions to enter. As in the Middle Ages, the sovereign has absolute control over who enters his territory. As a foreigner, the traveler must indicate that she is the subject of another sovereign and that she has subjugated those rights to the sovereign whose territory she is entering. The only exception to this rule is also incorporated into the discourse of sovereign statehood: refugees who argue that their "natural" state is acting against their interest to the extent that they cannot be repatriated. The passport represents a dialogue between two sovereigns: the sender recognizes the recipient as an equal entity, reaffirms the international legal principle of nonintervention, and finally requests that the sovereign temporarily take responsibility for the protection of the traveler (as long as the traveler makes a new, temporary contract to abide by the laws of the recipient sovereignty). Thus, the border becomes the only dangerous space where rights are abrogated. At the moment when foreigners are constituted as international actors by crossing borders and frontiers, the state moves to assert the dominance of its power to constitute every subject as a citizen—and even actors who *are* international—that is, refugees—must present themselves as being abnormal citizens.[28] Even if foreigners are inspected for a short time (between forty-five seconds and three minutes), they must feel the anxiety of being interrogated and potentially excluded in a display of the power of the state. The passport is not protection for the individual, just as the border guard cannot possibly defend the border (both of which require a much greater mechanism of population control). The passport, and its inspection, hint at the much greater security dilemma and institutional structure of the state—and, as argued previously, can provide only a limited and limiting promise of security for both individual and state.

The passport is presented by the traveler to the uniformed agent, who then interrogates the bearer to supplement the details that the passport does not reveal: residency, purpose of visit, length of stay, financial resources, and so on. Josiah Heyman describes the work of the immigration officer:

> In primary inspection, the inspector invades, with quick probing looks and questions the space of pedestrians or motorists and quickly classifies them by behavior and responses. Secondary inspection requires interrogation, a carefully aggressive process of mentally controlling the entrant, who is already under physical control, in order to determine admissibility.[29]

As indicated above, these are all questions that the passport application process ascertained in its earliest versions. These questions are necessary because of the form and function of the passport.

The passport must be unique, signifying a unique individual. It must also be replicable, so that citizens and examiners alike can recognize it as a valid document. Consequently, though the examiner is trained in the form of the passport, he must also determine if the passport is uniquely identical with the individual. In some border posts, the agent is able to pass a machine-readable passport through a reader, and the details of the passport are compared to a database of known or suspected dangerous individuals. At the Canadian border, officers are trained to read the visual clues of dissemblers.[30] Customs and immigration officials are under a great deal of bureaucratic pressure to process a large number of unproblematic travelers quickly and to catch dangerous travelers.[31] This has been emphasized in Britain, where the incomplete examination of entrants—which has led to the lack of an entry stamp—has serious consequences for illegal immigrants.[32] Immigration officers at the U.S.-Mexican border, one of the busiest, are pressured to process cars "at an average rate of 45 seconds per inspection."[33] At the U.S.-Canadian border between Detroit and Windsor, truck traffic is even more intense, forcing inspection of "one truck every 12 seconds."[34] Because of this high volume, inspectors come to develop and rely on a number of preconceived notions of who is dangerous and who is safe. As Matz Franzén contends, "The difference between risk profiles and stereotypes becomes difficult to sustain practically."[35] In the U.S. system, "inspectors share the belief that they should conduct the inspection of foreign nationals in two to three minutes. If a case requires more attention, 'secondary it'—refer it for more in-depth work properly left to the secondary inspection."[36] These secondary decisions are informed by individual experience and bureaucratic operating procedures that standardize national stereotypes and make practical foreign policy. Some foreign nationals are mandated for referral to a secondary inspection, whereas other foreign nationals are seldom referred.[37] Often, national categories are defined by a history of document fraud, to which immigration inspectors react particularly strongly.[38] This anxiety about false documents has been heightened since September 11, 2001. Recent measures include "'expedited removal' [that] allows an Immigration agent, with the concurrence of a supervisor, to bar non-citizens from the United States for five years if, in their judgment, the individuals presented false documentation or misrepresented themselves."[39] The prevalence of these anxieties was also evidenced recently in the case of *United States of America v. Chafat Al Jibori,* as a result of the first attack on the World Trade Center. Al Jibori, an Iraqi national, was caught with a falsified Swedish passport. He appealed his conviction under federal law (18 U.S. Code 1543; presentation of a false passport), because "section 1543 is a relatively uncommon statute upon which to premise a prosecution," and he was thus selectively prosecuted.[40] Although there had been a handful of prosecutions under this statute, this inspection and subsequent prosecution was based on a conviction of a Jordanian involved in the World Trade Center bombing. This other individual, using a similarly altered Swedish passport, presented an immediate precedent, which justified this rare prosecution of Al Jibori. The assistant U.S. attorney argued that "the decision to prosecute was based on the similarity between Al Jibori's case and that of the terrorist convicted in the World Trade Center bombing, both being middle easterners traveling on altered Swedish passports."[41] Thus, institutional history, national policy, and a sensitivity to fraudulent documents constructed a specific threat profile. Individual travelers are checked against this threat profile and accordingly treated as either safe or dangerous (subject to a cursory or more serious examination). State policy determines the characteristics of the populations that enjoy the two worlds of mobility.

Barring computerized or heuristic warnings, the passport does not reveal anything essential about the traveler's intentions. At least eleven of the terrorists who perpetrated the September 11 attacks were flagged by security or airport screening systems.[42] The weakness of this system is evidenced in the case of Richard Reid, the suspected terrorist on an American Airlines flight in December 2001. Reid was not charged with using a false passport because his passport was authentic, as was the nationality and identity he declared. Despite the fact that his passport did indeed raise red flags, and despite the fact that he was interrogated by French officials anxious about terrorism, his unflappable demeanor helped get him through security not once but twice.[43] Policymakers have responded to this bald indictment of the security profiling system by adding a new risk category to the system "to take into account British Muslims of this militant stripe."[44] Rather than draw the conclusion that Richard Reid represented an individual anomaly, officials concluded that a new population (of which Reid was a member) had to be added to the system. The U.S. National Security Entry-Exit Registration program was implemented on September 11, 2002. It attempts to supplement the passport system through registration of certain suspect nationals (e.g., from Iran, Iraq, Libya, Sudan, Syria, and Saudi Arabia and "certain nationals of other countries whom the State and Department and the Immigration Naturalization Service determine to be an elevated national security risk").[45] Plainly, then, national, racial, and religious stereotypes inform the profiling and inspection system.

Before September 11, only about 2 percent of the foreign nationals seeking entry as nonimmigrants were referred for secondary inspection, whereas 10 percent of those referrals were for fraudulent documents (32 percent were automatic referrals based on bureaucratically designated nationalities).[46] These figures illustrate the presumption that the majority of travelers are safe and that safety can be determined through a brief one- to two-minute interview. The form of the examination has changed, however, since the nineteenth century. The subject of examination was once the individual, but now the subject of examination is the document. The passport plays a limited role in identifying the traveler. The passport is dependent on breeder documents, which may be less than secure. Furthermore, a number of fraudulent, false, and stolen passports exist—to the extent that even an examination of passports as documents can never guarantee security for the state.

The interrogation regime shifted in the postwar period to an examination of documents. At the borders, machine-readable passports are compared to databases. There is a contemporary trend to read biometrics—reading the body again as a form of identity verification. Biometrics is the study of the physical body for unique identifiers, which are compared with a master record. Hence, fingerprints, retina patterns, and hand geometry—which are all unique to the individual—can be identified and corroborated with other governmental records. This assumes that the body cannot be altered in a way that the traveler can dissemble. The body testifies in concert with the government-issued documents to assure that identity is isomorphic. This displaced examination illustrates the ways in which a regime of surveillance has supplanted the previous regime of interrogation.

An important example of displaced interrogation comes from the examination of vehicles at the U.S.-Canadian border. The world's longest undefended border is portrayed alternately as the highlight of the friendly relationship between the two neighbors, or as a leaky backdoor into the United States, the mirror image of the U.S.-Mexican border. The dangerous aspect of this undefended border has been emphasized in light of the September 11 attacks. In the remainder of this section, I will look at the friendly aspect of this border.

Specifically, two complementary programs continue the trend toward machine-readable documents and self-examination. The U.S. PORTPASS initiative comprises several programs: INSPASS allows frequent low-risk travelers to forgo a face-to-face examination by a customs agent through a card reader at a number of airports; SENTRI allows frequent low-risk motorists to register themselves and their vehicles to bypass a face-to-face examination by a customs agent; and the Remote Video Inspection System was instituted to enable a face-to-video examination of entrants at remote border posts.[47] The Canadian equivalent of these programs (CANPASS) was instituted by the Canadian Customs and Revenue Agency to facilitate frequent low-risk travelers across the border.[48] This program has four aspects: air, boat, highway, and remote ports. In many cases, frequent visitors to Canada may simply phone in their arrival to a customs agent without the need for actual personal contact.[49] This status is based on a process of application, in which the CANPASS applicant submits his passport and supporting documentation. Following the Passport Office's initiative to include biometric information, Canadian Customs and Revenue Agency "as part of the enrollment process will take your photograph, record a sample of your signature, your fingerprint image, and your hand geometry."[50] The visitor is then pre-approved for entry, though subject to potential inspection. Should the visitor report any items that may be subject to duty, the customs official simply takes a credit-card number over the telephone.[51] The CANPASS highway program is extremely decentralized. CANPASS holders, after undergoing a similar application procedure, apply a decal to their windshield. They fill out a punch-card declaration for customs and duty, which is billed to their credit card. The sole "examination" takes place in the "special CANPASS–Highway lane for a visual examination by a customs officer, and after a signal from the officer, [the visitor] can enter Canada."[52] These take the place of a passport and substitute virtual examinations for actual examinations.

As a result of this program, the person never needs to be examined: the passholder's car is subject to a drive-by examination, or the visitor reports his arrival by boat or plane to an officer over the telephone. In this program, even the documents themselves are all but removed or are computerized. At several remote sites, the examination by a customs officer takes place via videophone. The Remote Video Inspection System was too expensive for Canada to implement, and so "a magnetic card reader, supported by extensive video camera surveillance [satisfied] Canadian requirements."[53] As part of the Alternative Inspection Services Program, an automatic, self-administered examination of one's identity papers substitutes for an examination of the person. Echoing the change in international epidemic policy, the frontier and border policies of these friendly neighbors have shifted from quarantine to surveillance. In both the U.S. and the Canadian programs, the face-to-face examination is replaced by a documentary check, either actual or electronic. Application to these programs involves a small fee and an extensive background check of other records (criminal, customs, tax, divorce, etc.). As a result, the passport proves itself to be identical to other state records. Yet the limits inherent in the other state records come to be replicated and exaggerated in the passport.

This discussion of the pragmatics of contemporary border crossing illustrates the implications resulting from changes in the inspection regimes described in the previous chapters. The regime of bodily inspection has been transformed to focus on the inspection of documents and is moving toward the inspection of the body through biometrics. Stealing across disciplinary boundaries and plundering the work of political anthropologists has revealed that immigration and passport officials—because of bureaucratic structures and the demands placed on their positions—rely on national stereotypes that reflect their personal experiences in addition to state policies. Finally, the structure of the transversal space reveals the presumption of the state that most travelers are unproblematic; the display of both bureaucratic and panoptic power; the construction of international space as dangerous; and the discursive necessity of withholding rights prior to being admitted at the border. Thus, sovereignty is enacted most visibly at the moment borders are passed. The penetration of the nation by a foreign body gives lie to the myth of homogeneity and completeness. A number of rites of passage are enacted to assert the control of the nation and its space.

Translocality, Transversality, and the Persistence of Borders

The question of the sovereignty territorial ideal has been approached critically from several disciplines. Scholars from international relations, human geography, cultural studies, anthropology, sociology, and postcolonial studies seemed to have formed a wide consensus that the territorial state is in decline. Akhil Gupta and James Ferguson put the issue succinctly:

> Something like a transnational public sphere has certainly rendered any strictly bounded sense of community or locality obsolete. At the same time, it has enabled the creation of forms of solidarity or identity that do not rest on an appropriation of space where contiguity and face-to-face contact are paramount.[54]

This premise has led to a recasting of the research agenda for the constitution of communities, translocality, and transborder communities. Sankaran Krishna illustrates the ways in which the life-worlds of frontier communities often ignore international borders or see them as largely administrative and decreasing in relevance.[55] We must remember that state borders are never natural or unproblematic, as well as that even so they remain important in the lives of those who cross them. One may argue that all frontiers are to some extent historically contingent and socially constructed, but once imbricated with the power of the state the borders come to be a real, experienced barrier, however porous, resisted, or transcended. On this point, works by scholars in anthropology and political geography have much to offer.[56]

An important contribution to this conversation has been by critical scholars who write under the rubric of territories, identity, and movement (TIM) theory and identities, borders, and orders theory.[57] These scholars displace the common statist focus of research and place deterritorialized identities and movement at the forefront of international relations theory. Peter Mandaville argues that Appadurai's concept of translocality grants international relations a greater capacity to understand deterritorialized identities, movements, and communities.[58] Appadurai argues that transversality recognizes "the growing disjuncture between territory, subjectivity and collective social movement and the steady erosion, principally due to the force and form of electronic mediation, of the relationship between spatial and virtual neighborhoods."[59] Elsewhere, he argues that scholars must question the placement of the state at the center of study, a project with which many critical scholars are sympathetic. He questions why states "are the only players in the global scene that really need the idea of territorially based sovereignty."[60] Nevzat Soguk and

Geoffrey Whitehall examine the importance of transversality, using the example of Merhan Karimi Nasseri, who was trapped in a transit area at Charles de Gaulle Airport for eleven years.[61] A similar case occurred in Egypt, although the traveler in question was kept for a few months, not years. The authors also retell an account by Krishna of life at the Indo-Bangladeshi border:

> Trade in staples such as fish, eggs, and clothing routinely move uninterrupted across the border, while marriages between parties on either side are frequent. As the journalist reporting on the region notes: "The bridegroom's part, accompanied by band music, crosses the border without hindrance and goes back with the bride and presents."[62]

The authors argue that these stories should be confined within the rubric of the sovereign state: "International Relations scholars would suggest that migrants, refugees, flows and movements are exceptions to the rules that grid their geopolitical imaginaries, [whereas we] suggest that migrant stories of transversal existence [point to] alternative trajectories to follow."[63] To supplement these accounts of the ephemeral, the moving, and the translocal, I would argue with Lothar Brock that "critical TIM relies on the assumption of deterriorialisation, [and] it should note the reterritorialising trends."[64] This call for studying reterritorialization has been made in other concerned disciplines.[65] Noting the trends toward reterritorialization does not discount movement or translocality. However, a serious study of the border as a practice of state power has yet to be undertaken. I would argue that the break, or the interruption, of territorialized power into the spatial or political imaginary of these translocal groups must also be theorized. We cannot take for granted that the border, because it is imagined out of existence, does not play an important role. As Amitava Kumar insists, we must "[return] the metaphor of the border to the material reality of barbed-wire fences, entrenched prejudices, and powerful economic interests that regulate the flow of human bodies across national boundaries."[66] Although Merhan Karimi Nasseri was able to create a life within the transit lounge, which indeed problematizes the usual conceptions within international relations of the nation-state and citizenship, his confinement was not a resistant or rebellious act but the result of his papers being misplaced.[67] And whereas certain practices ignore the border, other practices (such as smuggling and certain forms of corruption) are made possible by the border formalities.[68] The role of the state in making such a life not just possible but reasonable must be examined.

Borderlands—"sub-national areas whose economic and social life is directly and significantly affected by proximity to an international boundary"—are studied under the rubric of political anthropology as part of the larger study of community and nationality.[69] Many borders interrupt naturally occurring or prenational/nonnational communities, and in the majority of borderlands there is a prevailing economic interest in crossing the border (either legally or illegally). This chapter has used the U.S.-Canadian border to illustrate the deferral of bodily inspection, but the U.S.-Mexican border stands as an important case of a borderland in which the border is both reified and resisted simultaneously. Some agricultural sectors in the United States depend on the cheap labor of illegal Mexican migrants, yet federal law prevents them from immigrating to the United States. This configuration of the border as a control on the labor force has a long history in the United States and Great Britain. Although California withdraws social services from illegal migrants—making every state employee a potential collaborator—and greater amounts of money are devoted to patrolling the border, the hiring of illegal immigrants is facilitated by the establishment of roadside "depots" at which workers can be hired day to day for agricultural labor. Anthony Asiwaju argues that the "observable facts of interpenetration" and the two countries' mutual dependence lead to an acceptance of "co existence."[70] This narrative reflects a model of integration, made immediate at international borders, by which states develop along a linear path from nation-forming toward coexistence and, eventually, integration. In an attempt to avoid this developmental paradigm, which has garnered so much criticism elsewhere, I would argue that the two countries are in fact *codependent:* The United States needs cheap, illegal Mexican labor; Mexico needs the dollars that are returned in the form of remittances, and indeed many Mexicans benefit from a higher standard of living as a result of this arrangement.[71] As a consequence, in concert with policing procedures detailed below, the INS has set up a complex of documents that substitutes for the passport at the U.S.-Mexican border to accommodate a large population of unproblematic traffic. These border cards previously were used as a substitute for a passport and testified that an in-depth examination of the bearer and his/her documents had taken place. Thus, border cards represented the consignment of the bearer to a safe population who thus was able to enjoy an abridged examination. This complex of supplementary documents illustrates one of the main arguments of this book: there is a bifurcation of the modern mobility regime that is determined by membership in certain populations as defined and limited by state practices.

The policing of the border also illustrates codependency. The police function operates in the same bureaucratic department (the INS) as immigration and inspection at official border crossings. As Peter Andreas argues, "Border policing is not simply a policy instrument for deterring illegal crossings but a symbolic representation of state authority; it communicates the state's commitment to marking and maintaining the borderline."[72] Through this machinery the state attempts "a monopoly on the power to assign identities to those who enter this [national] space. It stamps or refuses to stamp passports and papers which are extensions of the person of the traveler who is required to pass through official ports of entry and exit."[73] However, newly constructed walls along the frontier have little deterrent or restrictive effect. Though the INS has erected physical barriers along certain high-visibility crossing points, they merely moved smuggling operations further into the hinterlands.[74] One urban geographer frames this argument as follows: "it is not so much a question of reducing crime, and other acts seen as harmful, as *redistributing in space*."[75] Despite increased border patrols, the economic incentives that make immigration desirous have not changed. This schizophrenia is reflected in the actual effect of increased policing: "there is no claim or evidence that overall levels of illegal immigration have actually declined as a result of tighter border controls."[76] Andreas suggests that "enhanced border policing has less to do with actual deterrence and more to do with managing the image of the border and coping with the deepening contradictions of economic integration."[77] Migrants are thus criminalized and marginalized not only in immigration legislation but also in the physical construction of the border.

This function is reinforced by the practices of the Border Patrol, which Josiah Heyman characterizes as a "voluntary-departure complex." It is the U.S. Border Patrol's tacit policy "whereby arrested aliens [especially at the Mexican border] are permitted (indeed encouraged) to waive their rights to a deportation hearing and return to Mexico without lengthy detention, expensive bonding, and a trial."[78] Illegal migrants who are caught are thus released to try their luck again until they evade the police, often on the same day. Michael Kearney argues that "the surveillance activities of the Border Patrol are not intended to prevent [the] entry [of illegal immigrants] into the United States to work, but instead are part of a number of ways of disciplining them to work hard and to accept low wages."[79] Heyman argues that this tacit policy reflects the image of the national borders as policed and allows for illegal immigration. Malcolm Anderson characterizes this as a "tidy" system of image control.[80]

The border appears more orderly because much greater control has in fact been imposed at the major urban crossing points that are most publicly visible. Unauthorized crossings are much less visible because they are more dispersed, more remote, and more hidden.[81]

This image management is a function of domestic pressure, governmental rationality, and economic pressures. Heyman illustrates this tension: "The U.S. government at once arrests many persons, thereby reinforcing the state idea of bounded citizenship for media sale and consumption, and negates the effectiveness of these arrests, thus permitting labor migration in numbers well beyond those permitted by law."[82] Put simply, the presence of the border—even when its transgression is an integral part of its practice—makes this geopolitical situation stable and maintains a docile immigrant labor force.

Other evidence from the borderlands of the Iberian Peninsula bear this conclusion out: borders create reasons for their transgression. William Kavanagh describes the effect of political borders on transborder village communities in Spain and Portugal. The border, which has been relatively stable since the twelfth century, runs through the village. He describes that "in some cases, the border actually divided houses, which would then have two doors, one giving onto Spain, the other door giving onto Portugal."[83] This bisection of the village did not lead to confusion of its residents regarding their nationality, allegiance, or taxes, but it did lead to a great deal of smuggling. Because of the economic differences between customs regulations and prices with the creation of national economies, "for people living on a border, smuggling on whatever scale is generally regarded as a completely natural activity, which often constitutes a way of life for many of the villagers on both sides."[84] The border police here function in the same way as the U.S. Border Patrol: not so much to prevent as to discipline and make difficult the economic transgressions.[85] In interviews with the villagers, however, what was illustrated was not a transborder community—a translocality or transversality—that ignored the border. Rather,

> for the people of these villages the border has always been, and still is, an obsession. It is nearly impossible to have an hour's conversation with anyone in either village without the subject of the border coming up. When they speak of the past, when they speak of the present, when they speak of almost anything, the border is always there somewhere.[86]

This experience is corroborated by another Spanish borderland: Catalonia. Peter Sahlins describes how a political boundary drawn down the middle of a valley in the Pyrenees led to the division of a once-united community. He argues that "the claims of French and Spanish identities put forth by the village communities gave significance to the political and administrative division of the valley. The arbitrary division had become a historical reality: not the states but the communities had defined the international boundary line."[87] The history of the creation of political identities illustrates the degree to which boundaries may be utilized by local communities to differentiate between self and other, even when there are no other predominant differences between the two groups. Following the example of the Spanish-Portuguese border (and examples throughout the world), the presence of the border does not separate the communities in any practical ways. Sahlins argues that the border actually *increases* the interaction between communities: "The demographic and social permeability of the frontier increased during the eighteenth and nineteenth centuries not because the Cerdans ignored the emerging territorial boundary line but because the differences introduced by the boundary created new reasons to cross it."[88] The simple fact of adjacent, different sovereignties creates certain opportunities, which in turn promote the transgression of the border. Thus, even as the administrative and imposed boundary came to have a real ideational effect on the differentiation between national communities, it also came to have real practiced effects on the ways of life in the border communities.

One example illustrates the complexities of this dynamic of borderlands: the Shabe border between Bénin and Nigeria. Similar to residents on the Spanish-Portuguese-French border, Shabe border residents claim "'we are the border.'"[89] Though Shabe residents have forged a transborder community that colludes to evade new Nigerian border instruments, Donna Flynn argues that the border has created

> a local sense of *deep placement* instead of displacement, *deep territorialization* instead of deterritorialization, which forges strong feelings of rootedness in the borderland itself and creates a border identity. . . . Shabe border residents are fully aware of how they can use their institial power—their borderland advantage—to benefit themselves.[90]

Since the imposition of colonial boundaries, the demarcation of interstate boundaries has created incentives for cross-border trade, smuggling, and movement. However, prior to 1990, Nigerian and Béninois customs posts were each located twenty-five kilometers from the border. As a result, the border was largely administrative, and residents of this region existed within a translocal community that enjoyed the advantage of being largely unregulated.[91] The new physical presence of a border post created a new governmental regime of the control of movement. The interruption of the local translocal community, which relied on the border and its lack of policing, has created a transborder community that is united in its distaste for and evasion of the border.[92] The ways in which residents now live with the border speaks to the importance of lived experience: locals act as mediators between customs agents and traders, erect tolls on the road, and charge for river transportation.[93] Precisely, it is the interruption of the border—however easy it may be to evade or the importance of the trade made possible by its presence—that has created this transborder community. In this case, the assertion of a governmental presence at the border has become the central feature of these transborder communities.

Just as the examination of papers has been replaced by the examination of individual travelers, so too has state exercise of power at the borders shifted: from exclusion toward discipline. What I wish to emphasize is not that the border is evaded, escaped, or resisted; rather, any evasion, escape, or resistance of the border has particular material effects both in the borderlands and in the national space that are functions of the border itself and, by extension, the national mobility regime. The actual break—the interruption of territorialized power into the spatial or political imaginary of these groups—must be taken seriously.

Conclusion: Narrating the Border

Within the discipline of international relations, a necessary level of abstraction often makes theorizing seem distant from the lived lives of international actors. In this chapter, I examined the most common experience of international relations—the crossing of borders—from the bottom up. This addition of real experiences to state practices at the border has led to several interesting arguments. The design of passport control spaces reveals that the state constructs international society as a source of danger and itself as the "creditor" of rights. The work of state agents at these borders is influenced by their own experiences, stereotypes, and prejudices as well as by bureaucratic embodiments of state and foreign policy. As Anderson argues, the function of state borders itself is not static: "beliefs, prejudices, contingencies, and calculations of interest determine the way in which governments use frontier controls."[94]

A consideration of these physical and thought spaces reveals that states, in most cases, are predisposed to admit the vast majority of travelers. Part of this implicit regime, however, is that restrictions on entry are a reflection of larger national and international politics and a reflection of the consent of the traveler to a kind of contract. The traveler gives up the protection of any state as she petitions entry and vouches that her papers are in order. In return, states generally facilitate admission procedures. However, in return for the right of return, or at least the right of admission to the country of issuance, the traveler is implicated in the international politics of the issuing country. For example, travelers from the Middle East have been subject to a much tighter review since the attacks of September 11, 2001. Travelers may be subject to interrogation based on national profiles, which are constituted by stereotypes as well as international imaginaries.

But a closer analysis of the examination process reveals another core weakness of the passport regime: no examination can be complete. Even close examination of terrorists has not revealed their intentions, and the creation of national or racial profiles will inevitably be incomplete and more than complete—stopping too many travelers but not necessarily the right ones. Thus, even though the passport regime cannot control the entrance of dangerous travelers, it may police them and structure the border space itself in such a way that travelers police themselves. The importance of the border is also relevant to those studying travelers who attempt to bypass it. The description of a border is both a cause and an effect of community definition. Even for transborder or transversal communities, the border represents a significant feature in their topography and lived lives. By redrawing the border into the consideration of translocal, transversal communities, we see that even in—if not especially in—its transgression the border plays an important psychic role.

In sum, the border plays a fundamental role in the constitution and practice of sovereign statehood and international relations. The passport is the key to crossing international space because it connects the individual to a sovereign state and the citizen to a nation.

Notes

1. Lothar Brock, "Observing Change, 'Rewriting' History: A Critical Overview," *Millennium: Journal of International Studies* 28 (1999): 483.

2. Alexander B. Murphy, "The Sovereign State System as a Political-Territorial Ideal: Historical and Contemporary Considerations," in *State Sovereignty as a Social Construct,* edited by Thomas J. Biersteker and Cynthia Weber (Cambridge, UK: Cambridge University Press, 1996), p. 82.

3. Robert H. Jackson and Mark W. Zacher, *The Territorial Covenant: International Society and the Stabilization of Boundaries*, Working Paper No. 15 (Vancouver, BC: Institute of International Relations, 1997), p. 6.

4. Friedrich Kratochwil, "Of Systems, Boundaries, and Territoriality: An Inquiry into the Formation of the State System," *World Politics* 39 (1986): 36.

5. Henri Lefebvre, *The Production of Space*, translated by Donald Nicholson-Smith (Oxford, UK: Blackwell, 1991), p. 281.

6. Joyce Carol Oates, "Customs," *Crossing the Border: Fifteen Tales* (New York: Vanguard, 1976), pp. 106–117.

7. Scott Peterson, "Checkpoint Charlies Dash British Convoy's Blithe Spirits," *Christian Science Monitor* (2 January 1996): 4.

8. Korea Telecom, "Inchon Airport," n.d.(accessed 15 February 2002), www.koreainfogate.com/travelguide/general.asp?src=new_b03.

9. Malcolm Anderson, *Frontiers: Territory and State Formation in the Modern World* (Cambridge, UK: Polity, 1996), p. 130.

10. Ernest R. May, "America's Berlin," *Foreign Affairs* 77 (June/July 1998): 154.

11. R. L. Garthoff, "Berlin 1961: The Record Corrected," *Foreign Policy* 84 (Fall 1991): 144.

12. Malcolm Anderson, Didier Bigo, and Eberhard Bort, "Frontiers, Identity, and Security in Europe: An Agenda for Research," in *Borderlands Under Stress,* edited by Martin Pratt and Janet Allison Brown (The Hague: Kluwer, 2000), p. 251.

13. Ibid., p. 160.

14. John Borneman, *After the Wall: East Meets West in the New Berlin* (New York: Basic Books, 1991), pp. 1–4.

15. John Borneman, *Subversions of International Order: Studies in the Political Anthropology of Culture* (Albany: State University of New York, 1998), p. 105.

16. Malcolm Anderson, "The Transformation of Border Controls: A European Precedent," in *The Wall Around the West: State Borders and Immigration Controls in North America and Europe,* edited by P. Andreas and T. Snyder (Lanham, MD: Rowman and Littlefield, 2001).

17. Clair Enlow, "New Gates for Asia," *Architecture Week* (6 June 2001): D1.

18. Brian Edwards, *The Modern Terminal: New Approaches to Airport Architecture* (New York: Routledge, 1998), chap. 9.

19. Christopher J. Blow, *Airport Terminals,* 2nd ed. (Oxford, UK: Butterworth-Heinemann, 1996), p. 142.

20. "Apartheid at Heathrow," *The Economist* (8 January 1993): 78; Jeff Goodell, "How to Fake a Passport," *New York Times* (10 February 2002): 44.

21. Jacques Derrida, "Foreigner Question," in *Of Hospitality,* edited by Jacques Derrida and Anne Dufoumantelle and translated by Rachel Bowlby (Stanford, CA: Stanford University Press, 2000), p. 15.

22. Josiah McC. Heyman, "Putting Power in the Anthropology of Bureaucracy: The Immigration and Naturalization Service at the Mexico–United States Border," *Current Anthropology* 36 (April 1995): 271.

23. Malcolm Anderson, "The Transformation of Border Controls."

24. For an interesting retelling of this genesis of the state as creditor and the citizen as debtor, see Friedrich Nietzsche, "Genealogy of Morals," in *The Birth of Tragedy and the Genealogy of Morals,* translated by Francis Golffing (New York: Anchor Press, 1956), pp. 203–205.

25. John Ashcroft, "Transcript of the Attorney General John Ashcroft Regarding the Transfer of Abdullah Al Muhajir (Born Jose Padilla) to the Department of Defense as an Enemy Combatant," U.S. Department of Justice, 10 June 2002.

26. Michel Foucault, "The Political Technology of Individuals," in *Technologies of the Self: A Seminar with Michel Foucault,* edited by Luther H. Mark, Huck Gutman, and Patrick H. Hutton (Amherst: University of Massachusetts Press, 1988), p. 146.

27. Derrida, "Foreigner Question," p. 27.

28. Nevzat Soguk, *States and Strangers: Refugees and Displacements of Statecraft* (Minneapolis: University of Minnesota Press, 1999), p. 218.

29. Heyman, "Putting Power in the Anthropology of Bureaucracy," p. 271.

30. Personal interview, Christina Tinson, 7 September 1999, Vancouver, Canada.

31. Janet A. Gilboy, "Deciding Who Gets In: Decisionmaking by Immigration Inspectors," *Law and Society Review* 25 (1991): 578.

32. Ramnik Shah, "Passport Control and Mistake," *New Law Journal* 142 (3 April 1992): 450–451.

33. Heyman, "Putting Power in the Anthropology of Bureaucracy," p. 271.

34. Stephen E. Flynn, "Beyond Border Control," *Foreign Affairs* 79 (December 2000): 58.

35. Matz Franzén, "Urban Order and the Preventive Restructuring of Space: The Operation of Border Controls in Micro Space," *Sociological Review* 9 (May 2001): 210.

36. Gilboy, "Deciding Who Gets In," p. 578.

37. Ibid., pp. 583–590.

38. Ibid., p. 589.

39. Government of Canada, Department of Foreign Affairs and International Trade, *Crossing the 49th: Advice for Canadians Travelling to the United States—2000* (Ottawa: Government of Canada, November 2000).

40. United States Court of Appeals for the Second Circuit, No. 1319—August term, 1995. Docket No. 95–1543.

41. Ibid.

42. Dan Eggen, "Airports Screened Nine of Sept. 11 Hijackers, Officials Say," *Washington Post* (2 March 2002): A11.

43. Gail Russell Chaddock and Francine Kiefer, "Lessons of Shoe-Bomb Incident," *Christian Science Monitor* (28 December 2001): 1.

44. Raymond Tanter, quoted in ibid.

45. U.S. Department of State, "Fact Sheet: National Security Entry-Exit Registration System" (5 June 2002), http://usinfo.state.gov/topical/pol/terror/02060509.htm.

46. Gilboy, "Deciding Who Gets In," pp. 574–575.

47. U.S. Immigration and Naturalization Service, "How Do I Apply for a PORTPASS?" 13 November 2001 (accessed 8 January 2002), www.ins.usdoj.gov/graphics/howdoi/portpass.htm.

48. Some of these facilities have been suspended after the September 11, 2001, attacks. See Canada Customs and Revenue Agency, "Suspension of Alternate Methods of Reporting to Customs," 26 February 2002 (accessed 1 March 2002), www.ccra-adrc.gc.ca/customs/individuals/canpass/canpass-e.html.

49. Canada Customs and Revenue Agency, "Memorandum D2-5-10: Transborder General Aviation—Telephone Reporting and CANPASS Programs" (7 May 1999), p. 2.

50. Canada Customs and Revenue Agency, "RC4062E (Rev 00) CANPASS—Airport Extending Facilities" (November 2000).

51. Canada Customs and Revenue Agency, "Memorandum D2-5-10," p. 2.

52. Canada Customs and Revenue Agency, "RC4197(E) CANPASS—Highway Extending Border Services" (June 2000).

53. Government of Canada, *Canada–United States Accord on Our Shared Border: Update 2000* (Ottawa: Ministry of Public Works and Government Services Canada, 2000), pp. 29–30 (Ci51-95-/2000E).

54. Akhil Gupta and James Ferguson, "Beyond 'Culture': Space, Identity, and the Politics of Difference," *Cultural Anthropology* 7 (1992): 9.

55. Sankaran Krishna, "Cartographic Anxiety: Mapping the Body Politic in India," *Alternatives* 19 (1994): 514–516.

56. Hastings Donnan and Thomas M. Wilson, *Borders: Frontiers of Identity, Nation, and State* (Oxford, UK: Berg, 1999); David Newman, "Boundaries," in *A Companion to Political Geography,* edited by J. Agnew and G. Toal (Oxford, UK: Blackwell, 2002), pp. 1–16.

57. See special issue of *Millennium: Journal of International Studies* 28 (1999); Mathias Albert, David Jacobson, and Yosef Lapids, eds., *Identities, Borders, Orders: Rethinking International Relations Theory* (Minneapolis: University of Minnesota Press, 2001).

58. Peter G. Mandaville, "Territory and Translocality: Discrepant Idioms of Political Identity," *Millennium: Journal of International Studies* 28 (1999): 653–654.

59. Arjun Appadurai, *Modernity at Large: Cultural Dimensions of Globalization* (Minneapolis: University of Minnesota Press, 1996), p. 189.

60. Arjun Appadurai, "Sovereignty Without Territoriality: Notes for a Postnational Geography," in *Geography of Identity,* edited by Patricia Yaeger (Ann Arbor: University of Michigan Press, 1996), p. 49.

61. Nevzat Soguk and Geoffrey Whitehall, "Wandering Grounds: Transversality, Identity, Territoriality, and Movement," *Millennium: Journal of International Studies* 28 (1999): 676.

62. Krishna, "Cartographic Anxiety," p. 516.

63. Ibid., p. 676.

64. Brock, "Observing Change," p. 488.

65. Gupta and Ferguson, "Beyond 'Culture,'" p. 20.

66. Amitava Kumar, *Passport Photos* (Berkeley: University of California Press, 2000), p. x.

67. Soguk and Whitehall, "Wandering Grounds," p. 676.

68. Krishna, "Cartographic Anxiety," p. 515.

69. A. Hansen, quoted in Anthony Asiwaju, "Public Policy or Overcoming Marginalization: Borderlands in Africa, North America, and Western Europe," in *Margins of Insecurity: Minorities and International Security,* edited by Sam C. Nolutshungu (Rochester, NY: University of Rochester Press, 1996), p. 251.

70. Ibid., p. 269.

71. Peter Andreas, *Border Games: Policing the U.S.-Mexico Divide* (Ithaca, NY: Cornell University Press, 2000), p. 35.

72. Ibid., p. 8.

73. Michael Kearney, "Borders and Boundaries of State and Self at the End of Empire," *Journal of Historical Sociology* 4 (1991): 58.

74. Peter Andreas, "The Escalation of U.S. Immigration Control in the Post-NAFTA Era," *Political Science Quarterly* 113 (Winter 1998/1999): 595.

75. Franzén, "Urban Order and the Preventive Restructuring of Space," p. 206 (emphasis in original).

76. Andreas, "The Escalation of U.S. Immigration Control," p. 595.

77. Ibid., p. 591.

78. Heyman, "Putting Power in the Anthropology of Bureaucracy," p. 266.

79. Kearney, "Borders and Boundaries," p. 61.

80. Malcolm Anderson, "Proceedings of an Expert Seminar," in *Policy Alternatives to Schengen Border Controls on the Future EU External Frontier*, edited by Malcolm Anderson, Joanna Apap, and Christopher Mulkins (Warsaw: Center for European Studies, 23–24 February 2001), p. 15.

81. Andreas, "The Escalation of U.S. Immigration Control," p. 600.

82. Heyman, "Putting Power in the Anthropology of Bureaucracy," p. 267.

83. William Kavanagh, "Symbolic Boundaries and 'Real' Borders on the Portuguese-Spanish Border," in *Border Approaches: Anthropological Perspectives on Frontiers*, edited by Hastings Donnan and Thomas M. Wilson (New York: University Press of America, 1994), p. 82.

84. Ibid., p. 82.

85. Ibid., p. 83.

86. Ibid., p. 86.

87. Peter Sahlins, "State Formation and National Identity in the Catalan Borderlands During the Eighteenth and Nineteenth Centuries," in *Border Identities: Nation and State at International Frontiers*, edited by Thomas M. Wilson and Hastings Donnan (Cambridge, UK: Cambridge University Press, 1998), p. 55.

88. Ibid., p. 52.

89. Donna K. Flynn, "'We Are the Border': Identity, Exchange, and the State Along the Bénin-Nigeria Border," *American Ethnologist* 24 (1997): 313.

90. Ibid., p. 312.

91. Ibid., p. 317.

92. Ibid., p. 318.

93. Ibid., pp. 321–322.

94. Malcolm Anderson, *Frontiers: Territory and State Formation in the Modern World* (Cambridge, UK: Polity, 1996), p. 129.

7

Conclusion: Passports, Identity, and International Relations

> *Our border controls will not just stop terrorists, but improve the efficient movement of legitimate traffic.*
> —U.S. national security strategy

> *But who is not a stranger?*
> —Michael Dillon, "The Sovereign and the Stranger," 1999

> *We remain necessarily strangers to ourselves.*
> —Friedrich Nietzsche, "Genealogy of Morals," 1956

At the heart of the international movement regime there lies a fundamental tension between two governmental desires: wealth and security. First, governments adhere to a liberal logic of economic interaction, whereby the reduction of border formalities increases trade, tourism, and migration. Second, governments adhere to a logic of state security, whereby the increase of border formalities decreases smuggling, illegal immigration, and terrorism (nonstate violence). A state must balance these two ideals: economic autarky is unfeasible, and the security state demonstrates nothing except its profound insecurity.[1] The passport operates at the nexus of this tension: It regulates entry, the expulsion of foreign nationals, and the increase of international trade; it defines and polices nationality; it guarantees citizens a home to which they can be repatriated; it operates as part of a system of documents that helps to regulate the health of the body politic; it certifies identity. In short, the passport distinguishes, albeit imperfectly, between the stranger and the native, between danger and safety.

In this book, I have made three main arguments: that the passport plays a limited and limiting role in the identity of travelers; that the passport system does not guarantee security, either to the bearer or to foreign states; and that there is a bifurcation in the modern mobility regime, in which two sets of populations enjoy greater or lesser freedom of movement. The September 11 terrorist attacks on the United States brought the vital importance of this topic into clear focus. These basic arguments have been substantiated through the history of the modern passport regime, examined through the themes of violence, health, cooperation, integration, and control.

The predecessors of the passport—the safe-conduct pass and letters of marque—helped consolidate the state's monopoly on legitimate violence. These documents also supported a geopolitical order in which the sovereign guaranteed the limitation of violence within the domestic sphere and ensured the presence of violence within the international sphere. As we have seen, letters of marque, the sovereign's use of private violent actors, and state-sponsored imperialism made the international realm violent. The transition from safe-conducts to passports occurred as sovereign states consolidated the geopolitical order. And though the passport is only one governmental tool among many, it illustrates the ways in which the bureaucratic control of individuals creates certain kinds of relationships and subjects. The passport created the sovereign subject by linking her directly to the sovereign's international legal personality. Government documents also reflected the variegated legal status of colonial subjects, offering limited protection but no right of return.

An examination of Britain's passport machinery demonstrates how the form of the passport came to be more important than the authenticity of the document and how different groups were afforded more or less protection. Because the government could not authenticate each recommender, the primary duty of the passport officer was to verify that the passport applicant was not immediately wanted for criminal charges, was not a particular danger to the state, or was not an imposter. The adjudication of the traveler's intentions was conducted within prevalent social scripts in which working women, artistes, criminals, and the poor were controlled to a greater extent than rich nobles, businessmen, and colonial officials. Increased travel and population mobility after World War II limited what the British Passport Office could accomplish. As a consequence, terrorists and spies—nonstate violent international actors—came to rely on passports to penetrate the domestic space of the target state.

And though the use of false passports is common, it has come to the world's attention as a result of September 11. In sum, the passport has acted as an instrument of the sovereign state to assert and police its monopoly of legitimate force, but recent events have emphasized that the promise of the passport is false. The passport may represent the subject, but it can never guarantee identity of the bearer or safety for the traveler or for the foreign state. The bearer is always subject to the revocation of rights at the border and is subject to the laws of the state in which he is present. The foreign state can never be sure that the bearer's identity is authentic and cannot discern intentions.

A complementary history of the passport illustrates how this governmental device is marshaled for other ends. To protect the health of the body politic, sovereigns and their delegates issued passports that certified identity and health: the health passport. The use of passports to enforce another geopolitical strategy—the quarantine—illustrated a government attempt to protect both itself and its community from the danger of contagious diseases. Contemporary social scripts found the causes of diseases in social ills. Consequently, groups that were already marginalized in society (the poor, immigrants, prostitutes, and colonial subjects) were controlled assiduously. This dynamic was also at play during the emergence of the HIV/AIDS crisis. The sovereign state must be capable of protecting its national population from disease—as much as from war—and it has mobilized the passport to control the spread of contagious diseases.

By examining these alternate uses of the passport, our focus shifted from the sovereign state as a singular entity to the sovereign state as a government that constitutes and controls a population, in part by distinguishing marginal groups from the majority. The promulgation of international regulations regarding the Health Organization of the League of Nations and the World Health Organization indicated the ways that the regime of disease control, and the concomitant movement control, has shifted from a system of quarantine and exclusion to a system of surveillance.

After World War I and the widespread introduction of the passport, the League of Nations convened the first international passport conferences. These early attempts at international cooperation expressed a conflict: a desire for freedom of movement and the anxiety of security. Early negotiations implied that the issuing state held a moral responsibility to the international community to certify its subjects and, more important, to accept its subjects if expelled.

As the Nansen passport managed refugees and stateless peoples, the passport became the essential proof of citizenship. This relationship between passport and nationality came to the fore during British decolonization. As the British colonies gained their independence, as the chief passport officer argues, the Passport Office became the primary adjudicator of nationality. The varied legal status of the colonies themselves was reflected in the varied legal status of the decolonized. Former British subjects could possess a British passport that did not grant them the right to return to Britain or to their home country—as in the case of Hong Kong and the Asians in Uganda. The question of nationality was brought into sharp focus by the passport, which is the documentary trace of governmental control over its population. The inability, or unwillingness, of the British state to protect British-protected persons meant that the passport served various functions for different individuals (and for some it served no function at all).

The disappearance of borders in the European Union challenged the function of the passport. However, we saw that the disappearance of formalities at the border (at least for some) created new formalities at the borders for foreigners and implied a wider surveillance system. Once the external border of Schengenland replaced the internal borders of states, anxiety was displaced to the leaking areas. These anxieties were framed with familiar social scripts according to labor, immigration, crime, and cultural infiltration.

The modern passport system represents the best attempt of states to regulate international mobility. This subject is understudied and would benefit from a research program that includes a study of the international visa regime and recent attempts by the U.S. and some European governments to supplement this system.

Problems of Citizenship, Nationality, and Documentation

In the first formulation of this project, I intended to analyze the bifurcation of the modern passport regime and hence the modern international mobility regime. Movement within Europe and between Canada, the United States, and Mexico had been facilitated by treaties and agreements and seemed barely regulated. The forty-five-second examination at the U.S.-Canadian border, or at Heathrow Airport, illustrates an ease of mobility that seems to reinforce globalization scholars' contention that international borders were decreasing in relevance. Movement within the developing and postcolonial worlds required a far more arduous journey of vaccinations, inoculations, bureaucracies, examinations, and interrogations. But a close examination of the dynamics of those border crossings indicates that it was not simply the borders that were different; different schema were applied to different kinds of travelers.

As a Canadian professional (and natural-born Briton), I received little examination. Despite my recurring anxieties that I would be excluded from the country, a far greater trial awaited others. Colleagues, friends, and fellow travelers of suspect nationality were detained, cross-examined, and given a far more rigorous interrogation. I came to understand that it was not only spaces that were controlled but also populations. I thus arrived at two conclusions. First, governments control the marginalized in international society more assiduously than privileged or normal travelers. Although I had assumed that this was true from a geopolitical perspective—reflecting one's citizenship in either the core or the periphery—it has become clear to me that an essential dynamic of the passport is the extent to which passports themselves were used to control and police the national body by state institutions.

Second, the passport represents a text that is interpreted by its examiners and, as such, is subject to the hermeneutics of interpretation. Institutions and individuals bring their assumptions and stereotypes to the examination booth. Although the body and documents may be exposed for examination, that evaluation takes place within a set of social scripts. In investigating the passport, we invariably investigate the national script that is being played out in the issuance, examination, and refusal of passports.

The first dynamic is clearest in the control of stigmatized groups such as sex workers, colonial workers, contagious travelers, and working women. Regardless of whether governments figure the threat that these travelers represent in terms of morality, health, labor, or security, each group is subject to a similar exclusionary and surveillance regime. Suspicion relies on a set of social scripts of high-risk national groups, reinforced by bureaucratic institutionalization. As Didier Bigo illustrates, there has been a shift

> from the control of and hunt for individual criminals to the policing of foreigners to the surveillance of so-called risk groups, defined by using criminology and statistics and which . . . focus attention on extra-community immigration and those diasporas which deem to constitute the origin of the most frequent and more serious threats to security.[2]

The second dynamic is clearest in the recent passport panic arising after September 11. This anxiety about identity and danger finds a focus in the passport precisely because of the illusion of control that it represents. The promise of the passport, however, is a false one. As recent history illustrates, the passport does not guarantee the traveler's intentions or that the traveler will not be a danger. The issuing agency is restricted even in finding out the personal history of the passport applicant. Previous criminal activity cannot restrict, in many cases, the issuance of a passport (although it may prevent the issuance of a visa). Most modern passport agencies verify identity only with reference to other forms of identification. There are more than 2 million blank passports in potential circulation—genuine passports stolen before any significant details have been entered, which are virtually undetectable as fraudulent unless the number has been noted and distributed to the various agencies.[3] Eberhard Bort notes that "in 1997 alone, German border police confiscated 1,700 passports at the Polish border."[4] Belgium, Canada, and the United States have all attempted to secure their identity documents since September 11, but this process is always incomplete. This is illustrated in the new Belgian passports, which "include instructions to border guards on some of the security features for which they should look."[5] The passport is thus inscribed with a test for its own identity. The passport does not need to be confirmed through other documents; it merely needs to be identical to itself. The great weakness in this system is the ease of obtaining authentic breeder documents that can be used to obtain fraudulent documents. The security apparatus of documentary checks has proven remarkably porous, as investigations after September 11 illustrate. Recent reports detail how "nine of the hijackers who commandeered jetliners on September 11 were selected for special security screenings, including two who were singled out because of irregularities in their identification documents."[6] Yet investigation, examination, and special screening did not prevent these nine September 11 terrorists, or Richard Reid, from being violent.

This history of the passport in international relations has related the importance of the documentary traces of individuals as constituted by a series of state institutions. The movement toward biometric measuring and computerized identity indicates the degree to which territorial security has become virtual security, in which our bodies are forced to testify against a database to verify an identity that has been assigned by other documents. This bureaucratic confirmation of national identity (both as sameness and as uniqueness) is supplemented by the ritual of the border crossing. A recent exhibition by the Australian Customs Agency at the National Maritime Museum indicates the ways that the construction of this national space can be pedagogical. The curator describes how "suspicious characters . . . lurk in niches along the hallway leading in to the exhibition. These characters just beg to be searched, and visitors have the opportunity to do just that."[7] Thus, even in the National Maritime Museum citizens are being educated in the role of the surveillance state and their roles as docile subjects. They play the role of both examined and examiner, citizens and smugglers.

It is a mistake to locate these anxieties at the border itself. Within the European Union, for example, "80 per cent of 'illegal' immigration is due to expiry of tourist visas, while only 20 per cent result from illegal frontier crossing."[8] This corresponds to figures in the United States, where "40–50 percent of all illegal immigrants in the United States entered the country legally (as tourists or students, for example) and then overstayed their visas."[9] As Malcolm Anderson points out, a great deal of frontier policing happens at a point prior to the border: "controls are now exercised in the consulates located in most countries of the world, by transportation companies through the use of carrier liability," as well as through policing of documents by employers.[10] Stephen Flynn argues that the sheer volume of cross-border trade, and the necessity of integration into the global economy, require that inspection shift from a regime of inspection to a regime of surveillance.[11] The border is deterritorialized—removed from the specific place at the territorial boundary of the state. This "remote policing" entails border inspections "outside the national territory . . . carried out further 'downstream,' within the border zone, or even 'upstream' with police collaboration in the immigrants' home country."[12] The United States will implement a similar scheme within the new Department of Homeland Security under the heading "smart borders."[13] Following the Schengen solution to the problem of porous internal borders, the borders of the state are supplemented by a general surveillance regime. The INS has put in place a regional version of a cross-border surveillance regime at the Mexican border.[14] Austrian border police have implemented a ten-kilometer-wide zone of increased surveillance while dismantling checks at the actual border.[15] Greek authorities have put in place a similar system of border zones, varying from twenty to fifty kilometers from the border.[16]

At present, "all of Bavaria is 'border zone'"—i.e., random spot checks are possible without cause of suspicion" as a result of Schengen countries' anxiety about the influx from the east.[17] And despite empirical evidence to the contrary, "the border is conveniently targeted as both the source of the problem and as the most appropriate site of the policing solution."[18] This deterritorialization and reterritorialization of the border highlight the relevance of the border in national discourses.

Despite the floating definitions of "security" in the post–Cold War era, it remains one of the most powerful rhetorical devices within nationalist imaginaries. Anxieties about nuclear apocalypse have been eclipsed by anxieties of cultural invasion or the return of the repressed. The defense of national borders presents a tidy example of governmental control. Security has shifted from grand geopolitical balances of power to the microbalances of the nation and its societal, cultural, and physical borders. There has been a securitization of culture and population, whereby the national populations have come to be objects of policing more assiduously than before. This securitization is expressed in anxieties over immigrant invasions—Turks in Germany, Algerians in France, Hispanics in the United States, and postcolonial returnees in Britain—and made real in the concomitant control of nationality, immigration, and passport policies. There is also the continuing trend toward the militarization of the border. Bigo comments on the use of military technology and military schema at the U.S.-Mexican border.[19] The same is true of the eastern border of Germany and the southern flank of the European Union. Not only are military metaphors being used to shore up the discourse of the border; military tactics and technologies are being mobilized.[20] Although military metaphors, and even military tactics, may not be matched for the task of policing the borders, the rhetoric of war and conflict may mobilize citizens. At its root, the passport regime provides an incomplete security guarantee for the state.

Constituting the Self as a National and International Actor

The sovereign state and the citizen are mutually constitutive. The state reinforces this sovereign personality by monopolizing the legitimate means of both moving and belonging in the mechanism of the passport. It is the necessary right of the sovereign state to define and demarcate its citizens. As a U.S. secretary of state clarified in 1893, "the universally admitted doctrine that a State is the sole ultimate judge of the citizenship of its own dependents, and is, in the sovereign capacity, competent to certify the fact."[21] But this sovereign right derives its authority from the very citizens that it constitutes. The passport represents an attempt to fix these international identities as sovereign and subject. For the state, the citizen who remains in the space of the nation replicates the boundaries of the nation-state only insofar as he/she remains in the state. It is the *foreign* national and the foreigner—the traveler, the bearer of the passport—that reifies the international presence of the nation-state, constructs the border in its crossing (whether legitimate or illegitimate), and consequently creates the sovereign character of the state in the international system. It is movement that is central to the state rather than being at home. As Jenny Edkins and Véronique Pin-Fat write, "The movement of people or peoples between and among states can be traced as a practice subversive of state identities and boundaries. It can also be seen as part of the way states script themselves through the regulatory mechanisms and practices they bring into being."[22] The policing of the border, the withholding and endowment of rights, the ascription and withdrawal of national protection—all signal the limits and depths of the power of the state and the citizen as a subject of the state. As Timothy Mitchell argues,

> By establishing a territorial boundary and exercising absolute control over movement across it, state practices define and help constitute a national entity. Setting up and policing a frontier involves a variety of fairly modern social practices—continuous barbed-wire fencing, passports, immigration laws, currency control and so on. These mundane arrangements, most of them unknown two hundred or even one hundred years ago, help manufacture an almost transcendent entity, the nation state.[23]

Michael Dillon emphasizes a parallel between "the suppliant and the stranger" that sheds new light on the border rite of passage.[24] Every citizen, foreign national, and refugee—as a stranger—must act as a suppliant, forgoing their rights while at the border in order that they may be granted entry and thus endowed with national rights once inside the territory. This notion is supplemented by Jacques Derrida's consideration of "conditional hospitality": "[the host] remains the master of the house, the country, the nation, he controls the threshold, he controls the borders, and when he welcomes the guest he wants to keep the mastery."[25] By this exercise of sovereign power, movement across the border becomes a reinscription of the power of the state.

Although the passport is not the only identity or travel document that is issued by modern governments, it often functions as a determinant of nationality. Because the national passport, and not a travel document or refugee passport, represents a promise by the state to accept the repatriation of the citizen, passports are issued only to nationals. In some postcolonial instances (e.g., citizens of the British Empire in interwar Canada, the non-British Asians expelled from Uganda, and the post-Soviet Russians in Lithuania), the state has defined the nation, through an issuance of differentiated passports, indicating who are true citizens and who are legacies of the colonial oppressors. Passports offer a trace of social construction of the nation as a homogeneous entity. They also indicate the multiplicity of identities that constitute the nation.

Borders and border crossings also play a primary, if not constitutive, role in the formation of translocal and transversal communities. The community may be formed in the shared experience of evading the border, or in its disparagement, but in both cases the border itself is a significant feature. We have seen that physical and juridical borders play a fundamental role in the constitution of the self-other dichotomy. As Anderson argues, "Whether or not corresponding with natural frontiers, the linear frontiers of Europe have become terrible realities."[26] This argument does not rely on any foundational notion of community, the nation, or the state. Although it is important to widen the scope of our analysis to include those groups and communities that do not fit neatly into the territorial state, it is folly to think that the presence of the border can be imagined away. As we have seen, the presence of the border—indicating two separate sovereignties and two jurisdictions—creates new opportunities for its transgression that would otherwise be absent.

Taking the "Inter-" Seriously

The international movement regime is saturated with the tension between the desire for free movement and the desire for security and homogeneity. As Bigo concludes: "Contradictions between liberal, economic, political and security logic become apparent. Free movement cannot be managed in the same way as goods and services."[27] The international mobility regime can be understood as having three regimes.

The first is the quarantine regime: the population is controlled through the application of state and bureaucratic power. Disease and violence are seen as two threats to the national body politic and are dealt with in similar ways. Passports, issued by the sovereign or his bureaucracy, legitimize certain kinds of travels and certain kinds of violence.

The second is the geopolitical regime: the population is controlled through the application of state and bureaucratic power in different ways in different spheres of international society. Freedom of movement and, indeed, movement without papers are touted as achievements of civilization, possible only within a civilized world. Passes are written for barbaric areas that have laws, but those laws are separate from European ones. And no passes are written for savage areas, in which movement is only possible through violence. Different regulations apply to members of each geopolitical sphere, which enable them to move more or less freely.

The third and final is the surveillance regime: the population is controlled indirectly through the application of institutional power rather than overt restrictions. As disease transmission and international trade are seen as increasingly unstoppable forces, state authorities move to control them through surveillance. This creates a network of discipline and self-discipline, in which force is applied through the physical and ideational structures of passports and borders.

I do not mean to imply here that each regime is part of a development or that the regime is equally applied or homogeneous within the globe. Indeed, different movement regimes exist within the developed North and different areas of the underdeveloped South. These models characterize three ways of conceiving and controlling movement in the world.

Placing movement and the international mobility regime at the center of our study rather than at the periphery grants a perspective whereby we can see the efforts of the state to sustain the myth of a stable, territorially bounded national community. Integrating the lived lives of individuals crossing borders illustrates the degree to which the state and the state border provide a very powerful interruption of imagined communities. In sum, the passport embodies changing modes of governmental power, changing international mobility regimes, and changing social attitudes. In each case, the passport operates at the nexus of the desire for wealth and mobility and the fear of violence and mobility.

Notes

1. One need only look at North Korea and Myanmar (Burma) for evidence of the former, and Israel and the Soviet Union for evidence of the latter.

2. Didier Bigo, "Landscape of Police Co-Operation," in *Boundaries of Understanding: Essays in Honour of Malcolm Anderson*, edited by Eberhard Bort and Russell Keat (Edinburgh: University of Edinburgh, International Social Sciences Institute, 1999), p. 70.

3. Thomas Fuller, "EU Passports: An Easy-to-Steal Tool for Terrorists," *International Herald Tribune* (8 January 2002).

4. Eberhard Bort, "The Frontiers of *Mittleeuropa*: Problems and Opportunities at the Eastern Frontier of the European Union," in *Schengen Still Going Strong: Evaluation and Update*, edited by Monica den Boer (Maastrict: European Institute of Public Administration, 2000), p. 96.

5. Thomas Fuller, "EU Passports: An Easy-to-Steal Tool."

6. Dan Eggen, "Airports Screened Nine of Sept. 11 Hijackers, Officials Say," *Washington Post* (2 March 2002): A11.

7. "Hands-On Customs Exhibition a Success," *Manifest* 4 (May 2000): 31.

8. Didier Bigo, "Frontiers and Security in the European Union: The Illusion of Migration Control," in *Frontiers of Europe*, edited by Malcolm Anderson and Eberhard Bort (London: Pinter, 1998), p. 152.

9. Peter Andreas, "The Escalation of U.S. Immigration Control in the Post-NAFTA Era," *Political Science Quarterly* 113 (Winter 1998/1999): 602.

10. Malcolm Anderson, "The Transformation of Border Controls: A European Precedent," in *The Wall Around the West: State Borders and Immigration Controls in North America and Europe*, edited by P. Andreas and T. Snyder (Lanham, MD: Rowman and Littlefield, 2001).

11. Stephen E. Flynn, "Beyond Border Control," *Foreign Affairs* 79 (December 2000): 62.

12. Bigo, "Landscape of Police Co-operation," p. 70.

13. U.S. Office of Homeland Security, "National Strategy for Homeland Security" (July 2002), p. 22.

14. Josiah McC. Heyman, "United States Surveillance over Mexican Lives at the Border: Snapshots of an Emerging Regime," *Human Organization* 58 (1999): 431.

15. Roberto Leo, "Schengen and Its Daily Practice on the Borders: The Particular Situation of the Borders in Friuli Venezia Giula," in *Schengen and the Southern Frontier of the European Union*, edited by Malcolm Anderson and Eberhard Bort (Edinburgh: University of Edinburgh, International Social Sciences Institute, 1998), p. 110.

16. Malcolm Anderson and Eberhard Bort, *Frontiers of the European Union* (London: Palgrave, 2001), p. 139.

17. Eberhard Bort, "200km Eastern Frontier of the EU," in *Boundaries and Identities: The Eastern Frontier of the European Union*, edited by Malcolm Anderson and Eberhard Bort (Edinburgh: University of Edinburgh, International Social Sciences Institute, 1996), p. 73.

18. Andreas, "The Escalation of U.S. Immigration Control," p. 600.

19. Bigo, "Frontiers and Security in the European Union," p. 159.

20. Andreas, "The Escalation of U.S. Immigration Control," p. 593.

21. P. Weis, *Nationality and Statelessness in International Law* (Germantown, MA: Sijthoff and Noordhoff, 1979), p. 228.

22. Jenny Edkins and Véronique Pin-Fat, "The Subject of the Political," in *Sovereignty and Subjectivity*, edited by Jenny Edkins, Nalini Persram, and Véronique Pin-Fat (Boulder: Lynne Rienner Publishers, 1999), p. 14.

23. Timothy Mitchell, "The Limits of the State: Beyond Statist Approaches and Their Critics," *American Political Science Review* 85 (1991): 94.

24. Dillon, "The Sovereign and the Stranger," p. 120.

25. Jacques Derrida, "Hospitality, Justice, and Responsibility," in *Questioning Ethics: Contemporary Debates in Philosophy*, edited by Richard Kearney and Mark Dooley (London: Routledge, 1999), p. 69.

26. Anderson, "The Transformation of Border Controls."

27. Bigo, "Frontiers and Security in the European Union," p. 150.

Bibliography

Abbott, Stephen. "The Official Government Website of the Republic of Howland and Baker Islands," n.d. (accessed 20 November 2001), users.metro2000.net/~stabbott/Visithowlandbaker.htm.
———. "Too Good to Be True: An Explanation of This Website," n.d. (accessed 20 November 2001), users.metro2000.net/~stabbott/RHBI explained.html.
Abeyratne, R.I.R. "The Development of the Machine Readable Passport and Visa and the Legal Rights of the Data Subject." *Annals of Air and Space Law* 17, no. 2 (1992): 1–31.
Abu-Lughod, Janet L. *Before European Hegemony: The World System, A.D. 1250–1350.* New York: Oxford University Press, 1989.
"Accra Mail, Extortion at Border." *Africa News* (1 October 2001).
"Afrabet Soup." *The Economist* (2 October 2001): 77.
Agar, Jon. "Modern Horrors: British Identity and Identity Cards." In *Documenting Individual Identity: The Development of State Practices in the Modern World,* edited by Jane Caplan and John Torpey, 101–120. Princeton, NJ: Princeton University Press, 2001.
Agnew, John. *Geopolitics: Re-visioning World Politics.* New York: Routledge, 1998.
Agnew, John, and Stuart Corbridge. *Mastering Space: Hegemony, Territory, and International Political Economy.* New York: Routledge, 1995.
Albert, Mathias, David Jacobson, and Yosef Lapids, eds. *Identities, Borders, Orders: Rethinking International Relations Theory.* Minneapolis: University of Minnesota Press, 2001.

Author's note: FO = Foreign Office; HO = Home Office.

Anderson, Benedict. "Exodus." *Critical Inquiry* 20 (Winter 1994): 314–327.

———. *Imagined Communities: Reflections on the Origin and Spread of Nationalism.* 2nd ed. London: Verso, 1991.

Anderson, Malcolm. *Frontiers: Territory and State Formation in the Modern World.* Cambridge, UK: Polity Press, 1996.

———. "Introductory Statement." In *Policy Alternatives to Schengen Border Controls on the Future EU External Frontier,* edited by Malcolm Anderson, Joanna Apap, and Christopher Mulkins, 4–8. Warsaw: Center for European Policy Studies, February 2001.

———. "Proceedings of an Expert Seminar." In *Policy Alternatives to Schengen Border Controls on the Future EU External Frontier,* edited by Malcolm Anderson, Joanna Apap, and Christopher Mulkins, 10–19. Warsaw: Center for European Studies, 23–24 February 2001.

———. "The Transformation of Border Controls: A European Precedent." In *The Wall Around the West: State Borders and Immigration Controls in North America and Europe,* edited by P. Andreas and T. Snyder. Lanham, MD: Rowman and Littlefield, 2001.

Anderson, Malcolm, Didier Bigo, and Eberhard Bort. "Frontiers, Identity, and Security in Europe: An Agenda for Research." In *Borderlands Under Stress,* edited by Martin Pratt and Janet Allison Brown, 251–274. The Hague: Kluwer, 2000.

Anderson, Malcolm, and Eberhard Bort. *Frontiers of the European Union.* London: Palgrave, 2001.

Andreas, Peter. *Border Games: Policing the U.S.-Mexico Divide.* Ithaca, NY: Cornell University Press, 2000.

———. "The Escalation of U.S. Immigration Control in the Post-NAFTA Era." *Political Science Quarterly* 113 (Winter 1998/1999): 591–616.

"Apartheid at Heathrow." *The Economist* 325 (8 January 1993): 78.

Appadurai, Arjun. *Modernity at Large: Cultural Dimensions of Globalization.* Minneapolis: University of Minnesota Press, 1996.

———. "Sovereignty Without Territoriality: Notes for a Postnational Geography." In *Geography of Identity,* edited by Patricia Yaeger, 40–58. Ann Arbor: University of Michigan Press, 1996.

Arnold, David. *Colonizing the Body: State Medicine and Epidemic Disease in Nineteenth-Century India.* Berkeley: University of California Press, 1993.

———. "Inventing Tropicality." In *The Problem of Nature: Environment, Culture, and European Expansion,* edited by David Arnold, 141–168. Oxford, UK: Blackwell, 1996.

———. "Modern Period in South Asia." In *The Cambridge World History of Human Disease,* edited by Kenneth F. Kiple, 418–425. Cambridge, UK: Cambridge University Press, 1993.

Ashcroft, John. "Transcript of the Attorney General John Ashcroft Regarding the Transfer of Abdullah Al Muhajir (Born Jose Padilla) to the Department of Defense as an Enemy Combatant." Washington, DC: U.S. Department of Justice, June 10, 2002.

Ashley, Richard. "The Achievements of Post-structuralism." In *International Theory: Positivism and Beyond*, edited by Steve Smith, Ken Booth, and Marysia Zalewski, 240–253. Cambridge, UK: Cambridge University Press, 1996.

Asiwaju, Anthony. "Public Policy or Overcoming Marginalization: Borderlands in Africa, North America, and Western Europe." In *Margins of Insecurity: Minorities and International Security*, edited by Sam C. Nolutshungu, 251–283. Rochester, NY: University of Rochester Press, 1996.

Baer, Joel H. "'The Complicated Plot of Piracy': Aspects of English Criminal Law and the Image of the Pirate in Defoe." *The Eighteenth Century* 23 (1982): 3–26.

Balińska, Marta Aleksandra. "Assistance and Not Mere Relief: The Epidemic Commission of the League of Nations, 1920–1923." In *International Health Organizations and Movements, 1918–1939*, edited by Paul Weindling, 81–108. New York: Cambridge University Press, 1995.

Bartelson, Jens. *A Genealogy of Sovereignty.* Cambridge, UK: Cambridge University Press, 1995.

Benyon, John. "The Politics of Police Co-operation in the European Union." *International Journal of the Sociology of Law* 24 (1996): 353–379.

Bigo, Didier. "Frontiers and Security in the European Union: The Illusion of Migration Control." In *Frontiers of Europe,* edited by Malcolm Anderson and Eberhard Bort, 148–164. London: Pinter, 1998.

———. "Landscape of Police Co-Operation." In *Boundaries of Understanding: Essays in Honour of Malcolm Anderson,* edited by Eberhard Bort and Russell Keat, 59–74. Edinburgh, Scotland: University of Edinburgh, International Social Sciences Institute, 1999.

Bishop, Ryan, and Lillian S. Robinson. *Night Market: Sexual Cultures and the Thai Economic Miracle.* New York: Routledge, 1998.

Black, Jeremy. *The British Abroad: The Grand Tour in the Eighteenth Century.* New York: St. Martin's, 1992.

Blaut, J. M. *The Colonizer's Model of the World: Geographical Diffusionism and Eurocentric History.* New York: Guildford, 1993.

Bloore, R. "Minute Sheet 'Refusal of Passports,'" 12 April 1947 (FO 612 244).

Bloore, R., to J. Keith. "Correspondence." 9 April 1947 (FO 612 244).

Bloore, R., to Under Secretary of State for the Colonies. "Refusal of Passports." Misc: 14288, 21 April 1947 (FO 612 244).

Blow, Christopher J. *Airport Terminals.* 2nd ed. Oxford, UK: Butterworth-Heinemann, 1996.

Blunker, L. H. "Reports on Passport Office Organisation and Procedures by Treasury Organisations and Methods Division." 1947 (9233/35) (FO 612 267).

Bond, Brian. *War and Society in Europe, 1870–1970.* London: McGill-Queens, 1998.

Borneman, John. *After the Wall: East Meets West in the New Berlin.* New York: Basic Books, 1991.

———. *Subversions of International Order: Studies in the Political Anthropology of Culture.* Albany: State University of New York Press, 1998.

Bort, Eberhard. "The Frontiers of *Mittleeuropa:* Problems and Opportunities at the Eastern Frontier of the European Union." In *Schengen Still Going Strong: Evaluation and Update,* edited by Monica den Boer, 85–104. Maastrict: European Institute of Public Administration, 2000.

———. "200km Eastern Frontier of the EU." In *Boundaries and Identities: The Eastern Frontier of the European Union,* edited by Malcolm Anderson and Eberhard Bort, 71–80. Edinburgh, Scotland: University of Edinburgh, International Social Sciences Institute, 1996.

Boudreau, Frank G. "International Health Work." In *Pioneers in World Order: An American Appraisal of the League of Nations,* edited by Harriet Eager Davis, 193–207. New York: Columbia University Press, 1944.

———. "International Health Work." *Proceedings of Academy of Political Science* 12 (1926).

Brandt, Allan M. "Acquired Immune Deficiency Syndrome (AIDS)." In *The Cambridge World History of Human Disease,* edited by Kenneth F. Kiple, 547–551. Cambridge, UK: Cambridge University Press, 1993.

"Brief for the Committee of Ministers on the Establishment of a European Passport." 15 October 1949 (IOC [49] 255) (FO 612 290).

Brock, Lothar. "Observing Change, 'Rewriting' History: A Critical Overview." *Millennium: Journal of International Studies* 28 (1999): 483–497.

Britain, Aliens Department, Home Office. "General System of Alien Control." 7 July 1939 (HO213 331).

Brown, David, and Jon Jeter. "Hundreds Walk Out on Mbeki." *Washington Post* (10 July 2000).

Bull, Hedley. *The Anarchical Society: A Study of Order in World Politics.* London: Macmillan, 1977.

Burns, Robert I. "The *Guidaticum* Safe-Conduct in Medieval Arago-Catalonia: A Mini-institution for Muslims, Christians, and Jews." *Medieval Encounters* 1 (1995): 51–113.

Burton, Richard F. *Personal Narrative of a Pilgrimage to Al-Madinah and Meccah.* Edited by Isabel Burton. New York: Dover, 1964.

Buzard, James. *The Beaten Track: European Tourism, Literature, and the Ways to Culture, 1800–1918.* Oxford, UK: Clarendon, 1993.

Cammett, Melani. "Defensive Integration and Late Developers: The Gulf Cooperation Council and the Arab Maghreb Union." *Global Governance* 5 (July–September 1999): 379–402.

Canada Customs and Revenue Agency. "Memorandum D2–5–10: Transborder General Aviation—Telephone Reporting and CANPASS Programs." 7 May 1999.

———. "RC4062E (Rev 00) CANPASS—Airport Extending Facilities." November 2000.

———. "RC4197(E) CANPASS—Highway Extending Border Services." June 2000.

———. "Suspension of Alternate Methods of Reporting to Customs." 26 February 2002 (18 December 2001). Available online at www.ccra-adrc.gc.ca/customs/individuals/canpass/canpass-e.html.

Canadian Passport Order (SI/81–86). Section 9b and 10b. "Canada Gazette," part 2, vol. 115, no. 12. Ottawa: Queen's Printers, 1981, 1852–1857.

Carmichael, Ann G. "Diseases of the Renaissance and Early Modern Europe." In *The Cambridge World History of Human Disease,* edited by Kenneth F. Kiple, 279–287. Cambridge, UK: Cambridge University Press, 1993.

———. *Plague and the Poor in Renaissance Florence.* Cambridge, UK: Cambridge University Press, 1986.

———. "Plague Legislation in the Italian Renaissance." *Bulletin of the History of Medicine* 57 (1983): 508–525.

Chaddock, Gail Russell, and Francine Kiefer. "Lessons of Shoe-Bomb Incident." *Christian Science Monitor* 93 (28 December 2001): 1.

Chirimuuta, Richard, and Rosalind Chirimuuta. *AIDS, Africa, and Racism.* 2nd ed. London: Free Association Books, 1989.

Chirimuuta, Richard C., and Rosalind J. Harrison-Chirimuuta. "AIDS from Africa: A Case of Racisms vs. Science?" In *AIDS in Africa and the Caribbean,* edited by George C. Bond, John Kreniske, Ida Susser, and Joan Vincent, 165–180. Boulder: Westview, 1997.

"Classes of Passports." *The Times* (2 June 1967).

Cohen, Jon. "AIDS Debate Declared Dead." *Science Now* (25 April 2001): 1.

———. "The Hunt for the Origins of AIDS." *Atlantic Monthly* 286 (October 2000).

"Control of Aliens: Permanent Legislation Demanded." *The Times* (25 November 1955).

Conway, W, to Downing. "Council of Europe European Passport." 13 March 1951 (WU 10713/13/6) (F0 612 290).

Cox, R. C. *Notes on United Kingdom Nationality Law.* Examiners Circular No. 470, 1950 (FO 612 275).

Dalby, Simon. "The Environment as Geopolitical Threat: Reading Robert Kaplan's 'Coming Anarchy.'" *Ecumene* 3 (1996): 472–496.

Davis, John M. "Passport Fraud: Protecting U.S. Passport Integrity." *FBI Law Enforcement Bulletin* 67 (July 1998): 9–13.

DeLaRue, PLC. "Global Services." N.d. (Accessed on 26 December 2001), www.delarue.com/global.

Der Derian, James. "Spy Versus Spy: The Intertextual Power of International Intrigue." In *International/Intertextual Relations: Postmodern Readings of World Politics,* edited by James Der Derian and Michael J. Shapiro, 163–187. New York: Lexington Books, 1989.

DeRosa, James D. "The Immigrant Investors Program: Cleaning Up Canada's Act." *Case Western Reserve Journal of International Law* 27 (Spring/Summer 1995): 359–406.

Derrida, Jacques. "Foreigner Question." In *Of Hospitality,* edited by Jacques Derrida and Anne Dufoumantelle and translated by Rachel Bowlby, 3–73. Stanford, CA: Stanford University Press, 2000.

———. "Hospitality, Justice and Responsibility." In *Questioning Ethics: Contemporary Debates in Philosophy,* edited by Richard Kearney and Mark Dooley, 65–83. London: Routledge, 1999.

———. *Of Grammatology.* Translated by Gayatri Chakravorty Spivak. Baltimore: Johns Hopkins University Press, 1976.

Devonshire, Duke. "Telegram to Lord Byng, the Gov-Gen of Canada: Personal." 25 July 1924 (32812/24) (FO 612 129).

Dillon, Michael. "The Sovereign and the Stranger." In *Sovereignty and Subjectivity,* edited by Jenny Edkins, Nalini Persram, and Véronique Pin-Fat, 117–140. Boulder: Lynne Rienner Publishers, 1999.

Dixon, M.G. "Order Book Amendments: P/Misc. 16348." 9 April 1968 (FO 612 349).

———. "Revision of Form A 1969." 12 October 1969 (FO 612 346).

Donnan, Hastings, and Thomas M. Wilson. *Borders: Frontiers of Identity, Nation, and State.* Oxford, UK: Berg, 1999.

Doty, Roxanne Lynn. "Sovereignty and the Nation: Constructing the Boundaries of National Identity." In *State Sovereignty as Social Construct,* edited by Thomas J. Biersteker and Cynthia Weber, 121–147. Cambridge, UK: Cambridge University Press, 1996.

Driessen, Henk. "The 'New Immigration' and the Transformation of the European-African Frontier." In *Border Identities: Nation and State at International Frontiers,* edited by Thomas M. Wilson and Hastings Donnan, 96–116. Cambridge, UK: Cambridge University Press, 1998.

Dubin, Martin David. "The League of Nations Health Organization." In *International Health Organizations and Movements, 1918–1939,* edited by Paul Weindling, 56–80. New York: Cambridge University Press, 1995.

Duckett, Margaret, and Andrew J. Orkin. "AIDS-Related Migration and Travel Policies and Restrictions: A Global Survey." *AIDS* 3 (1989): S231–S252.

Economic Community of West African States, "Mini Summit of Heads of State and Government on the Creation of a Borderless ECOWAS: Final Communique." March 2000.

Edkins, Jenny, and Véronique Pin-Fat. "The Subject of the Political." In *Sovereignty and Subjectivity,* edited by Jenny Edkins, Nalini Persram, and Véronique Pin-Fat, 1–18. Boulder: Lynne Rienner Publishers, 1999.

Edwards, Brian. *The Modern Terminal: New Approaches to Airport Architecture.* New York: Routledge, 1998.

Eggen, Dan. "Airports Screened Nine of Sept. 11 Hijackers, Officials Say." *Washington Post* (2 March 2002): A11.

Ejime, Paul. "ECOWAS: Appraising Sub-Regional Integration Process." *Financial Times* (2 December 2001).

Emmett, Nicholas. "Norway's Rejection of the European Union." *Contemporary Review* 268 (June 1996): 287–288.

Enloe, Cynthia. *Bananas, Beaches, and Bases: Making Feminist Sense of International Politics.* Berkeley: University of California Press, 1990.
Enlow, Clair. "New Gates for Asia." *Architecture Week* (6 June 2001): D1–3.
Espionage Unlimited. "British Honduras Passports." N.d. (accessed 18 December 2001), www.espionage-store.com/passport.html.
European Union (Justice and Home Affairs). "Incorporating the Schengen *Acquis* into the European Union." 10 January 2002 (accessed 14 December 2001), europa.eu.int/scadplus/leg/en/lvb/l33020.htm.
Fahrmeir, Andreas. "Governments and Forgers: Passports in Nineteenth-Century Europe." In *Documenting Individual Identity: The Development of State Practices in the Modern World,* edited by Jane Caplan and John Torpey, 218–234. Princeton, NJ: Princeton University Press, 2001.
Farmer, Paul. *AIDS and Accusation: Haiti and the Geography of Blame.* Berkeley: University of California Press, 1992.
Feinstein, Dianne. "Demonstrations of Biometric Technologies Senate Panel to Examine How Biometric Data Can Be Used to Help Prevent Terrorism." FDCH Press Release (13 November 2001).
"Findings." *Wilson Quarterly* 25 (Autumn 2001): 12–16.
Finor Associates. "Camouflage Passports." N.d. (accessed 18 December 2001), www.finor.com/en/camouflage_passports.htm.
"First Bahraini Enters UAE Using ID Card." *Financial Times* (4 July 2000).
Flynn, Donna K. "'We Are the Border': Identity, Exchange, and the State Along the Bénin-Nigeria Border." *American Ethnologist* 24 (1997): 311–330.
Flynn, Stephen E. "Beyond Border Control." *Foreign Affairs* 79 (December 2000): 57–69.
Foreign Office, *British Protection of Anglo-Chinese, Mr. Fraser's Despatch No. 64 of 30th April, 1878* (FO 612 61).
———. "Circular No. 052." 14 June 1962 (TNN 3542/1) (FO 612 320).
———. "Instructions to Delegate at 1926 Passport Conference." (FO 612 355).
———. "Passports Within the Empire." 6 August 1926 (Cor. 6826.HSM) (FO 612 129).
———. *Regulations Respecting Passports.* 28 March 1892 (FO 612 61).
"Forum Interview with Szeming Sze." *World Health Forum* 9 (1988): 29–34.
Foucault, Michel. *Discipline and Punish: The Birth of the Prison.* Translated by Alan Sheridan. New York: Vintage, 1977.
———. "Governmentality." In *The Foucault Effect: Studies in Governmentality,* edited by Graham Burchell, Colin Gordon, and Peter Miller, 87–104. Chicago: University of Chicago Press, 1991.
———. "Nietzsche, Genealogy, History." In *Aesthetics, Method, and Epistemology: Essential Works of Michel Foucault, 1954–1984,* vol. 2, edited by James D. Faubion, 369–392. New York: New Press, 1998.
———. "The Political Technology of Individuals." In *Technologies of the Self: A Seminar with Michel Foucault,* edited by Luther H. Mark, Huck

Gutman, and Patrick H. Hutton, 145–162. Amherst: University of Massachusetts Press, 1988.

———. "Security, Territory, Population." In *Ethics: Subjectivity and Truth: Essential Works of Michael Foucault,* vol. 1., translated by Robert Hurley et al. and edited by Paul Rabinow, 67–72. New York: New Press, 1997.

———. "Society Must Be Defended." In *Ethics: Subjectivity and Truth, Essential Works of Michael Foucault,* vol. 1, translated by Robert Hurley et al. and edited by Paul Rabinow, 59–65. New York: New Press, 1997.

———. "Truth and Power." In *Power/Knowledge: Selected Interviews and Other Writings, 1972–1977,* edited by Colin Gordon and translated by Colin Gordon, Leo Marshall, John Mepham, and Kate Soper, 109–133. New York: Pantheon, 1980.

Franzén, Matz. "Urban Order and the Preventive Restructuring of Space: The Operation of Border Controls in Micro Space." *Sociological Review* 49 (May 2001): 202–218.

Frey, Linda S., and Marsha L. Frey. *The History of Diplomatic Immunity.* Columbus: Ohio State University Press, 1999.

Fuchs, Barbara. "Faithless Empires: Pirates, Renegados, and the English Nation." *English Literary History* 67 (2000): 45–69.

Fuller, Thomas. "EU Passports: An Easy-to-Steal Tool for Terrorists." *International Herald Tribune* (January 8, 2002), available online at www.iht.com.

Fussell, Paul. *Abroad: British Literary Traveling Between the Wars.* Oxford, UK: Oxford University Press, 1980.

Garthoff, R. L. "Berlin 1961: The Record Corrected." *Foreign Policy* 84 (Fall 1991): 142–157.

"GCC Leaders Welcome Iranian President's Offer of Talks About Islands," British Broadcasting Company, 24 December 1997.

Geselle, Andrea. "Domenica Saba Takes to the Road: Origins and Development of a Modern Passport System in Lombardy-Veneto." In *Documenting Individual Identity: The Development of State Practices in the Modern World,* edited by Jane Caplan and John Torpey, 199–217. Princeton, NJ: Princeton University Press, 2001.

Gilboy, Janet A. "Deciding Who Gets In: Decisionmaking by Immigration Inspectors." *Law and Society Review* 25 (1991): 571–599.

Goldbart, Albert. "Fetishes of Passport." *Virginia Quarterly Review* 72 (Winter 1996): 92.

Goldberg, Suzanne B. "Immigration Issues and Travel Restrictions." In *Encyclopedia of AIDS: A Social, Political, Cultural, and Science Record of the HIV Epidemic,* edited by Raymond A. Smith. New York: Fitzroy Dearborn Publishers, 1998.

Goldgeier, James M., and Michael McFaul. "A Tale of Two Worlds: Core and Periphery in the Post–Cold War Era." *International Organization* 46 (Spring 1992): 467–491.

Gong, Gerrit W. *The Standard of "Civilization" in International Society.* Oxford, UK: Clarendon, 1984.

Goodell, Jeff. "How to Fake a Passport." *New York Times* (10 February 2002): 6, 44.

Gordon, April A. "Population, Urbanization, and AIDS." In *Understanding Contemporary Africa,* 3rd ed., edited by April A. Gordon and Donald L. Gordon, 189–216. Boulder: Lynne Rienner Publishers, 2001.

Government of Canada. *Canada–United States Accord on Our Shared Border: Update 2000.* Ministry of Public Works and Government Services Canada, 2000 (Ci51-95-/2000E).

Government of Canada, Department of Foreign Affairs and International Trade. "Bon Voyage, but . . . : Information for the Canadian Traveller 2000." 1998. Available at http://www.voyage.gc.ca/Consular-e/Publications/bon_voyage_but-e.htm

———. *Crossing the 49th: Advice for Canadians Travelling to the United States, 2000.* November 2000.

Grabbe, Heather. "The Sharp Edges of Europe: Extending Schengen Eastwards." *International Affairs* 76 (July 2000): 519–527.

Groebner, Valentin. "Describing the Person, Reading the Signs: Identity Papers, Vested Figures, and the Limits of Identification, 1400–1600." In *Documenting Individual Identity: The Development of State Practices in the Modern World,* edited by Jane Caplan and John Torpey, 15–27. Princeton, NJ: Princeton University Press, 2001.

Grotius, Hugo. *De Jure Belli ac Pacis Libri Tres,* vol. 1, translated by Francis W. Kelsey. Buffalo, NY: William S. Hein, 1995.

"Gulf Interior Ministers' Meeting Discusses Freedom of Travel, Iran, Women," British Broadcasting Corporation. 27 October 2000.

Gupta, Akhil, and James Ferguson. "Beyond 'Culture': Space, Identity, and the Politics of Difference." *Cultural Anthropology* 7 (1992): 6–23.

Gutteridge, Frank. "The World Health Organization: Its Scope and Achievements." *Temple Law Quarterly* 37 (Fall 1963): 1–14.

Hacking, Ian. *The Emergence of Probability: A Philosophical Study of Early Ideas About Probability, Induction, and Statistical Inference.* New York: Cambridge University Press, 1975.

"Hands-On Customs Exhibition a Success." *Manifest* 4 (May 2000): 31.

Hannum, Hurst. *The Right to Leave and Return in International Law and Practice.* Boston: Martinus Nijhoff Publishers, 1987.

Haste, Cate. *Keep the Home Fires Burning: Propaganda in the First World War.* London: Penguin, 1977.

Hatty, Suzanne E., and James Hatty. *The Disordered Body: Epidemic Disease and Cultural Transformation.* Albany: State University of New York Press, 1999.

Heyman, Josiah McC. "Putting Power in the Anthropology of Bureaucracy: The Immigration and Naturalization Service at the Mexico–United States Border." *Current Anthropology* 36 (April 1995): 261–287.

———. "United States Surveillance over Mexican Lives at the Border: Snapshots of an Emerging Regime." *Human Organization* 58 (1999): 430–438.
Higgens, Lesley, and Marie-Christine Leps. "'Passport, Please': Legal, Literary, and Critical Fictions of Identity." *College Literature* 25 (Winter 1998): 94–138.
Holsti, K. J. "Governance Without Government: Polyarchy in Nineteenth-Century European International Politics." In *Governance Without Government: Order and Change in World Politics*, edited by James N. Rosenau and Ernst-Otto Czempiel, 30–57. Cambridge, UK: Cambridge University Press, 1992.
Home Office. "Draft Booklet for Issuance to Police Consolidating All H.O. Circulars on National Registration Identity Cards." September 1944 (HO Circular 700,600/17) (HO 213 754).
Immigration Services International. "Camouflage Passports." N.d. (accessed 18 December 2001), www.tcfb.com/secondpassport/camouflage_english.htm.
International Civil Aviation Organization. "Proposed New Section III to Appendix D of the Consolidated State of Continuing ICAO Policies in the Air Transport Field" (June 2001), A33-WP/12 EC/7.
———. "Report by the Council on the Progress of Implementation of Resolution A32–18: International Cooperation in Protecting the Security and Integrity of Passports" (June 2001), A33-WP/12 EC/7.
International Solutions Incorporated. "Camouflage Passports." N.d. (accessed 18 December 2001), www.ptclub.com/Campassport.html.
Irwin, Mary Ann. "'White Slavery' as Metaphor: Anatomy of Moral Panic." *Ex Post Facto: History Journal* 5 (1996) (accessed 20 December 2001), www.walnet.org/csis/papers/irwin-wslavery.html.
Jackson, Robert H., and Mark W. Zacher. *The Territorial Covenant: International Society and the Stabilization of Boundaries*. Working Paper No. 15. Vancouver, BC: Institute of International Relations, 1997.
Jain, Rajendra K. "Fortifying the 'Fortress': Immigration and Politics in the European Union." *International Affairs* 34 (1997): 163–192.
Javaid, Makbool. "Passport Control." *People Management* 5 (6 March 1999): 28.
Johnson, Maryfran. "The Biometrics Age." *Computerworld* 35 (8 October 2001): 24.
Johnson, Paul. *The Birth of the Modern: World Society 1815–1830*. New York: HarperCollins, 1991.
Kamen, Henry. *Early Modern European Society*. London: Routledge, 2000.
Kaplan, Robert D. "The Coming Anarchy." *Atlantic Monthly* 360 (February 1994): 44–76.
———. *The Ends of the Earth: From Togo to Turkmenistan, from Iran to Cambodia—a Journey to the Frontiers of Anarchy*. New York: Vintage, 1996.

Kaprielian-Churchill, Isabel. "Rejecting 'Misfits': Canada and the Nansen Passport." *International Migration Review* 28 (1996): 281–306.
Kavanagh, William. "Symbolic Boundaries and 'Real' Borders on the Portuguese-Spanish Border." In *Border Approaches: Anthropological Perspectives on Frontiers*, edited by Hastings Donnan and Thomas M. Wilson, 76–87. New York: University Press of America, 1994.
Kearney, Michael. "Borders and Boundaries of State and Self at the End of Empire." *Journal of Historical Sociology* 4 (1991): 52–74.
Keegan, John. *A History of Warfare*. London: Pimlico, 1993.
Kern, Stephen. *The Culture of Time and Space, 1880–1918*. Cambridge, MA: Harvard University Press, 1983.
Kohn, George F. *The Organization and the Work of the League of Nations*. London: P. S. King and Son, 1924.
Kratochwil, Friedrich. "Of Systems, Boundaries, and Territoriality: An Inquiry into the Formation of the State System." *World Politics* 39 (1986): 27–52.
Kraut, Alan M. *Silent Travellers: Germs, Genes, and the "Immigrant Menace."* New York: Basic Books, 1994.
Krishna, Sankaran. "Cartographic Anxiety: Mapping the Body Politic in India." *Alternatives* 19 (1994): 507–521.
Kumar, Amitava. *Passport Photos*. Berkeley: University of California Press, 2000.
Kutty, Faisal. "Canadian Press Calls for Inquiry into Allegations Regarding Mossad Use of Passports." *Washington Report on the Middle East* (January/February 1998) (accessed 19 July 2000), www.washingtonreport.org/backissues/0198/9801026.htm.
Lancy, Robert S. "The Evolution of Australian Passport Law." *Melbourne University Law Review* 13 (June 1982): 428–452.
Lane, Frederick C. "Economic Consequences of Organized Violence." *Journal of Economic History* 17 (December 1958): 401–417.
League of Nations "Passport" 1925 (FO 655 1880).
League of Nations, Advisory and Technical Committee for Communications and Transit, Subcommittee on the Passport Regime. "Minutes of the 3rd Session, Held in Paris, October 2nd to 5th, 1925" (C.699.M.252. 1925 8), (FO 612 355).
League of Nations, Health Organization. *Health*. Geneva: League of Nations, Information Section, 1931.
League of Nations, Provisional Committee on Communications and Transit. *Conference on Passports, Customs Formalities, and Through Tickets*. November 1920 (FO 612 354).
League of Nations, Secretariat. *Ten Years of World Co-operation*. London: Hazell, Watson, and Viney, 1930.
Le Carré, John. *The Spy Who Came in from the Cold*. New York: Coward-McCann, 1963.
———. *Tinker, Tailor, Soldier, Spy*. New York: Bantam, 1974.

Lefebvre, Henri. *The Production of Space.* Translated by Donald Nicholson-Smith. Oxford, UK: Blackwell, 1991.

Leo, Roberto. "Schengen and Its Daily Practice on the Borders: The Particular Situation of the Borders in Friuli Venezia Giula." In *Schengen and the Southern Frontier of the European Union,* edited by Malcolm Anderson and Eberhard Bort, 109–112. Edinburgh, Scotland: University of Edinburgh, International Social Sciences Institute, 1998.

Lindenbaum, Shirley. "AIDS: Body, Mind, History." In *AIDS in Africa and the Caribbean,* edited by George C. Bond, John Kreniske, Ida Susser, and Joan Vincent, 191–194. Boulder: Westview, 1997.

Lloyd, T. O. *The British Empire, 1558–1995.* 2nd ed. Oxford, UK: Oxford University Press, 1996.

Lucassen, Leo. "A Many-Headed Monster: The Evolution of the Passport System in the Netherlands and Germany in the Long Nineteenth Century." In *Documenting Individual Identity: The Development of State Practices in the Modern World,* edited by Jane Caplan and John Torpey, 235–255. Princeton, NJ: Princeton University Press, 2001.

Lyon, David. "Under My Skin: From Identification Papers to Body Surveillance." In *Documenting Individual Identity: The Development of State Practices in the Modern World,* edited by Jane Caplan and John Torpey, 291–310. Princeton, NJ: Princeton University Press, 2001.

Machiavelli, Niccolo. *The Prince.* Translated by George Bull. New York: Penguin Books, 1981.

Mandaville, Peter G. "Territory and Translocality: Discrepant Idioms of Political Identity." *Millennium: Journal of International Studies* 28 (1999): 653–673.

Manderson, Lenore. "Wireless Wars in the Eastern Arena: Epidemiological Surveillance, Disease Prevention, and the Work of the Eastern Bureau of the League of Nations Health Organization, 1925–1942." In *International Health Organizations and Movements, 1918–1939,* edited by Paul Weindling, 109–133. New York: Cambridge University Press, 1995.

Manzo, Katherine. *Creating Boundaries: The Politics of Race and Nation.* Boulder: Lynne Rienner Publishers, 1996.

Mardini, Ahmad. "Iran Turns Towards U.S., Gulf States." *Inter Press Service* (26 December 1997).

Martin, H. S. "Issuance of Passports to Criminals." 28 March 1929 (FO 612 105).

———. "Refusal of British Passports." 1926 (FO 612 355).

———. "Technical Sub-Committee on the Passport Regime." 14 May 1926 (FO 612 355).

———. "Validity of British Passports." T.3889/21 (FO 612 355).

Matthews, Glenn. "Forests of the Night: The Moralized Topography of Mau Mau." In *At the Edge of International Relations: Postcolonialism, Gender, and Dependency,* edited by Phillip Darby, 106–124. London: Continuum, 1997.

May, Ernest R. "America's Berlin." *Foreign Affairs* 77 (June/July 1998): 148–161.
McNeill, William H. *Plagues and Peoples.* New York: Anchor, 1976.
Meehan, Michael. "Canada to Use Iris Scans for Customs IDs." *Computerworld* 34 (4 December 2000): 7.
———. "Iris Scans Take Off at Airports." *Computerworld* 34 (1 July 2000): 1–2.
Mendez, Antonio J. "CIA Goes Hollywood: A Classic Case of Deception." *Studies in Intelligence* 43 (Winter 1999), available online at http://www.cia.gov/csi/studies/winter99–00/art1.html.
"Minutes of Meeting in Foreign Ministry to Discuss Council of Europe Questionnaire." (WU 10713/11) (FO 612 290).
Mitchel, Timothy. *Colonising Egypt.* Berkeley: University of California Press, 1988.
———. "The Limits of the State: Beyond Statist Approaches and Their Critics." *American Political Science Review* 85 (1991): 84–96.
Mitchener, Brandon. "Dutch Airport Experiments in Trading Privacy for Speed." *Wall Street Journal* 238 (30 October 2001): A20.
Mitrany, David. "The Functional Approach to World Organization." *International Affairs* 24 (July 1948): 350–363.
Mongia, Radhika Viyas. "Race, Nationality, Mobility: A History of the Passport." *Public Culture* 11 (1999): 527–556.
The Monitor. "Mushega Tells Investors to Go into Politics." *Africa News Service.* 21 December 2001.
———. "Regional Passport Useless, Say MPs." *Africa News Service.* 20 November 2001.
Moore, Robert, and Tina Wallace. *Slamming the Door: The Administration of Immigration Control.* London: Martin Robertson, 1975.
Murphy, Alexander B. "The Sovereign State System as a Political-Territorial Ideal: Historical and Contemporary Considerations." In *State Sovereignty as a Social Construct,* edited by Thomas J. Biersteker and Cynthia Weber, 81–120. Cambridge, UK: Cambridge University Press, 1996.
Murphy, Craig N. *International Organization and Industrial Change: Global Governance Since 1850.* Cambridge, UK: Polity, 1994.
Musto, David F. "Quarantine and the Problem of AIDS." In *AIDS: The Burdens of History,* edited by Elizabeth Fee and Daniel M. Fox, 67–85. London: University of California Press, 1988.
Nadelmann, Ethan A. "Global Prohibition Regimes: The Evolution of Norms in International Society." *International Organization* 44 (Autumn 1990): 479–526.
Neff, James, Duff Wilson, and Hal Bernton. "Few Resources Spent on Guarding Canada Border." *Seattle Times* (23 September 2001): A1.
Nelson, Leonard J. III. "International Travel Restrictions and AIDS Epidemic." *American Journal of International Law* 81 (January 1987): 230–236.

Neumann, Iver B. *Uses of the Other: "The East" in European Identity Formation.* Minneapolis: University of Minnesota Press, 1999.

"New Caution on Passports: Liberal Peer's Anxiety." *Manchester Guardian* (26 October 1955).

Newman, David. "Boundaries." In *A Companion to Political Geography,* edited by J. Agnew and G. Toal, 1–16. Oxford, UK: Blackwell, 2002.

Nietzsche, Friedrich. "Genealogy of Morals." In *The Birth of Tragedy and the Genealogy of Morals,* translated by Francis Golffing, 147–299. New York: Anchor, 1956.

Norden, Daniel. "Sauf-conduits et passeports, en France, à la Renaissance." In *Voyager à la Renaissance: Actes du colloque de Tours,* edited by Jean Céard and Jean-Claude Margolin, 145–158. Paris: Maisonneuve et Larose, 1987.

Norway. "Norway and Schengen: How Will This Affect You?" Government of Norway, Ministry of Justice and Police (G-0303 B). Oslo: Algard Offset, 2001.

O'Byrne, Darren J. "On Passports and Border Controls." *Annals of Tourism Research* 28 (2001): 399–416.

Oates, Joyce Carol. "Customs." In *Crossing the Border: Fifteen Tales,* 106–117. New York: Vanguard, 1976.

Otis, Leah Lydia. *Prostitution in Medieval Society: The History of an Urban Institution in Languedoc.* Chicago: University of Chicago Press, 1985.

Paolini, Albert. "Globalization." In *At the Edge of International Relations: Postcolonialism, Gender, and Dependency,* edited by Phillip Darby, 33–60. London: Continuum, 1997.

Parry, Clive, ed. *A British Digest of International Law, Part 6: The Individual in International Law.* London: Stevens and Sons, 1965.

Passport Office. "Applications for Passports." 1916 (FO 737 24).

———. *British Nationality and Status of Aliens Act, 1933. 4&5 Geo.5. Ch. 17.* 26 November 1946 (FO 612 257).

———. "Business Plan, 1993–94." Department of Foreign Affairs and International Trade, 1993, 2.

———. "Form A." 1915 (FO 737 24).

———. *The History of Passports.* 2001. Available online at www.dfait-maeci.gc.ca/passport/history_e.asp.

———. "Memo: British Nationality and Status of Aliens Acts 1914 to 1943." 1943 (T. 10741/75/378) (FO 612258).

———. "Passport Registers, 1841–1850." (FO 610 3).

———. "Refusal of Passports to British Subjects Going Abroad." (FO 612 273).

———. *Revision of Form A.* 1934/5 (FO 612 181).

———. "Revision of Passport Application Forms: Minute Sheet." 1946 (FO 612 246).

———. "Specimens of Passports." 15 September 1938 (FO 612 198).

Passport Office, Consular Instructions. "Passports and Visas." October 1921 (FO 612 265).

Passport Office, Passport Office Reorganization. 1922 (FO 612 232).

"Passport-Free Trips to Germany: Council of Europe Citizens." *Manchester Guardian* (9 September 1955).
Pendleton, G. "Immigration: Canada Joins US in Limiting Admission of People with AIDS." *AIDS Policy and Law* 16 (20 July 2001): 3.
Peterson, Scott. "Checkpoint Charlies Dash British Convoy's Blithe Spirits." *Christian Science Monitor* 88 (2 January 1996): 4.
Potts, Lydia. *The World Labour Market: A History of Migration.* Translated by Terry Bond. London: Zed Books, 1990.
Qureshi, Sarah N. "Global Ostracism of HIV-Positive Aliens: International Restrictions Barring HIV-Positive Aliens." *Maryland Journal of International Law Trade* 18 (1995).
Reale, Edigio. "Passport." In *Encyclopaedia of Social Sciences, Volume 12*, edited by Edwin R.A. Seligman, 13–16. New York: Macmillan, 1934.
Rediker, Marcus. "Life Under the Jolly Roger." *Wilson Quarterly* 12 (Summer 1988): 154–166.
Risse, Geunter B. "Epidemics and History: Ecological Perspectives and Social Responses." In *AIDS: The Burdens of History,* edited by Elizabeth Fee and Daniel M. Fox, 33–66. Berkeley: University of California Press, 1988.
Rivlin, Helen Anne B. *The Agricultural Policy of Mohammed 'Ali in Egypt.* Cambridge, MA: Harvard University Press, 1961.
Robertson, A. H. *The Council of Europe: Its Structures, Functions, and Achievements,* New York: Praeger, 1961.
Rosenberg, Justin. *The Empire of Civil Society: A Critique of the Realist Theory of International Relations.* London: Verso, 1994.
Ruggie, John Gerard. "Territoriality and Beyond: Problematizing Modernity in International Relations." *International Organization* 47 (Winter 1993): 139–174.
Russo, Robert. "Canadian Passports Easily Obtained." 14 March 2001. Available online at www.canoe.ca/CNEWSLaw0103/14_ressam-cp.html.
Ryan, Chris, and C. Michael Hall. *Sex Tourism: Marginal People and Liminalities.* New York: Routledge, 2001.
Sahlins, Peter. "State Formation and National Identity in the Catalan Borderlands During the Eighteenth and Nineteenth Centuries." In *Border Identities: Nation and State at International Frontiers,* edited by Thomas M. Wilson and Hastings Donnan, 31–61. Cambridge, UK: Cambridge University Press, 1998.
Said, Edward W. "The Mind of Winter: Reflections on Life in Exile." *Harper's* 269 (1984): 49–55.
———. *Culture and Imperialism.* New York: Vintage, 1993.
———. *Reflections on Exile and Other Essays.* Cambridge, MA: Harvard University Press, 2000.
Said, Mohamed. "Premodern Period in South Asia." In *The Cambridge World History of Human Disease,* edited by Kenneth F. Kiple, 413–417. Cambridge, UK: Cambridge University Press, 1993.

Salter, Mark B. *Barbarians and Civilisation in International Relations.* London: Pluto Press, 2002.
Schneider, Howard. "Canada Pulls Ambassador from Israel." *Washington Post* (3 October 1997): A29.
Schraeder, Peter J. "African International Relations." In *Understanding Contemporary Africa,* 3rd ed., edited by April A. Gordon and Donald L. Gordon, 143–187. Boulder: Lynne Rienner Publishers, 2001.
Schuman, Frederick L. "The Council of Europe." *American Political Science Review* 45 (September 1951): 724–740.
Shah, Ramnik. "Passport Control and Mistake." *New Law Journal* 142 (3 April 1992): 450–451.
Sibley, N. W. "The Passport System." *Journal of Comparative Legislation and International Law* 7 (1906): 26–33.
Simmel, Georg. "The Stranger." In *On Individuality and Social Forms,* edited by Donald E. Levine, 143–149. Chicago: University of Chicago Press, 1971.
Smith, Paul J. "The Terrorists and Crime Bosses Behind the Fake Passport Trade." *Jane's Intelligence Review* (1 July 2002).
Smith, Roy. "Fit to Govern?" *World Today* 56 (October 2000): 14–16.
Smith, Stephen. "Always Alone with a British Passport: Britons in Cuba Suspected of Being Spies." *New Statesman* 129 (6 November 2000): 31–32.
Soguk, Nevzat. *States and Strangers: Refugees and Displacements of Statecraft.* Minneapolis: University of Minnesota Press, 1999.
Soguk, Nevzat, and Geoffrey Whitehall. "Wandering Grounds: Transversality, Identity, Territoriality, and Movement." *Millennium: Journal of International Studies* 28 (1999): 675–698.
Sohn, Louis B., and Thomas Buergenthal, eds. *The Movement of Persons Across Borders.* Washington, DC: American Society of International Law, 1992.
Sontag, Susan. *AIDS and Its Metaphors.* New York: Farrar, Strauss, Giroux, 1988.
Sparaco, Pierre. "IATA Advocates Biometric Security." *Aviation Week and Space Technology* 155 (12 November 2001): 50.
Spruyt, Hendrik. *The Sovereign State and Its Competitors.* Princeton, NJ: Princeton University Press, 1994.
Stafford, J. W. (Correspondence with J. C. Crombie). "Passport Office Reorganisation." 19 February 1945 (FO 612 231).
Stoddard, Lothrop. *The Rising Tide of Color Against White World-Supremacy,* New York: Charles Scribner's Sons, 1920.
Stoler, Ann Laura. *Race and the Education of Desire: Foucault's History of Sexuality and the Colonial Order of Things.* Durham, NC: Duke University Press, 1995.
"Sultan Qaboos of Oman on Private Visit to UAE." *Deutsche Presse-Agentur* (6 May 1996).

Teitelbaum, Michael S., and Jay Winter. *A Question of Numbers: High Migration, Low Fertility, and the Politics of National Identity.* New York: Hill and Wang, 1998.
Thomson, Janice E. "Sovereignty in Historical Perspective: The Evolution of State Control over Extraterritorial Violence." In *The Elusive State: International and Comparative Advantages,* edited by James A. Caporaso, 227–254. London: Sage, 1989.
———. *Mercenaries, Pirates, and Sovereigns.* Princeton, NJ: Princeton University Press, 1994.
Tilly, Charles. *Coercion, Capital, and European States.* Cambridge, UK: Blackwell, 1990.
Tollefson, Harold. *Policing Islam: The British Occupation of Egypt and the Anglo-Egyptian Struggle over the Control of the Police, 1882–1914.* Westport, CT: Greenwood Publishers, 1999.
Torpey, John. "Coming and Going: On the State Monopolization of the Legitimate Means of Movement." Center for the Study of Democracy, University of California–Irvine, 1998. Available online at http://www.democ.uci.edu/democ/papers/torpey.htm.
———. "The Great War and the Birth of the Modern Passport System." In *Documenting Individual Identity: The Development of State Practices in the Modern World,* edited by Jane Caplan and John Torpey, 256–270. Princeton, NJ: Princeton University Press, 2001.
———. *The Invention of the Passport: Surveillance, Citizenship, and the State.* Cambridge, UK: Cambridge University Press, 2000.
Treasury Office. "Passport Office Reorganisation." (4933/54/505) (FO 612 230).
Treverton, Gregory F. *Covert Action: The CIA and the Limits of American Intervention in the Postwar World.* London: I. B. Tauris, 1987.
Trexler, Richard C. *Public Life in Renaissance Florence.* New York: Academic Press, 1980.
United Nations, Department of Economic and Social Affairs, Population Division. "International Migration Policies." New York: United Nations, 1998 (ST/ESA/Ser.A/161).
United Nations, Economic and Social Council Official Records. "Report of the Meeting of Experts to Prepare for a World Conference on Passports and Frontier Formalities." April 1947.
United Nations, UNAIDS. "Technical Update: Population Mobility and AIDS." February 2001.
UNAIDS and the World Health Organization. "AIDS Epidemic Update." UNAIDS (UNAIDS/00.44E—WHO/CDS/CSR/EDC/2000.9) December 2000 (accessed 22 December 2001), www.unaids.org/wac/2000/wad00/files/WAD_epidemic_report.htm.
U.S. Department of Health and Human Services. "International Certificate of Vaccination." PHS-731 (Rev. 11-91). Washington, DC: U.S. Government Printing Office: 1997—430-384.

U.S. Department of Justice, Office of the Inspector General. "The Potential for Fraud and INS's Efforts to Reduce the Risks of the Visa Waiver Pilot Program." March 1999.

U.S. Department of State. "Human Rights Report 2000: Oman." February 2001 (accessed 8 January 2002), www.humanrights-usa.net/reports/oman.html.

———. DSP-11. (9 July 2001). Available online at travel.state.gov/dsp11.pdf.

U.S. Immigration and Naturalization Service. "How Do I Apply for a PORTPASS?" (24 December 2000). Available online at www.ins.usdoj.gov/graphics/howdoi/portpass.htm.

U.S. Office of Homeland Security. *National Strategy for Homeland Security.* July 2002.

Urwin, Derek W. *Historical Dictionary of European Organizations.* London: Scarecrow, 1994.

Verhovek, Sam Howe. "Vast U.S.-Canada Border Suddenly Poses a Problem to Patrol Agents." *New York Times* (4 October 2001).

Virilio, Paul. "The State of Emergency." In *The Virilio Reader,* edited by James Der Derian, 46–57. Oxford, UK: Blackwell, 1998.

Vogel, Dita. "Identifying Unauthorized Foreign Workers in the German Labour Market." In *Documenting Individual Identity: The Development of State Practices in the Modern World,* edited by Jane Caplan and John Torpey, 328–344. Princeton, NJ: Princeton University Press, 2001.

Walker, R.B.J. *Inside/Outside: International Relations as Political Theory.* Cambridge, UK: Cambridge University Press, 1993.

Walkowtiz, Judith R. *Prostitution and Victorian Society: Women, Class, and the State.* Cambridge, UK: Cambridge University Press, 1980.

Watts, Sheldon. *Epidemics and History: Disease, Power, and Imperialism.* New Haven, CT: Yale University Press, 1997.

Weber, Max. "Politics as a Vocation." In *From Max Weber: Essays in Sociology,* edited by H. H. Gerth and C. Wright Mills, 77–128. London: Routledge, 1991.

Weis, P. *Nationality and Statelessness in International Law.* Germantown, MA: Sijthoff and Noordhoff, 1979.

Wendt, Frantz. "Nordic Cooperation." In *Nordic Democracy: Ideas, Issues, and Institutions in Politics, Economy, Education, Social, and Cultural Affairs of Denmark, Finland, Iceland, Norway, and Sweden.* Copenhagen: Det Danske Selskab, 1981.

White, G. Edward. "The Marshall Court and International Law: The Piracy Cases." *American Journal of International Law* 83 (1989): 727–735.

Wight, Martin. "Why Is There No International Theory?" In *Diplomatic Investigations,* edited by Herbert Butterfield and Martin Wight, 17–34. London: Allen and Unwin, 1966.

World Health Organization. "The Global Risk of Infectious Diseases." WHO, Department of Communicable Disease, Surveillance and Response. Available online at http://www.who.int/emc/pdfs/GlobalhealthsecurityE.pdf.

———. Article 81. "International Health Regulations (1969)."

———. Weekly Epidemiological Report, vol. 61 (1985): 27.

Zill, Orianne. "Crossing Borders: How Terrorists Use Fake Passports, Visas, and Other Identity Documents." *Frontline*. N.d. (accessed 12 December 2001), www.pbs.org/wgbh/pages/frontline/shows/trail/etc/fake.html.

Index

Abbot, Stephen, 38
Abel, Rudolf, 35
Abu-Laghod, Janet, 14
Aliens, 26; control of, 78
Aliens Act (1905), 81, 82
Aliens Act (1920), 82, 86
Aliens Restriction Act (1914), 82
Alternative Inspection Services Program, 134
Amin, Idi, 91
Anderson, Malcolm, 127, 139, 142, 155
Andreas, Peter, 101, 138
Antidiplomacy, 33–34
Antipassports, 33–39
Appadurai, Arjun, 61, 122, 135
Arnold, David, 58
Ashcroft, John, 127
Asiwaju, Anthony, 114, 137
Aureshi, Sarah, 65
Australia: restricted exit policies, 8n9
Austro-Hungarian Empire, 103–104
Authority: across space, 11, 122; in Middle Ages, 11; secularization of, 52

Baer, Joel, 18
Bahrain: in passport unions, 101; regional security concerns by, 113

Bartelson, Jens, 17
Belarus: entry testing by, 65
Belgium: elimination of passports in, 102, 104, 108; new passports in, 154
Benin: borderlands in, 140; cross-border trade in, 141; open-border policy, 114; in passport unions, 101
Benyon, John, 110
Berlin Wall, 124, 125
Bigo, Didier, 153, 156, 159
Billeta de sanità, 3
Birth certificates, 26, 29, 35, 92
Bishop, Ryan, 68
Blaut, J. M., 14
Boards of health, 51; assignment of color coding for marginal groups, 53–54
Bond, Brian, 31–32
Bonfire of the vanities, 52
Borderlands, 137, 139, 140
Border(s): analysis of, 122; anxiety over spies and, 32; bilateral agreements on, 82; cards, 137, 138; changing, 122; checks, 105, 107; closed, 2; contested function of, 123; as control on labor force, 137; controls, 32, 80, 105, 111; crossing, 158; crossing difficulties, 113;

decrease in relevance of, 135; dismantling, 79; elimination of, 115; emergence of, 121; formalities, 137, 149; importance of, 122; inspection, 155; internal, 115; interruption of, 137, 141; inviolable location of, 122; leaky, 8; legitimate, 122; medieval, 12; micropolitics of, 123; narrating, 142–143; open, 2; permeability of, 2; persistance of, 122, 134–141; policing, 138; political, 139; porous, 77; regulation of, 25; relevancy of, 122; removal of controls, 79; revocation of rights at, 151; sacrosanct functions of, 122; stability of, 122; tension at crossings, 123–134; theories of state of, 122; trade across, 136; U.S.-Canadian, 35, 130, 132, 137; U.S.-Mexican, 130, 137
Borges, Jorge Luis, 38
Borneman, John, 125
Bort, Eberhard, 111, 154
Botswana: HIV/AIDS in, 66
Bottomley, Horatio, 32
Boundaries: colonial, 122, 141; cultural, 122; discursive, 122; disease and, 50; firm, 14; micropolitics of, 123; policing, 122; state juridical, 122. *See also* Borders
Brandt, Allan, 65
British Nationality Acts, 87, 90–91, 91, 95
British Nationality and Status of Aliens Acts, 87, 88, 90
British Passport Office, 22, 27, 40–41, 91, 95, 150; Certificates of Identity for Aliens and, 26; control of international movements of nationals, 80; control of movement of criminals by, 31; denial of passports, 29; innovations by, 77; issuance of passports as extension of royal prerogative, 28–29; paternal role of, 29; as policing agency of state, 88; postwar function, 89; role of, 89; tourism and, 103; wartime duties, 89

Brock, Lothar, 136
Brugiere, Jean Louis, 35
Burkina Faso: in passport union, 101

Canada, 4; Alternative Inspection Services Program, 134; bans on entry from noncitizens with HIV/AIDS, 65; CANPASS system, 133; citizenship laws in, 90; fraudulent use of passports, 34, 35; immigration inspections in, 130; immigration restrictions in, 59; Passport Office, 94; refugee passports in, 84; Remote Video Inspection System, 133, 134; restricted exit policies, 8n9; restrictions on Indian immigration, 24
CANPASS system, 133
Cape Verde: in passport union, 101
Capital: promotion of interests of, 79; in trade for safety, 14
Carmichael, Ann, 51, 53
Certificat de nationalité, 18, 19
Certificates of health, 59–60, 69
Certificates of Identity for Aliens, 26
Checkpoint Charlie, 124, 126
China, 35, 38, 39; bans on entry from noncitizens with HIV/AIDS, 69; entry testing by, 65
Cholera, 49, 55–62, 69; British attitudes on causes of, 56–57; imperial rule and, 57; natural isolation in India, 57; as political disease, 57; social ills and, 57; transmission by military forces, 58
Citizenship, 86–93; camouflage passports and, 37; categories of, 92; colonial/national, 87; by descent, 88; by domicile, 88; dual, 5; as modern invention, 89; nationality as problem of, 90; naturalized, 9n12; paternity and, 7; problem of colonies and, 89; problems of, 152–156; as recompense for wartime mobilization, 25; second, 37; social, 108
Colonialism: cholera and, 55–62; civilizing mission of, 21, 57, 58; illegality of, 122; passports and,

55–62; problem of citizenship and, 89; war and, 102
Colonial subjects: incorporation of as dangerous objects, 20; legal status of, 150; visual identification of, 32
Colonies: banishment to as punishment, 30; control over, 21; extraction of resources/labor from, 20, 23; government treatment of, 20; imperial anxiety over fertility of populations in, 57; passports in, 43n42; regulation of travel within, 20; safety of, 56
Commonwealth Immigration Act (1968), 91
Concert of Europe, 102
Conference on Passports and Frontier Formalities (1920), 78
Congress of Vienna, 40
Conscription, 24, 40; impact of, 31; loyalty and, 32; mass, 31, 32; in World War I, 31
Cook, Thomas, 22, 102–103
Cooperation: economic, 113; international, 102, 104, 151; invention of passport and, 3; police, 109; technical, 85
Cordon sanitaire, 40, 58, 62
Corvée, 23
Côte d'Ivoire: in passport union, 101
Council of Europe, 105–106
Cowley, E. R., 26
Cox, R. C., 89, 106
Crimean War, 104
Criminality, 56; border controls and, 115; control of, 153; surveillance and, 153; transborder, 109
Customs controls, 32

Declaration of Paris (1856), 19
DeLaRue, 38
Denmark: first passports in, 18; in passport unions, 101
Der Derian, James, 33, 34
Derrida, Jacques, 126–127, 128, 157
Deterritorialization, 136, 156
de Vattel, Emmerich, 16
Dillon, Michael, 149, 157
Diplomacy, 4; use of terror in, 33–34

Discipline: institutional, 25
Disease: armies and, 50; association with nonnormative characteristics, 71; association with social ills, 51, 52; control regime, 151; control through control of social body, 51, 52; discourse of, 52; geopolitics of, 67, 68, 69; germ theories of, 56; in global South, 63; information regarding, 61; invention of passport and, 3; marginalized groups and, 52, 70, 151; miasma theories of, 50; migration as factor, 64; mobility and transmission of, 68; population control and, 49–71; of poverty, 69; proliferation of, 50; social ills and, 151; surveillance programs for, 60; threat of, 49; threats to public order and, 53; trade routes and, 56; transmission of, 50, 65, 66, 67, 68; tropical, 64; vaccination and, 61; vectors of, 60
Documents: breeder, 2, 35, 132, 154; checks on, 2; examination of, 132; fraudulent, 111, 130; on legal status of colonial subjects, 150; of nationality, 2, 96; problems of, 152–156; state-issued, 2
Dominion of Melchizedek, 37
Duckett, Margaret, 65
Dufferin, Lord, 21
Dutch East Indies Company, 20
Dutch Guiana, 36

East African Community, 101–102; passport union in, 67, 112, 114–115
Eastern Bureau, 61
East India Company, 20
Economic: autarky, 149; cooperation, 113; development, 69, 114; integration, 79, 82, 113, 114; interaction, 149; recovery, 79; union, 113
Economic Community of West African States, 101, 112, 113–115
Economy: global, 155; national, 19
Edkins, Jenny, 157
Egypt: entry testing by, 65; identity cards in, 23; mobility passes in, 23; movement control in, 22, 23

Ejime, Paul, 114
Ellis Island, 60, 63
Enloe, Cynthia, 7
Epidemic Commission, 62
Epidemics: blame for, 59; control of, 49, 61; immigration and, 52; prevention of exit for afflicted individuals, 55; surveillance and, 61, 63
Espionage International, 36
European Convention on Establishment (1955), 81
European Union: elimination of border checks, 105, 107; External Frontiers Convention, 108; fear of East by, 111; membership rejection by Norway, 110; passport union, 87, 101; Schengen Agreement and, 3, 101, 105–112
External Frontiers Convention, 108

Fahrmeir, Andreas, 103
Farmer, Paul, 66
Ferguson, James, 135
Fingerprints, 84, 94, 132
Finor Associates, 36
Flynn, Donna, 141
Flynn, Stephen, 155
Forgery, 104
Foucault, Michel, 24, 25, 49, 51, 56, 70, 109, 128
France: early passports in, 25; elimination of passports in, 102, 104, 108; entry testing by, 68; exit permits in, 13; French revolution in, 25, 34, 40, 102; imperial expansion of, 89; World War I conscription in, 31
Franco-Prussian War, 104
Franzén, Matz, 130
French Revolution, 25, 34, 40, 102
Frontiers: controls at, 62; limits of jurisdiction and, 12; relevancy of, 122; sovereignty of, 121–123; stability of, 122; as transition zones, 14. *See also* Borders
Fuchs, Barbara, 17
Fussell, Paul, 27

Gambia: in passport union, 101
Garthoff, R. L., 124
Gender, 6, 7, 103, 113
Germany: border control in, 124, 125, 126; East/West Berlin, 124, 125; elimination of passports in, 102, 103, 108; Friedrichstrasse, 124
Geselle, Andrea, 103
Ghana: in passport union, 101
Globalization: criticisms of, 63–64; disease transmission and, 63
Gong, Gerrit, 21
Gorbachev, Mikhail, 125
Government(s): control of disease by, 50–55; motivations in movement of people, 2, 3; right of refusal to passport issuance, 5
Grabbe, Heather, 111
Grand tours, 26, 102
Great Britain: categories of citizenship in, 92; colonial issues and, 55–62; emigration of poor and sick from, 60; English fluency requirement for entry, 87, 88; entry testing by, 68; first passports in, 18; Foreign Office, 27; Home Office, 27, 82, 83; Immigration Branch, 26, 27; immigration restrictions in, 59; imperial expansion of, 89; importance of colonial trade to, 58; Ministry of Labour, 83, 92; need for passports for Commonwealth members, 86; problem of postcolonial returnees in, 91; refugee passports in, 84; refusal to implement quarantine regulations, 58; rejection of European passport, 107; restricted exit policies, 8n9; restrictions on entry into, 82, 91, 107; travel to outer islands from, 27. *See also* British Passport Office
Great Depression, 83
Groebner, Valentin, 53
Grotius, Hugo, 18
Guidaticum, 13, 15
Guinea: in passport union, 101
Guinea-Bissau: in passport union, 101

Gulf Cooperation Council (GCC), 101, 112, 113
Gupta, Akhil, 135

Hand geometry, 132
Hatty, James, 52
Hatty, Suzanne, 52
Health issues, 49–71; concern for in domestic and international communities, 54–55; plagues, 50–55
Health Organization of the League of Nations, 49, 61, 62, 70, 151
Heyman, Josiah, 129, 138, 139
HIV/AIDS, 49, 151; effects on Africa, 65; entry restrictions for, 65; in gay men, 66, 68; global response to, 65; in Haitian patients, 66; myths of origin, 65–66; refugees and, 67; tourism and, 67–68; travel restrictions and, 65, 66, 67, 68; United Nations joint program for, 64; vectors of, 65, 66; zone patterns of transmission, 68
Hong Kong, 38, 39, 92, 152
Howland and Baker islands, 37, 38
Hungary: entry testing by, 65; European Union membership and, 111

Iceland: in passport unions, 101
Identity: deterritorialized, 135; European, 105–112; passports as markers of, 2, 4, 5, 20, 28, 35, 80, 85, 86, 96; political, 140; regional, 115; as relationship of allegiance and responsibility, 89
Identity cards: control of colonial populations and, 55, 56; national, 29
Immigration, 4, 86–93; anticholera measures and, 59; controls, 31, 91; false documentation and, 130, 131; female, 31; illegal, 155; importance of visual examinations in, 60; legislation, 58; medical exams and, 60; officers, 129–130; of postcolonial subjects, 91–93; prevention for health purposes, 52; race and, 59, 88, 91, 92; restrictions based on secondary race characteristics, 24, 88, 91, 92; restrictions on, 92; Schengen Agreement of the European Union and, 109
Immigration Act (1971), 91
Immigration Act (1990), 65
Imperialism: economic logic of, 23; justification for, 21; state-sponsored, 150
India, 35, 94; British control of, 56–59; cordon sanitaire around, 58; restrictions on entry to Great Britain, 86, 87; as source of disease, 56
Indonesia: bans on entry from non-citizens with HIV/AIDS, 69
INSPASS system, 133
Inspection, 3; anxiety at, 130; border, 155; change in form, 132; of documents, 63, 94; immigration, 129, 130; of individual, 63, 94; passport, 121–143; preconceived notions of dangerous applicants, 130; secondary, 130; security profiling system and, 131, 132; of vaccination certificates, 70
Integration: economic, 79, 82, 113, 114; into global economy, 96, 155; invention of passport and, 3; market, 82; security and, 81
International Air Transportation Association, 94
International Certificate of Vaccination, 63, 64, 70, 85
International Civil Aviation Organization, 85
International Committee of the Red Cross, 70
International Conference on Passports, Customs Formalities and Through Tickets, 78
International Congress on Hygiene, 58
International Covenant on Civil and Political Rights (1966), 81
International Health Regulations, 64
International Sanitary Conference, 59
Iran, 34, 132
Iraq, 132

Ireland, 106
Isle of Man, 27
Isle of Wight, 27
Israel, 2, 34, 160$n1$
Italy: documentation regime in, 103; elimination of passports in, 102, 104

Jackson, Robert, 122
Japan, 35; bans on entry from noncitizens with HIV/AIDS, 69
Jaume (King of Arago-Catalonia), 15
Joint United Nations Programme on HIV/AIDS, 64
Jus sanguinis, 88
Jus soli, 88

Kaplan, Robert, 63, 64, 113
Kavanagh, William, 139
Kean, Thomas, 128
Kearney, Michael, 139
Kenya: HIV/AIDS in, 66; in passport union, 101, 114, 115
Kratochwil, Friedrich, 122
Kraut, Alan, 59
Krishna, Sankaran, 135, 136
Kumar, Amitava, 2, 136
Kuwait, 35; in passport unions, 101; regional security concerns by, 113

Labor: colonial extraction of, 22, 23; coolie, 23, 24; demand for, 23; domestic, 83; forced relocation of, 23; foreign, 82; market, 78, 82, 83; movement, 83; permits, 83; unpaid, 23; unregulated, 105; unrest, 83; unskilled, 23; wartime, 83
League of Nations, 26, 77, 84, 151; Conference on Passports and Frontier Formalities, 78; control of epidemics and, 61; control of refugees by, 77; Covenant, 79
Lebanon, 35
Le Carré, John, 34
Lefebvre, Henri, 123
Letters of marque, 16–20, 39, 150; sanctioning of violence and, 17
Liberalism: in interwar period, 79
Liberia: in passport union, 101

Libya, 132
Lightner, Allan, 124
List, Friedrich, 20
Locke, John, 20
Lucassen, Leo, 104
Luxemburg: elimination of passports in, 108

Machiavelli, Nicolo, 50, 52
Magna Carta (1215), 13
Mali: in passport union, 101
Malthus, Thomas, 20, 57
Mandaville, Peter, 135
Manderson, Lenore, 61
Market: common, 113; integration, 82; labor, 78, 82, 83
Mauritania: in passport union, 101
May, Ernest, 124
McNeill, William, 57
Mental illness, 56
Mexico: immigration inspections in, 130
Middle Ages: authority in, 11; borders in, 12; control of movement in, 11
Migration: forced, 23
Militärpass, 16
Mitchell, Timothy, 157
Mobility, 2–3; class, 83; continental regime, 82; freedom of, 64; gender and, 103; government motivations and, 2, 3; international, 3, 58; lack of international regime, 62; modern regimes, 77; policies, 125–126; restrictions, 124; sovereign's monopoly on, 13; upward, 83; wartime regime, 81. *See also* Movement
Mongia, Radhika, 24, 59, 88
Morality: public, 31, 81; threats to, 31
Movement: between colonies, 23–24; control of, 15, 23, 39, 49, 80; coordination of, 21; dangers in, 8; in developed countries, 2; freedom of, 2, 81, 84, 104, 105, 109, 114, 115, 149–150; health concerns, 49–71; illicit, 105; incomplete state control over, 36; in infected individuals, 49; international, 6, 96,

149, 158–160; labor, 83; legal foundation for controlling, 13; legitimate/illegitimate, 2, 5, 6, 39; for marginalized groups, 51, 52; in Middle Ages, 11; population, 80, 90; restricted, 2, 70; safe, 14; social, 135; between states, 4; travel permits and, 27; violent, 39–41; in wartime, 32
Mozambique: HIV/AIDS in, 66
Murphy, Craig, 79
Myanmar, 160$n1$

Nadelmann, Ethan, 18, 109
Nasseri, Merhan Karimi, 136
Nationality, 152; determinants of, 158; problems of, 152–156
National Registration Identity Card, 92
Nation-states: control of movement and, 15; evolution as unit, 12–13; formalization of relations of violence in, 12; functions of, 12, 16; as international actors, 11; organization of communities into, 122; sealed boundaries, 124; security of, 81
Naturalisation Act (1870), 89
Naturalization, 9$n12$, 87
Ne exeat regno, 13, 29
Nelson, Leonard, 67
Netherlands: elimination of passports in, 108
Netherlands East Indies, 36
Nietzsche, Friedrich, 149
Niger: open-border policy, 114; in passport union, 101
Nigeria: borderlands in, 140; cross-border trade in, 141; National Boundary Commission, 114; in passport union, 101
Nordic Council, 101, 105, 106, 108, 109, 110
North Korea, 160$n1$
Norway, 110
Nyassaland, 115

Oman: in passport unions, 101; regional security concerns by, 113

Orkin, Andrew, 65

Pakistan, 90, 94
Palestine, 2
Paolini, Albert, 63
Passport, British: development of, 26; issuance as extension of royal prerogative, 28–29; lack of grounds for denial of, 30–31; lack of necessity for, 29; rationale for, 29; restrictions on issuance of, 29; restrictions on use of, 40–41
Passport, camouflage, 36, 37, 115
Passport, diplomatic, 124; immunity and, 4
Passport, European Union, 105; rejection by Great Britain, 107
Passport, health, 3, 49, 151; necessity for in travel, 54; prevention of exit for afflicted individuals and, 55; as stand-in for body of traveler, 71; vaccination certificate as, 63
Passport, military, 26, 27
Passport, refugee, 4, 84
Passport, regional, 114
Passport, virtual, 37, 38
Passport regimes: colonial space and, 55; contemporary, 85; economic aims of, 82; evolution of, 77–96; during French Revolution, 25, 26, 34; international, 3, 77–96; justifications for, 78; modern, 3; Nansen, 77, 84, 151; securitized, 84
Passport(s); based on personal connections, 22, 26, 28; biometric information on, 94, 132; breeder documents and, 2, 35, 132, 154; class dynamics and, 7, 44$n71$; colonialism and, 20–24, 55–62; commodification of, 38; control and, 3; control of criminals and, 84; control of epidemics and, 49–71; control of refugees and, 84; control space, 123–134; cooperation and, 3; criminal behavior and, 45$n78$; disappearance of, 3, 25–26, 85, 101–116; disease and, 3; as document of

movement control, 21; as document of nationality, 2, 81, 96; duration of, 80; electronic, 113; examination of, 3–6; false, 34, 35, 36, 37, 131, 150; form/function, 3–6; fraudulent use of, 34; gender and, 6, 7, 113; as guarantee of repatriation, 4; health perspectives, 49–71; inability to absolutely verify identity, 27–28; inspection, 3, 93–95, 121–143; integration and, 3; international model, 85; international society and, 77–96; lack of obligation of foreign sovereigns and, 5; machine-readable, 85, 93–95, 113, 130, 132; as marker of identity, 2, 4, 5, 20, 28, 35, 80, 85, 86, 96, 149; as mechanism to prevent immigration, 59; military service and, 24–33; movement control and, 80; in periphery, 112–115; photographs on, 93, 94; population control and, 25, 77; race and, 7, 88, 91, 92; relinquishing, 125; reluctance of international community to issue, 78; restrictions, 8*n*9, 29; Schengen Agreement and, 101; security and, 2, 5–6, 85, 104; single-use, 22, 26, 28, 40, 80; social marginalization and, 25, 151; standardization of, 107; as tool of surveillance, 101; tracking role of, 80; traveler's intentions and, 131; types of, 4; use of photographs on, 27; violence perspective of development, 3, 11–41; vulnerability to falsification, 35; as weapons, 35. *See also* Safe-conduct instrument

Passport unions, 115; East African Community, 67, 101–102, 112, 114–115; Economic Community of West African States, 101, 112, 113–115; Gulf Cooperation Council, 101, 112, 113; Nordic Council, 101, 108, 109, 110

Paternity, 7

Peace of Westphalia (1648), 11

Padilla, Jose, 127–128

Perestroika, 125

Philippines: bans on entry from noncitizens with HIV/AIDS, 69; sex tourism in, 68

Pin-Fat, Véronique, 157

Piracy, 16–20, 39, 40

Plague, 49; association with social ills, 52; boards of health and, 51; centralization of victims of, 51; governmental mechanisms to control, 50–55; marginalized groups and, 51, 52; mobility regimes and, 51; origins in divine punishment, 52; political control and, 53; quarantine and, 51; use of military to limit transmission, 54

Poland: European Union membership and, 111

Political: identity, 140; instability, 67; revolutions, 11

Portugal: transborder communities in, 139

Privateers, 16–20, 39; commissioning of, 17

Protocapitalism, 14

Protosovereignty, 17

Provisional Committee on Communications and Transit Conference, 77

Qatar: in passport unions, 101; regional security concerns by, 113

Quarantines, 49, 50, 51, 54, 60, 159; abandonment for surveillance, 62; ineffectiveness of, 61–62; rejection of, 58, 59; unacceptability of, 63

Race: colonial discourse and, 7; immigration and, 59, 88, 91, 92

Raison d'état, 50

Reagan, Ronald, 125

Reale, Edigio, 32, 78

Refugees, 4; African, 67; control of, 77, 78, 84; repatriation and, 129; sovereign obligation to protect, 6; stigmatization of, 67; temporary residence for, 77

Reid, Richard, 112, 131, 154

Repatriation, 4, 5; in European Union, 106–107; monetary deposit

against, 31; refugees and, 129; regulation of, 6
Ressam, Ahmed, 35
Reterritorialization, 136
Retina patterns, 132
Revolution identificatoire, 33
Rhodesia, 36, 115
Risse, Geunter, 70
Rivlin, Helen, 23
Robinson, Lillian, 68
Rosenau, James, 122
Rousseau, Jean-Jacques, 20
Ruggie, John, 14

Safe-conduct instrument, 13, 39, 150; creation of new market towns and, 15; creation of revenues and, 13; development of commerce and, 14; expansion of sovereign realms and, 15; extraction of capital and, 15; multiple uses of, 15; precursor to passport, 13; for protection of envoys, 13
Sahlins, Peter, 140
Said, Mohamed, 56
Saudi Arabia, 132; entry testing by, 65; in passport unions, 101; regional security concerns by, 113
Sauf-conduit, 13
Savonarola, Girolamo, 52, 53
Schengen Agreement of the European Union, 3, 105–112, 108, 115; electronic transmission of information and, 109–110; immigration and, 109; need to carry identification under, 110, 115; transborder crime and, 109
Schengen Information System, 109, 110
Schengenland, 115, 152, 156; defining, 109; leaks in, 110, 111
Schwarzenberger, Georg, 16
Sea briefs, 18
Sealand, 37, 38
Security, 2–3, 77; floating definitions of, 156; generalization of, 13; infrastructure, 115; integration and, 81; lack of guarantees for, 39; national, 7, 79, 81; of nation-states, 81; role of passport in, 2; safe-conduct instrument and, 13; state, 149; vaccination certificate and, 63
Senegal: in passport union, 101
SENTRI system, 133
Sexuality, 56
Sibley, N. W., 13
Sierra Leone: in passport union, 101
Single European Act, 105
Slavery, 23; white, 31, 82
Smuggling, 137
Snow, C. P., 56
Soguk, Nevzat, 78, 84, 135–136
Sorge, Richard, 35
South Africa: HIV/AIDS in, 66
South Korea: sex tourism in, 68
Sovereign: ascendance of, 11; control of entrance to territory by, 128–129; establishment of international legal structure by, 18; legitimatization of violence and, 11; monopolization of use of violence by, 15, 39; need for permission to exit territory, 13; obligation to protect refugees, 6; overlapping rights, 106; power, 33; prohibitions on, 11; protection, 13; right to determine exit and reentry, 6, 13; treatment of foreigners by, 16
Sovereignty: challenges to, 17; criticisms of, 64; ecclesiastical foundation, 17, 52; frontiers of, 121–123; international doctrine of, 4; intervention in another country's, 4; natural, 89; polity-centered paradigm of, 17; Renaissance, 52; secular notion of virtue and, 52
Sovereignty territorial ideal, 121, 134, 135; naturalization of cultural borders of nations and, 123; universality of, 122
Space: authority across, 11; colonial, 20–24, 21, 55, 56; control of, 32, 50, 56; dangerous, 12, 15–16, 17, 19, 20, 24, 26, 40, 49, 79, 129, 134; discrete division of, 11; domestic, 12, 17, 19, 32;

geopolitical, 33, 122, 159; global, 11; international, 12, 17, 19, 55, 56, 79, 134; of interrogation, 123–134; liminal, 22; multilateral, 79; national, 56; nationalization of, 19; of overlapping authority structures, 12; passport control, 123–134; redistributing in, 138; safe, 3, 12, 17, 19, 20, 24, 40, 49, 79, 104; transversal, 134
Spain: elimination of passports in, 102, 104; exit permits in, 13; transborder communities in, 139, 140
Statelessness, 90
State(s): authority, 127; bureaucratic, 26; decline of, 135; dominance of, 6; equality in law of, 4; expansion as necessary activity of, 20; inability to control piracy, 19; legal norms and, 21–22; movement between, 4; need for international systems, 12; secularization of, 53; security, 149; spatial geopolitics of, 19; taming of violence in, 11; technology undermining of, 121; territorial, 135; virtual, 37; Westphalian, 11. *See also* Nation-states
Stoddard, Lothrop, 58
Sudan, 132
Surveillance, 58, 60, 159; of borders, 138, 139; capabilities of, 101; criminality and, 153; for detection of unwanted aliens, 104; epidemics and, 61, 63; international, 110; preferred to quarantine, 62; role of World Health Organization in, 63; safe populations and, 112; target groups and, 112
Sweden: entry testing by, 68; in passport unions, 101
Syria, 132

Tanganyika, 115
Tanzania, 114, 115; in passport union, 101
Territories, Identity, and Movement Theory, 135, 136

Terrorism, 2, 8, 35, 112, 130, 131, 149, 150, 154
Thailand: HIV/AIDS in, 68; sex tourism in, 68
Thomson, Janice, 18, 19
Togo: in passport union, 101
Torpey, John, 25, 33, 55, 56, 87, 103
Tourism, 22, 67–68, 102, 149
Trade: barriers, 113; colonial, 58, 59; cross-border, 136, 141, 155; desire for, 77; disease and, 56; increase in, 61, 149; international, 17, 149; safety of, 17; in staples, 136
Translocality, 134–141
Transversality, 134–141
Travel: accessibility of, 102; basic assumptions on, 24; desire for, 77; gender and, 103; increase in, 61; marginalized groups and, 54; permits, 26, 27; post–World War I encouragement of, 29; restrictions, 2, 54; as threat to national interest, 32
Travelers: class status and, 22; commercial agents, 22; government agents, 22; health passports as stand-ins for actual body of, 71; intentions of, 28, 33; personal recognizance of, 22, 26, 28; tourists, 22; uncertainty of identity of, 53
Treaty of Amsterdam (1997), 108
Treaty of Rome, 105
Trexler, Richard, 53
Trotsky, Leon, 35
Trusteeship, 89
Tuberculosis, 69
Turack, Daniel, 6
Typhus, 62

Uganda, 7, 91, 152; in passport union, 102, 114, 115
UNAIDS, 64, 66, 67
United Arab Emirates: in passport unions, 101; regional security concerns by, 113
United Nations, 106; Meeting of Experts, 84–85
United States: bans on entry from noncitizens with HIV/AIDS, 65;

Central Intelligence Agency, 128; cordon sanitaire around, 59; Department of Homeland Security, 155; Department of Justice, 128; Ellis Island, 60; Federal Bureau of Investigation, 128; Immigration and Naturalization Service, 127, 132, 137, 138, 155; immigration law in, 60; immigration restrictions in, 59, 60; INSPASS system, 133; Public Health Service, 60; refugee passports in, 84; SENTRI system, 133

United States National Security Entry-Exit Registration program, 131–132

United States PORTPASS initiative, 133

United States v. Chafat Al Jibori, 130–131

U.S. Centers for Disease Control and Prevention, 65, 67

Vaccinations, 61; certificates of, 63, 64, 70, 85; proof of, 63

Vietnam: bans on entry from noncitizens with HIV/AIDS, 69

Violence: anxiety about, 33; arbiters of, 19; authorization through issuance of state documents, 16; colonial economy of, 21; delegitimation of nonstate, 21; development of passports and, 11–41; formalization of relations of, 12; implementation of, 12; international, 17; invention of passport and, 3; justification for, 21; legitimate, 11, 12, 16, 17, 19, 39; letters of marque and, 17; limitation of, 150; in maintenance of colonial rule, 21; monopolization by sovereign, 15, 39; monopoly of, 19; nonstate, 41, 149; passport development and, 11–41; private, 17, 19, 150; reduction within domestic territory, 16; unauthorized, 33–39

Visas, 3, 107, 113; expiry of, 155

Vogel, Dita, 110

Walkowitz, Judith, 31
Watts, Sheldon, 51
Weber, Max, 39
Whitehall, Geoffrey, 136
Wilde, Oscar, 121
World Health Organization, 62, 70, 151; Certificate of Vaccination, 63, 66; dissemination of information role of, 63; surveillance role of, 63
World War I, 24–33, 26, 29, 40, 77, 86; anxiety over presence of spies, 32; conscription in, 31; control of movement in, 32; passport development during, 27; tracking combatants, 78; verification of deserters from, 78
World War II, 87; control of movement in, 32
Worthington, Peter, 34

Yugoslavia, 35

Zacher, Mark, 122
Zambia: HIV/AIDS in, 66
Zanzibar, 36
Zimbabwe: HIV/AIDS in, 66

About the Book

From the fourteenth century to the twenty-first, the passport has been one of the essential means of identification—and control—of peoples in the international system. Despite predictions that it would soon become an anachronism, it continues to be a central feature of international relations. Mark Salter's narrative of the history of the passport adds a vital perspective to the understanding of world politics.

Rights of Passage explores shifting notions of sovereignty, citizenship, and identity, as well as changing concerns with issues of race, class, gender, and nation. Ranging from such topics as health, war, and migration to the current mood of vigilant surveillance, the book sheds new light on the role of borders in the age of globalization.

Mark B. Salter is assistant professor of political science at the American University in Cairo. He is author of *Barbarians and Civilisation in International Relations*.